New Ways in Teaching Speaking

SECOND EDITION

Julie Vorholt, Editor

This book has a companion website. Go to www.tesol.org/teachingspeaking for additional resources.

www.tesol.org/bookstore

TESOL International Association
1925 Ballenger Avenue
Alexandria, Virginia, 22314 USA
www.tesol.org

Director of Publishing: Myrna Jacobs
Copy Editor: Tomiko Breland
Production Editor: Kari S. Dalton
Cover Design: Citrine Sky Design
Design and Layout: Capitol Communications, Inc.
Printing: Gasch Printing, LLC

ISBN 9781945351280
Library of Congress Control Number 2017954007

This book is dedicated
to the spirit of relentless determination
instilled in me by my mother,
encouraged in me by my loved ones, and
observed and respected by me in my students.

Contents

Note: The activities in each section are arranged alphabetically within each section.

Part III. Developing Pronunciation

Segmental Phonemes

Suprasegmental Phonemes

Game-Based Learning

Miscellaneous

Part IV. Speaking in Specific Contexts

Interviews and Questioning

Part V. Speaking and Technology

Developing Fluency and Accuracy Using Technology

Developing Pronunciation Using Technology

Spoken English for Academic and Professional Purposes Using Technology

INTRODUCTION, WITH A USER'S GUIDE TO ACTIVITIES

Welcome to *New Ways in Teaching Speaking Second Edition*!

The purpose of the New Ways series remains the same as when it began, ". . . to publish ideas written by teachers for teachers." This is the first line of the introduction from the first edition of *New Ways in Teaching Speaking* (Teachers of English to Speakers of Other Languages, 1994, p. viii), which was coedited by Dr. Kathleen M. Bailey and Lance Savage. Also remaining the same in this specific volume is the focus on teaching speaking, an essential skill for many language learners.

Both editions contain more than 100 activities, submitted by English language teaching professionals from around the world. They volunteered to share their expertise from their perspectives as instructors in English as a second language and English as a foreign language contexts and as native and nonnative English speakers themselves. Their submissions constitute a wide array of engaging activities that have succeeded when taught in their own classrooms. Their contributions represent different approaches and techniques in language teaching in a multitude of situations. Successful instruction can occur in diverse ways (Cook, 2016), and these activities illustrate that. For ease of use, the book is organized into major categories. The sections, however, were not planned in advance for either the first edition (Bailey & Savage, 1994) or this one. Instead, the contributions from the teachers were used to determine the major categories and smaller subsections.

More than 100 brand new activities are in this new edition. They are divided into five major categories: Developing Fluency (Part I), Developing Accuracy (Part II), Developing Pronunciation (Part III), Speaking in Specific Contexts (Part IV), and Speaking and Technology (Part V).

The widespread use of technology in teaching is evident by the addition of the extensive new category Speaking and Technology, in which teachers incorporate a variety of technological tools, such as tablets, internet-connected projectors, and smartphones. These tools allow students to create podcasts, film movies, record other video or audio clips, time themselves, and more—all to improve their speaking skills while utilizing their digital literacy skills. This experience supports students' development as "effective and independent learners who can take advantage of the tools and resources for language learning in authentic contexts" (Son, Park, & Park, 2017, p. 95). In this new Speaking and Technology category, more than 20 activities are divided into three subsections. The first and largest is Developing Fluency and Accuracy Using Technology. These activities vary in their aims. Some activities concentrate on improving fluency, some on accuracy, some on both, and some can be adapted to shift the concentration. The second subsection is Developing Pronunciation Using Technology and the third is Spoken English for Academic and Professional Purposes Using Technology.

This new edition includes an expanded subsection with career-focused content. Speaking in Specific Contexts contains a subsection titled Spoken English for Academic and Professional Purposes. The new career-focused activities connect to work in business, law, and more, illustrating the value of additional instruction in speaking even when learners' English skills reach an advanced proficiency level. In a survey completed by 229 international students, 343 domestic students, and 125 professors at a Canadian university, MacGregor and Folinazzo (2018) asked about challenges encountered by international students in higher education; "communication, language" (p. 313) was the top response from the international students' professors and native-English-speaking classmates and the third most-cited response from the international students themselves. This subsection offers activities to support these students learning and working in English.

In this new edition, there are also four entirely new subsections. Game-Based Learning and a Miscellaneous section (for teaching repeatable techniques and activities for student practice) have been added to Developing Pronunciation. In Speaking in Specific Contexts, Oral Presentation Skills includes activities to improve students' nonverbal communication, transitions, sentence-level errors, and conclusions, and a teacher assessment method. Also in Speaking in Specific Contexts, Young Speakers consists of a diverse grouping of activities intended for learners from kindergarten through Grade 12. However, some of these activities may also work well with adults. Conversely, many of the activities in other sections of the book could work well with younger learners, especially with students in middle school and high school. When read in its entirety, this book includes activities that represent students at all proficiency levels and of all ages.

USER'S GUIDE TO ACTIVITIES

Each activity is organized according to its major category and subsection and then arranged alphabetically by title. All activities state the proficiency level that is suggested for the students, the aims of the activity, the estimated time needed in class, the estimated time needed by the teacher for preparation, and the resources needed. Note that estimated times for preparation do not include how long it may take to become familiar with the activity and organize materials.

Next, each activity provides an introduction with some background information, followed by step-by-step instructions to lead students in the activity. That procedure is followed by Caveats and Options, such as any tips, suggestions, or alternate ideas about teaching or extending the activity. Some activities end with a list of references that are cited or suggested for further reading. An appendix, if included, is the final section.

> **R** This "R" stands for "Resources." This "R" icon is a sign to go to:
> **www.tesol.org/teachingspeaking** to access valuable resources. There, the appendixes are available, including handouts, PowerPoint presentations, and more. You can also find an annotated list of Online Resources: websites that are useful for classroom teachers who want more information or materials about teaching speaking.

Following are some additional points to consider.

> - Teachers know their students, context, and environment better than anyone. Please carefully preview each activity and make any necessary changes. Note that some activities may be developed for students at a certain proficiency level, but they can be adapted. As stated by van Lier, "Successful teaching is a blend of planning and improvisation . . ." (1996, p. 9). If they might work better for your students, use the suggestions found in the Caveats and Options section and use your own ideas.
>
> - The materials and resources available to each educator vary; however, for the sake of simplicity, the activities in this book assume that all teachers have access to a blackboard or whiteboard, paper, and writing utensils. Thus, those materials are not listed as resources. Activities that list smartphones, tablets, and other digital devices as necessary resources are found in Speaking and Technology.

Although these activities are designed for English language classrooms in an English as a second language or English as a foreign language context, some can be used to teach speaking to native English speakers and many, with a few modifications, can be used to teach speaking in other languages.

To my readers, I hope that using these diverse activities developed by language teachers worldwide encourages us to continue collaborating and supporting each other as we teach speaking in new ways.

ACKNOWLEDGMENTS

Without the contributors, a volume like this could not be created. I am grateful to the many English language teaching professionals from around the world who submitted their activities. The response to the call for contributions was tremendous, with more than 200 activities received. Even though not every submission could be published, I greatly appreciate your enthusiasm and support. Your response shows how meaningful this book is to our field.

I would like to express my thanks to those who assisted me during the editing process. Delia Russo-Savage assisted with word processing and organizing the submissions into categories. Lara Ravitch created detailed activities to increase diversity and inclusion in a submission. Valuable feedback on drafts of the Table of Contents came from Dr. Renee Jourdenais and Hisako Yamashita as well as Robyn Brinks Lockwood, who also provided steadfast support from the start. Finally I would like to thank TESOL Press for giving me this opportunity and for providing editorial support.

Julie Vorholt, Editor

REFERENCES

Bailey, K., & Savage, L. (Eds.). (1994). *New ways in teaching speaking*. Alexandria, VA: Teachers of English to Speakers of Other Languages.

Cook, V. (2016). *Second language learning and language teaching* (5th ed.). New York, NY: Routledge.

MacGregor, A., & Folinazzo, G. (2018, June). Best practices in teaching international students in higher education: Issues and strategies. *TESOL Journal, 9*, 299–329.

Son, J-B., Park, S-S., & Park, M. (2017). Digital literacy of language learners in two different contexts. *The JALT CALL Journal, 13*(2), 77–96.

van Lier, L. (1996). *Interaction in the language curriculum: Awareness, autonomy, and authenticity*. London, England: Longman.

Part I

Developing Fluency

- **Conversation**
- **Interaction**
- **Group Work**
- **Dialogues and Role-Plays**
- **Game-Based Learning**

3-2-1 Icebreaking

Thi Ngoc Yen Dang

Levels	*All*
Aims	*Develop fluency*
	Help students get to know each other at the beginning of a course
Class Time	*30–60 minutes*
Preparation Time	*10 minutes (first time only)*
Resources	*Timer*
	1 card per student (see Appendix)

T his activity is based on the 4/3/2 technique (Arevart & Nation, 1991; Nation & Newton, 2009), which helps to foster speaking fluency. In a 4/3/2 activity, a student talks about a familiar topic with three different students, giving the same speech within a gradually reduced time. The speaker talks with the first student for 4 minutes, with the second student for 3 minutes, and with the third student for 2 minutes. Delivering the speech with the same content in reduced amounts of time enables students to improve their speaking fluency.

Icebreaking is a useful activity at the beginning of a course. It helps students get to know each other so that a friendly and cooperative environment can be created. This activity focuses on students introducing themselves to their peers. Note that the time for this activity has been adapted to 3/2/1 because a 4-minute talk about oneself may be too long.

PROCEDURE

1. Prepare the cards (Appendix).
2. Explain the purpose of the activity to the students.
3. Give students 1 minute to plan a speech about themselves, with the option of writing it down. Suggest some information that can be included, such as nationality, hobbies, and reasons to study English.
4. Give each student one card. Tell them to find one partner holding the card with the same color as theirs. In pairs, one student talks about him- or herself for 3 minutes while the other listens and tries to remember that information. The speaker can look at their notes but should not read the notes aloud. The listener may take notes when listening.
5. When 3 minutes have passed, ask the students to change roles.

6. When another 3 minutes have passed, ask the students to change partners by finding a student holding a card with the same shape as theirs. In this round, each student talks for 2 minutes.

7. When both 2-minute rounds have passed, ask the students to change partners again by finding a student holding the card with the same letter. In this round, each student talks for 1 minute.

8. Ask the students to return to their desks for a class discussion. Each student speaks to the whole class and introduces one student they met. Other students who also talked to the same person can add any information that is missing.

CAVEATS AND OPTIONS

1. Some students may cut down the information in their speech to deal with the time reduction. Teachers should remind students to avoid this so that they can develop their speaking fluency. They should repeat the same ideas within a shorter period of time.

2. This activity can be used with other topics.

3. Depending on the levels of the students and the topics, the allotted time for each turn can be longer or shorter.

4. Shrinking-time condition (4/3/2 or 3/2/1) focuses solely on pushing fluency. To develop students' complexity and accuracy rather than fluency, a constant-time condition (3/3/3 or 2/2/2) may be more suitable (Thai & Boers, 2016).

REFERENCES AND FURTHER READING

Arevart, S., & Nation, P. (1991). Fluency improvement in a second language. *RELC Journal, 22*, 84–94.

Nation, I. S. P., & Newton, J. (2009). *Teaching ESL/EFL listening and speaking*. New York, NY: Routledge.

Thai, C., & Boers, F. (2016). Repeating a monologue under increasing time pressure: Effects on fluency, complexity, and accuracy. *TESOL Quarterly, 50*, 369–393.

At the End of the Rainbow

Leticia Araceli Salas Serrano

Levels	*All*
Aims	*Develop fluency*
	Enhance interaction among students
Class Time	*30 minutes*
Preparation Time	*None*
Resources	*A picture of a rainbow or markers in the seven colors of the rainbow*

An old Irish tale tells that a pot of gold can be found at the end of a rainbow. However, there are also other stories and symbols connected to rainbows. For example, some people say that rainbows represent the future. What would you like to find at the end of that rainbow? This activity guides students in discussion about some personal goals. Students interact with their peers and share their plans or projects for the future. This is a great activity to wrap up a unit or a course.

PROCEDURE

1. Ask the class, "What are the seven colors of the rainbow?" and write them on the board as the students say them: red, orange, yellow, green, blue, indigo, and violet. Then show a picture of a rainbow or draw one using colorful markers.

2. Ask the class, "Do you know what object is at the end of the rainbow?" Tell the Irish legend about the pot of gold found at the end of the rainbow.

3. Explain that a rainbow can also represent the future and then encourage the class to think about their hopes and dreams for the future. Write on the board, "What goals would you like to reach? What would you like to find at the end of the rainbow?" Give an example, such as learning English or receiving an award. Seeing it at the rainbow's end means the goal was achieved.

4. Students copy the questions written on the board. For a few minutes, students discuss in pairs what their goals are and what they would like to find at the end of the rainbow.

5. Lead a class discussion in which students share their goals.

6. After the discussion, young learners draw what they would like to find at the end of the rainbow. Adults can listen to the song "At the End of the Rainbow" and sing along.

CAVEATS AND OPTIONS

1. Because the activity might be very personal or emotional, some students might prefer not to share their real plans or projects. In that case, tell them to make up a goal. Another option is to tell them to choose a popular character from a book or movie and make up a goal for that character. If they do that, they should tell their partner the name of the character.

2. To extend the activity, students could discuss how they're going to reach their goals, or they can create a plan of action.

REFERENCES AND FURTHER READING

To read more about Irish myths: www.celtic-weddingrings.com/celtic-mythology /myth-of-the-leprechaun.aspx

For young learners, watch this video, "The Ancient Rock at the End of the Rainbow!": www.youtube.com/watch?v=wKUnq-KaLeE

For adults, watch this video with the lyrics to "At the End of the Rainbow," and sing along with Earl Grant: www.youtube.com/watch?v=NdkfJbSidzs

Conversation Champions

Eleanora S. Bell (Nonie) and Amanda Strickland

Levels	*High beginner to advanced*
Aims	*Use multimodal integrative language skills in practice of targeted vocabulary and language functions*
	Increase fluency in creative oral production
Class Time	*90 minutes*
Preparation Time	*15–30 minutes (plus 10 minutes first time only)*
Resources	*Handouts (Appendixes A–F)*

Conversation Champions is a scaffolded task-based extension activity for instruction of targeted vocabulary and language structures. It begins with recognition of these vocabulary and language structures in a listening activity, continues with dialogue creation, and concludes with dialogue presentations that showcase the forms in authentic, original conversations. As a culminating activity, such as at the conclusion of a unit, Conversation Champions works well for either practice, reinforcement, assessment, or all three.

PROCEDURE

1. If desired, prepare an audio recording of the sample conversation (Appendix A). Once the recording is made, preparation time in the future is dedicated to assembling handouts.

Phase One: Listening Activities (25 minutes)

2. Divide students into two groups. Distribute the Info Gap Questions handout (Appendix B). Students receive only the part/column designated for their group.

3. Prepare students to listen and fill in the Info Gap Questions handout. Direct them to take notes on the paper while listening, paying special attention to the vocabulary words used and their context.

4. Present a brief sample conversation including target vocabulary. Either play the audio recording or read the text. If the text is read, ask for student volunteers to read the two parts of bank teller and customer aloud to the class. Remind each group to listen for different vocabulary items.

5. Repeat the listening to allow students to check their handout.

6. Distribute the Cloze of Sample Conversation handout (Appendix C). Pair students from Group 1 with Group 2. Tell them to review their notes and complete

the handout based on the combination of the content from their respective Info Gap Questions sheets.

7. Lead the class in a review of the answers, highlighting use of target structures.

Phase Two: Dialogue Creation Activity (45 minutes)

8. The same student pairs choose from preselected topics to create a meaningful, real-life dialogue including a required number of target vocabulary words and grammar structures. Distribute the handout Student Instructions (Appendix D) and review the directions and requirements with the class.

9. Move around the room, clarifying or offering assistance as needed. While students are working, prepare rubrics with student names.

Phrase Three: Dialogue Presentation Activity (20 minutes)

10. Student pairs present their dialogues before an audience of peers. The audience members use student rubrics (Appendix E) to note the number of vocabulary words and structures used by each pair. Simultaneously, the instructor evaluates the dialogue presented by each pair using the teacher rubric (Appendix F).

11. The audience then votes on the pair that best demonstrates targeted forms.

12. The selected student pair is recognized as "Conversation Champions."

CAVEATS AND OPTIONS

1. Instructors should introduce, review, and quiz students on a limited list of target vocabulary and grammar structures at least one week in advance of this culminating activity.

2. Pair students sensitively across language capability levels and culture groups.

3. While student pairs are collaborating on dialogues to present, they're naturally using the targeted forms repeatedly in authentic, original conversations that could be graded separately from the final product.

4. Students can provide a recording and text of their performed dialogue via a class website. It can be used as an assessment or sample conversation for future use.

5. This activity can be based on a range of topics at any level, such as household chores, directions, housing issues, a job search, or academic research.

Finding Commonalities in Conversations

Jacqueline Foster

Levels	*High beginner to low intermediate*
Aims	*Develop speaking fluency*
Class Time	*30–35 minutes*
Preparation Time	*10–15 minutes*
Resources	*Pictures of 2 famous people*
	Classroom space for students to move around and change group formations
	Handout (Appendix)

This activity is designed for students who have studied the language structures for introducing, describing, and speaking about themselves and friends. Students should be familiar with using adjectives to describe themselves and using the present simple tense for speaking about habits, routines, and interests.

PROCEDURE

1. Show pictures of two famous people that the students will most likely know.

2. Ask the students who the famous people are and why they are famous. Add information if needed.

3. Ask the students what the famous people have in common. Check that the students understand *in common*.

4. List some of the similarities on the board.

5. Explain that the students are going to find out what they have in common with their classmates.

6. Distribute the handout (Appendix). Explain that each student will find a partner (or be assigned a partner).

7. Tell students that they have 5 minutes to speak to their partner, identify five commonalities, and list them in the "Partner 1" circle on the handout. Students may write in phrases.

8. After 5 minutes, move to the next phase. Group each pair of students with another pair to form a group of four.

9. Students have 5 minutes to identify five commonalities shared among all four members of the group, which can be the same or different from the first conversation, and list them in "Circle 2" on the handout.

10. After 5 minutes, move to the next phase. Tell the students to follow your instructions to form a final group of six students. Split some groups of four into pairs. Tell each pair which group of four to join, resulting in newly formed groups of six.

11. Within their new group, students have 5 minutes to identify five commonalities shared among all six members of the group and list them in "Circle 3" on the handout. The similarities can be the same or different from the previous conversations.

12. After 5 minutes, tell students to return to their desks for a class discussion.

13. Have the students look at "Circle 3" and ask for examples of what their last group has in common. To guide the responses, write a few sentence stems on the board.

    - We are
    - We like
    - We have

14. Record the examples on the board. Circle or identify commonalities shared by the entire class.

15. Conclude by directing the students to write five class-wide commonalities in sentences at the bottom of the handout. An example sentence could be, "We like listening to music in English." Students can read their sentences to a partner and/or share them with the class.

CAVEATS AND OPTIONS

1. If there are not enough students to form groups of six, then groups of five or other group sizes can work.

2. High beginner and low intermediate students may want to use "Our class" instead of "We" when forming sentences. Remind them that "Our class" requires a singular rather than a plural verb.

3. This activity can also be used as an icebreaker for intermediate and upper level students.

4. Upper level students can be asked to find unusual commonalities.

Highs and Lows

Jelena Danilovic Jeremic

Levels	Intermediate to advanced
Aims	Practice conversation
	Develop fluency
	Prompt interaction
Class Time	No set time
Preparation Time	None
Resources	None

Setting the mood for English class and creating a positive learning environment is not always an easy task. This activity was initially conceived as a warm-up, to help learners relax and interact with the teacher in a casual atmosphere. It is based on the idea that learners like to share their daily experiences with other people in an informal speaking context, when the focus is on an exchange of meaningful, personal information and not accuracy. Performed on a regular basis, the activity can not only help learners improve their speaking skills but also foster the development of an amicable, trusting relationship with the teacher and fellow learners.

PROCEDURE

1. At the very beginning of the class, tell the learners your best (or "high") and worst (or "low") moments of the day. In case of an uneventful day, invent an interesting story or retell the high and low moments of the week, month, or year. Make sure the vocabulary and grammar are appropriate for your learners' proficiency levels. Provide opportunities for the learners to pose questions and actively participate in the conversation.

2. Invite the class to think about their high and low moments of the day.

3. Choose a talkative learner and ask them about the highs and lows of the day. Ask questions about how they felt or reacted to the situation. Encourage others to become engaged in the conversation.

4. Explain to the learners that they are going to share their personal experiences with their classmates. Organize them into pairs or small groups, depending on the size of the class. Try to mix very confident and less confident speakers so the discussion about highs and lows of the day actively involves everyone. Monitor the course of the activity and, if necessary, provide encouragement to the learners by joining in the discussions. Remind the class that the goal of the activity is to keep the conversation going and that any errors that might occur should be overlooked.

5. Invite the learners to report to the whole class if anything particularly interesting has happened to their classmates. Praise their efforts to speak fluently.

CAVEATS AND OPTIONS

1. The activity presumes that the learners are familiar with past tenses so they can effortlessly follow a story or retell an event. With lower level learners, present tenses (e.g., the historical present) can be used instead.

2. If the students are reluctant to speak, the activity can be introduced through prompt cards that contain fictional information about a day in the life of famous people. As a class, discuss a "high of the day" and a "low of the day" for a celebrity who is known by your students.

3. In large classes, students can be invited to actively listen to their classmates' accounts and try to remember as many details as possible. Once they finish with discussions in their pairs/groups, have them retell the goings-on to members of other pairs/groups. Thus, the learners may become more engaged in the activity and simultaneously practice both speaking and listening.

4. The activity can be expanded with a different focus. Learners can be asked to take notes of their classmates' high and low moments of the day and then write a short story or dialogue based on them. This can be done individually or in pairs, in class or at home.

5. The activity can be modified to serve various lexico-grammatical purposes and parts of a lesson plan, such as the introduction of a new teaching unit, revision of previously taught vocabulary items, practice of indirect speech or sequence of tenses, overview of narrative tenses, and so on.

Note: This activity idea was inspired by the movie *The Story of Us*, in which the main characters play the family conversation game "High-Low" with their children at the dinner table.

Reflecting With Art Cards: Expressing Thoughts and Feelings

Hisako Yamashita

Levels	*All*
Aims	*Practice expressing thoughts and feelings*
	Develop awareness of current and future self
Class Time	*30–45 minutes*
Preparation Time	*0–5 minutes*
Resources	*A wide variety of postcard-sized art cards (Appendix A)*
	Handout (Appendix B)

R

Being able to have the opportunity to project one's "voice that speaks one's words" (van Lier, 2004) in a student's learning process not only gives them authentic speaking opportunities but also facilitates their development of self-reflective skills, one of the key characteristics of autonomous learners. This fun and easy-to-do classroom activity immediately grabs students' attention and leads them to reflect on their thoughts, feelings, and learning paths. Furthermore, based on their self-reflection, students will then express their "voices" in English. This activity helps create a supportive learning community as students share their situation and feelings with each other.

PROCEDURE

1. Purchase a wide variety of postcard-sized art cards. They are available at different locations, including in bookstores and online (Appendix A).

2. Ask the students to sit in groups of four to six. Place many art cards in front of them, on the desk.

3. Ask each student to pick a card that best illustrates their current situation/ feelings.

4. Each student will first describe the art on the card and then talk about the reasons they chose that particular one. To facilitate deeper reflection, have them write their thoughts on the worksheet before speaking (Appendix B).

5. When everyone is finished talking, ask each student to pick another card that best depicts their ideal future selves. Each student will then describe the art of the card and talk about how the card describes their ideal future.

CAVEATS AND OPTIONS

1. Beginning students could benefit from being introduced to vocabulary and phrases necessary to describe their feelings at the beginning of the activity.

2. If the students cannot find the appropriate card on their table, they can walk around the class and check art cards available in other groups.

3. As an additional final step, students can think about what actions they can take to come closer to their future goals, especially in terms of language learning.

4. This activity can be done on the spot or as a project in which the learners prepare by looking up necessary vocabulary and phrases in advance.

REFERENCES AND FURTHER READING

van Lier, L. (2004). *The ecology and semiotics of language learning: A sociocultural perspective.* Boston, MA: Kluwer Academic.

Speed Chatting Circles

Heather Yoder and Nicholas Hogg

Levels	*High beginner to intermediate*
Aims	*Develop conversational fluency in discussing familiar topics*
Class Time	*10 minutes*
Preparation Time	*10–30 minutes*
Resources	*Conversation cards*
	Timer

Students enjoy Speed Chatting Circles because of its fast pace. We first started using speed chatting as a review activity for our high school students in Japan. As more topics are covered in class, they can be added into the speed chatting repertoire. In addition, we sometimes joined the activity to conduct individual interview assessments with students.

PROCEDURE

1. Before class, prepare conversation cards with topic ideas on them. At the top of the conversation card, write the topic, such as "The Weekend." Then write a prompt, such as, "What did you do last weekend?"

2. Organize the classroom. Have students arrange themselves in one inner circle and one outer circle, so that each student has a partner in the other circle. If students have desks, they can move the desks to make the circles. Each pair gets one conversation card. Only the person in the outer circle can look at it.

3. Set the timer for 1 minute. Students have a conversation following the prompts on the card. The students in the outer circle, who have the conversation cards, lead the discussion. After 1 minute, the outer-circle students give their card to the inner-circle students and move to their right.

4. Set the timer for 1 minute. Now, the inner-circle students lead the conversation with a new partner. When the timer goes off, the inner-circle students pass the conversation card to the outer-circle students and move to their right. Continue following this pattern for as long as you like.

5. If there are an odd number of students, you can join the activity to ensure that students always have a partner, or one pair of seats/desks can be set up as a self-directed workstation where students could complete a supplementary worksheet or a questionnaire.

CAVEATS AND OPTIONS

1. The conversation cards can contain as much or as little guidance as your students need, depending on their level. Using the example of "The Weekend," here is an example with additional guidance.

Example

- "What did you do last weekend?" (said by the discussion leader)

- "I went to _____." (expected response from the listener)

- "That's nice. Who did you go with?" (said by the discussion leader)

2. Using Speed Chatting Circles for review includes a variety of topics that students have learned over the semester or year. For a class of 20–30, two conversation cards for each topic works well.

3. This activity can go for as long as needed, but students are usually ready to stop when they meet their first partner again.

4. This activity can be used for an interview assessment. If there are two teachers, one joins the group in the inner circle and the other joins in the outer circle. Teachers can do 1-minute assessments by rotating around the circles with the students. If they do 2-minute assessments, the teachers don't move and the students simply go around them. If there is only one teacher, assessments can still be done, but this may require one student per round to spend 1 minute at a self-directed workstation.

5. Implementation of this activity can take a while. Therefore, it works better if done for a longer time, such as half a class period or even a full class period. It also improves as the students do it more often. Once or twice a semester is a good amount.

I

CONVERSATION

Speed Conversing

Robyn Brinks Lockwood

Levels	*High intermediate to advanced*
Aims	*Practice spontaneous speaking*
	Learn to sustain small talk
	Develop fluency
Class Time	*Variable*
Preparation Time	*None*
Resources	*Bell*
	Video clips of speed dating or speed networking events (optional)

Speed dating has grown in popularity and has been featured on a variety of television and news shows. The concept of participants meeting many people over a series of "dates" lasting from 3–8 minutes has spun off into other settings, such as business speed networking in which participants meet potential business contacts. The concept focuses on some skills that high-intermediate and advanced students find challenging if they want to work or study in English-speaking settings—speaking and responding spontaneously, sustaining small talk, and developing fluency.

In this version, students participate in a speed conversing party. Students usually feel more at ease because they speak to just one person at a time while other pairs are participating in their own conversations, so the focus is not on them.

PROCEDURE

1. Arrange the class so that pairs of students sit across from each other and each pair has its own desk or table.

2. Explain speed dating and speed networking. Make sure students understand the idea is to meet many people in a short time and that pairs talk for a few minutes before rotating to talk to someone else. At the end of each time period, the organizer (the teacher) rings a bell and the participants rotate to talk to someone new.

3. If desired, show clips of speed dating or speed networking as shown on television shows such as *Gilmore Girls*, *Frasier*, or *House* or information featured on news shows such as *60 Minutes*.

4. Talk about the challenges and benefits of talking to someone for longer than a minute or two.

5. Explain that the class is going to participate in a speed conversing party. Pair students and challenge them to talk to their conversation partner for a set period of time. Most speed events range between 3 and 8 minutes. At the end of the set time, ring the bell.

6. After each bell, ask students to rotate to a new partner and start the timer again.

7. Hold a group discussion session at the conclusion of the entire conversing party. Ask students what topics they covered, how they handled any lulls in conversations, if they were disappointed when the time actually went faster than they expected, and so on. Develop a list of small talk strategies based on their answers for them to use to participate in small talk outside of class.

CAVEATS AND OPTIONS

1. Timing can vary depending on the level, comfort level, and class time available. More advanced students might be able to converse for 8 minutes whereas lower level students might prefer shorter conversations. Time can also increase with each conversation as students build confidence.

2. Remind students the goal of the activity is fluency and not perfect pronunciation or grammatical accuracy.

3. Ask students to record one of the conversations and summarize the topics and their own performance in a written report or a one-on-one meeting with the instructor.

4. This activity can be done in a variety of classes or revolve around different topics. For example, students can pretend they are at a department party, an office party, or a social holiday party or event, such as a wedding.

Cats vs. Dogs Debate

Channing Dodson

Levels	*High beginning to intermediate*
Aims	*Introduce students to key features of debate organization, strategy, and language*
Class Time	*90 minutes–2 hours*
Preparation Time	*10 minutes*
Resources	*Handouts (Appendixes A and B)*

The importance of debate in improving students' academic communication proficiency cannot be overstated. For students in U.S. college classrooms, the ability to organize information into structured arguments and debate it, whether formally or informally, is a necessary skill.

In addition to their value as a tool for enhancing academic speaking and listening skills, debates are also a helpful tool at the beginning stage of teaching persuasive essay writing because there is considerable overlap in the techniques that are employed.

PROCEDURE

1. Divide the class into two teams. If dividing them by counting off into 1s and 2s, make sure that each team includes students from a variety of linguistic/cultural backgrounds (if applicable) and skill levels.

2. Distribute the two handouts, "Debate Information and Academic Word List Wordbank" (Appendix A) and "Debate Rubric" (Appendix B). (Ideally, you can fit these on two sides of one sheet of paper, allowing students to reference both during the activity.) Explain that the two teams will engage in a debate on the topic of "cats vs. dogs." Discuss the handout, starting with an outline for the debate. Each side will have 2 minutes for opening statements and 2 minutes for closing statements. The time period for open debate in the middle can be determined based on student numbers and class time, but 20 minutes is often a good minimum to start from.

3. Explain that students will need to formulate a thesis statement plus a minimum of three supporting arguments to support their team's position. Each member of the debate team is expected to contribute to both the debate preparation and the debate itself. Each team will also need to incorporate a certain number of words and phrases from the wordbank.

4. Call representatives from each team to the front for a coin toss. The team who wins gets to choose their side's position.

5. Allow students an appropriate amount of prep time. Circulate and offer feedback about students' arguments while they prepare. Encourage students to not only focus on supporting arguments, but also consider opposing arguments that the opposite side may use in response.

6. During the debate itself, be sure to only allow students who raise their hand to talk and allow the opposing side an opportunity for rebuttal afterward. Make strict use of a timer, and don't allow anyone to go over their allotted time.

7. Take notes and fill out the rubric during the debate to determine the winner. Use copies of the rubric that you made to record your assessment. Meanwhile, encourage students to look at their copies of the rubric to confirm that they are on target in meeting the activity's goals.

CAVEATS AND OPTIONS

1. The actual debate topic is somewhat arbitrary and can be replaced with something different if many of your students come from a culture where keeping dogs as pets is not common. Similar to the famous "Latke-Hamantash Debate" at the University of Chicago, the goal is to get students to engage in debate on a topic that may be silly and not require extensive research but still requires them to use complex debate strategies and appropriate academic vocabulary.

2. Prior to introducing this activity, it is helpful for students to have seen and discussed the process of debate in action so as to have a better frame of reference. TED (ted.com) contains several good examples of debates on a variety of topics that may serve as a good reference.

3. As an optional extension, you could have each team go around campus to interview students on the topic. They could then cite student responses in their arguments.

4. Length for both preparation and the debate itself may vary, but, generally, budget at least one class session for preparation plus one for the debate itself.

5. If you have an odd number of students in your class, you can also deputize one of the students to moderate with you.

6. Once your students have some debate experience under their belts, you can utilize this activity to explore more academically focused subjects, such as nuclear power, GMOs, and educational policy.

7. Though this activity was initially developed for college-level English to speakers of other languages students, it can easily be adapted for classes from Grades 6–12.

REFERENCES AND FURTHER READING

Academic Word List: www.victoria.ac.nz/lals/resources/academicwordlist

TED Talks (for examples of debates): ted.com

Circumlocution Challenge

Chanchal Singh and Sohani Gandhioke

Levels	*All*
Aims	*Find ways around difficult and unfamiliar words*
	Enhance fluency
	Practice speaking spontaneously
	Active listening
Class Time	*No set time*
Preparation Time	*None*
Resources	*One strip of paper per student*

During a conversation, English as a second/foreign language students are known to suddenly stop speaking because they are searching for the right word. Circumlocution Challenge is an activity to help students get around lexical gaps to overcome untranslatability or lack of vocabulary. They learn to describe the difficult word and give information until the listener understands what the speaker is trying to say, without stopping to use the dictionary or add fillers. Learners are compelled to use their knowledge of English and apply it with effective results, encouraging critical thinking on the part of the listener and creativity on the part of the speaker.

PROCEDURE

1. Introduce the activity. Explain circumlocution and this activity's focus on fluency.

2. Review the directions for the activity and share an example, such as the following:
   - Student A writes (but does not say) the word, "Trousers."
   - Students A and B meet.
   - Student A says, "Both men and women own it."
   - Student B responds, "Is it a vehicle?"
   - Student A says, "No, it isn't a vehicle. Men use it more than women."
   - Student B asks, "What does it do?"
   - Student A says, "It gives warmth."
   - . . . and so on, until . . .
   - Student B guesses the word and takes Student A's paper.

3. Encourage very attentive listening, because the students will exchange papers and explain their new word to a different classmate.

4. Direct each student to take a strip of paper, write a word on it, and fold it to cover the word. The student should know the word well enough to be able to describe it to a classmate.

5. Ask the students to mingle, find a classmate, and describe the word they have written.

6. After a student has correctly guessed the word or has given up, both students exchange their papers and find new classmates who will be their new partners. Students move from one student to another until the end of the activity or until the end of the time you have set.

7. Circulate to help students if they are stuck, assess progress, help with pronunciation, and so on.

CAVEATS AND OPTIONS

1. This activity may be modified for all levels, based on the difficulty of the vocabulary.

2. Tell students to describe the word in two to four turns. The description should not be so easy that students can guess the word from the first try and it should not be so difficult that students need more than four tries to correctly guess the word.

3. In larger classes, students could get into groups and think of challenging words to describe to another group.

4. To continue this activity further, at the end of the activity, ask the students which word they felt was the most difficult and how they overcame the challenge. A longer impromptu class discussion could be sparked.

5. Each student could write their words on the board. The teacher could then randomly ask the students their opinion about the new words and their usage. This provides an opportunity to correct pronunciation and grammar with the class.

6. The activity could be presented as a game in which scores are kept, adding an element of fun and competition.

Confidence Day

Riah Werner

Levels	*Intermediate to advanced*
Aims	*Increase confidence*
	Minimize the fear of mistakes
Class Time	*10–15 minutes (plus 1–2 minutes per student)*
Preparation Time	*2 minutes*
Resources	*Ball*

Students often feel intimidated when speaking English in front of others, particularly in formal or academic settings. This shyness can lead to mumbling or unclear speech, which makes it even harder for listeners to understand a student's speech. When students speak clearly and at an appropriate volume, they are more likely to be understood. By declaring a "Confidence Day," teachers can encourage students to set aside their fear of mistakes and focus on confident communication.

PROCEDURE

1. In the previous class, tell your students that the next class will be "Confidence Day" and ask them to prepare a short speech of 1–2 minutes on a topic that is important to them. Explain that the focus of the next class will be on speaking confidently, so they do not need to worry about making mistakes. The focus is on being understood.

2. Begin the next class by reminding students that it is Confidence Day. Encourage them not to worry about any mistakes during that day's class.

3. Explain that not having confidence can make it harder to understand someone, even if they do not make any mistakes with their English. Demonstrate by slouching, mumbling and looking away from your students as you describe an important day in your life. Ask your students what you were talking about and if you made any mistakes. Students should not have been able to understand you clearly enough to answer these questions.

4. Stand with good posture, face your students and speak to them clearly on the same topic, but deliberately include a few grammatical errors. Ask your students what you were talking about. This time, they should be able to tell you. Ask them if you made any mistakes. Explain that speaking clearly and confidently makes it more likely that listeners can understand, even if there are grammar or vocabulary errors.

5. Ask students to describe the difference between the first and second stories. For each suggestion, show students an example and ask them to copy you, either by mirroring your body language or repeating a sentence after you.

6. Have students make two lines facing each other, with as much space between them as your classroom allows.

7. Standing in one line, throw a ball to a student in the opposite line, while saying the first line from your story. Ask that student to throw the ball to a different student across from them, while saying the first line of their speech or story. Throwing the ball while speaking should help students project their voices. If they are not loud or clear enough, ask the student who caught the ball to throw it back and have them try again. Continue until all students have thrown the ball and said their first line clearly.

8. Have students return to their seats. Ask one student to stand at the front and share their speech, focusing only on speaking clearly and confidently, without worrying about mistakes. Tell the other students that their job is to listen for the main idea. After each student's presentation, elicit the main idea from the listeners. Have each student present their speech, for 1–2 minutes. Remind them that if their classmates were able to tell them their main idea correctly, it meant that they were successful communicators, even if they made some mistakes.

CAVEATS AND OPTIONS

1. When choosing a topic for this activity, focus on themes that will instill pride in your students or encourage genuine communication. "The most important day in my life was . . ." or "My proudest achievement is . . ." are good starters.

2. This activity can be adapted for beginning learners as well. For beginners, ask them to use body language rather than verbal descriptions to demonstrate the difference between the first and second stories you modeled.

3. It can be useful to end the class with a discussion of how students felt during Confidence Day.

Solve My Problem!

Sasha Wajnryb

Levels	Pre-intermediate +
Aims	Develop fluency within the problem-solution context
Class Time	30 minutes
Preparation Time	None
Resources	None

The following activities provide valuable prompts for creating engaging lessons because learners are more likely to become engrossed in English language learning activities that are rooted in their own life experiences than in fabricated ones. In this activity, students brainstorm and discuss common problems that they face and offer solutions.

PROCEDURE

1. Elicit and brainstorm common problems that students face. Examples may include what to study, peer pressure, relationships, employment, financial pressures, becoming independent, or time management.

2. Discuss what types of people give the best advice and how their advice may differ. Examples may include parents, counselors, and agony aunt columns in newspapers and online.

3. Direct students to write their own problem(s) on a piece of paper. Encourage them to choose a problem that they are comfortable discussing with everyone in the class. They should be interested in hearing their classmates' solutions.

4. Students mix and mingle in pairs. Each student describes their own problem(s) and asks for suggestions on how to solve it/them.

5. Students offer solutions.

CAVEATS AND OPTIONS

1. Providing scaffolding through functional language to create controlled practice for describing problems and offering solutions is particularly useful for lower-level students.

   Examples
   - Describing problems: "I need some help . . . What should I do?"
   - Advice functions, including "If I were you, I'd [base verb]," "You should/could [base verb]," "[Verb + –*ing*] may help you to solve this issue."

2. Provide a letter-writing structure so students can write different types of letters (e.g., agony aunt letters, IELTS General Training Task 1).

3. Assign different roles (e.g., parent, friend, counselor) to each student. Students must give the type of advice that is appropriate to their role.

4. Turn this activity into a sequence of lessons. It can become a "thread" that is woven through the entire semester, creating continuity. It can be used as a conversation warmer each morning, with students solving a problem or two.

5. After mixing and mingling, students can give a short presentation and describe the best piece of advice they received.

6. Electronically savvy learners may enjoy completing the activity online. Some classes may be willing to create online groups (e.g., Facebook private groups or WhatsApp groups) where all members can see the problems and advice offered. This creates the opportunity for students to provide written feedback on their classmate's problem as well as critique the quality of advice offered by other classmates. Alternatively, students may record and send each other voicemail messages with advice via voice messaging services, such as WhatsApp.

7. Students can act out their problem in front of the class and have their classmates guess what the problem is.

Note: Some students may be reluctant to discuss personal problems. Discussion of these topics may be a trigger (particularly for those student cohorts from disadvantaged/ traumatic backgrounds). Your knowledge of the class is vital in determining whether this activity is appropriate. Careful monitoring of the class' brainstorming will ensure students choose problems that are appropriate for discussion. It is advised that you prepare a number of uncontroversial problems (e.g., my roommate is too noisy, I always oversleep) to distribute when required. In addition, you can encourage students to discuss problems that are experienced by many students, rather than a particular personal problem.

REFERENCES AND FURTHER READING

Lazar, G. (2006). Unit 6: Taking steps. Life is a journey. In *Meanings and metaphors* (pp. 23–25). Cambridge, United Kingdom: Cambridge University Press.

Wajnryb, R. (2003). *Stories: Narrative activities in the language classroom*. Cambridge, United Kingdom: Cambridge University Press.

Speak 1-2-3

Alice Llanos and Amy Tate

Levels	*Intermediate to advanced*
Aims	*Improve speaking quality, clarity, and confidence*
Class Time	*20–30 minutes*
Preparation Time	*2 minutes*
Resources	*Countdown timer*

Class discussions are lost opportunities when only one or two students speak and there is little meaningful feedback. Speak 1-2-3 takes discussion questions off the page and into a lively interchange where all students speak, offer feedback, and improve their responses. Students answer the same prompt three times, for three different listeners. The amount of time is decreased with each repetition. After speaking each time, the partners give helpful feedback, which the speakers incorporate into their next answer. This approach allows each speaker to find individual ways to improve. The repetition boosts speaker confidence and improves fluency and accuracy.

PROCEDURE

1. Provide an open-ended question or prompt.
2. Students stand in pairs around the room in a circle.
3. In each pair, designate a Student A (a speaker) and B (a reviewer).
4. In the first cycle, Student A responds to the prompt for the full time limit (1 minute).
5. Student B listens and then asks clarifying questions to help Student A improve their answer (1 minute).
6. All of the As rotate to a new Student B.
7. In the second cycle, Student A answers the prompt again for the new partner with a decreased amount of time (55 seconds). Student A incorporates the previous partner's feedback to make the response clearer and more concise.
8. Student B listens and then asks clarifying questions (55 seconds). All of the As rotate to a new Student B.
9. In the third and final cycle, Student A answers the prompt again (50 seconds).
10. Student B listens and then summarizes the response to Student A.

11. Student A confirms the accuracy of Student B's summary or discusses discrepancies.

12. Repeat the process with three cycles so all of the Bs are now speakers.

CAVEATS AND OPTIONS

1. Remind speakers to use the full amount of time to respond. Reviewers should wait to ask questions after the speaker finishes.

2. The countdown timer should be visible to students, so they can manage their time.

3. Clarifying questions will vary depending on the prompt and each speaker's individual needs. Reviewers can ask about unclear information, unfamiliar vocabulary, and mispronounced words. They can offer suggestions about adding or subtracting details and improving organization.

4. As a variation, speaking time can be increased with each repetition to encourage elaboration.

5. Students can be given a specific focus. It could be a grammatical form (e.g., past tense), specific vocabulary, or an aspect of pronunciation (e.g., linking). The speaker should use that focus and the reviewer should listen for it.

6. Textbook discussion questions and TOEFL or IELTS prompts work well. Students can also summarize a text or lecture with this activity.

Speed Debating

Gena Saldaña and Kisha C. Bryan

Levels	Intermediate to advanced
Aims	Improve fluency in speaking
	Practice listening skills
Class Time	Variable
Preparation Time	5 minutes
Resources	Timer
	Sample debates (available online)

Debating is a great way to help students become confident in their English language skills. In this activity, students practice supporting the same topic in four rounds. Similar to speed dating, students change partners with each round. They must also repeat their key points within a shorter time period. This activity supports students as they work to increase their speaking speed and to gain confidence.

PROCEDURE

1. Choose a topic that interests your students. See the References and Further Reading for websites with various debate topics. Consider class demographics when selecting topics.

2. Check background knowledge by asking students to define the term *debate*. Explain what a debate is and why people debate certain topics. Ask them about topics that people have debated in their countries/cultures. Discuss the importance of an *opening statement* and *supporting arguments*.

3. Examine the structure of a debate by viewing a demonstration as an example. Watch video clips or attend a debate and discuss its structure in class.

4. Introduce the topic of the debate and verify that students understand it.

5. Arrange desks so they are facing each other, arranged in two rows for each pair of students. Assign each student as "For" or "Against" the topic. This may be done in advance or on the spot using your specific method for randomly selecting students for activities.

6. Allow each group to sit together for 5–10 minutes to discuss their side of the argument. Students may write important points on a small index card.

7. Ask all "For" students to sit on one side of the row of desks. Ask all "Against" students to sit across from the "For" students facing them. Pairs are now formed.

8. Set the timer for 5 minutes and begin Round 1. One student talks about their side of the argument. Then announce that the other student should begin speaking and set the timer for 5 minutes. Be sure that students have an opening statement that briefly outlines their position and at least three supporting arguments that support their case. Round 1 ends after 10 minutes.

9. Ask students to move to the next student. Let each side make their argument for 4 minutes. Round 2 lasts 8 minutes.

10. Ask students to rotate again. Each speaker gets 3 minutes. Round 3 lasts 6 minutes.

11. For the last time, ask students to rotate. Set the timer for 2 minutes. Round 4 lasts 4 minutes.

CAVEATS AND OPTIONS

1. Students can be given the topic the previous night for homework so that they can conduct research.

2. Lower proficiency students might be grouped together or with higher proficiency students. Higher proficiency students might be grouped together and asked to take notes as they listen. When speaking, higher proficiency or advanced students may include more supporting arguments or details.

3. Consider having the students take turns recording each other during the debate session. They can then view their performance and concentrate on vocabulary, fluency, accuracy, and other aspects of speaking and listening.

REFERENCES AND FURTHER READING

These websites include debate topics:
- ProCon.org: www.procon.org/debate-topics.php
- Debate Motions Headquarters: www.debate-motions.info/best-debatable -topics/
- Debate.org: www.debate.org/big-issues/
- International Debate Education Association: idebate.org/debatabase

Visualizing Ideal Second Language Classmates

Yoshifumi Fukada, Joseph Falout, Tetsuya Fukuda, Tim Murphey

Levels	*High beginning to advanced*
Aims	*Create a better social classroom atmosphere*
	Develop fluency through interactive output
Class Time	*5–15 minutes (in two classes a week apart)*
Preparation Time	*5 minutes (first session), 15–20 minutes (second session)*
Resources	*Handout of the "Ideal Classmates Question" (optional; teacher created)*
	Handout of all students' comments, without student names (teacher created)

Visualizing a possible self or ideal self has become a mainstay classroom application of motivation theory, namely that of the second language motivational self system (Dörnyei, 2009). Although such visualizations can enhance motivation, Lockwood and Kunda (1999) caution that an over-focus on academic ideal selves can actually hinder motivation by preventing learners from visualizing even better possible selves that could be inspired by others as role models. This activity helps students to visualize possible ideal others, specifically possible ideal classmates (Murphey, Falout, Fukuda, & Fukada, 2014; Murphey & Iswanti, 2014). These visualizations are shared across the classroom, possibly inspiring students to see greater potential in themselves to 1) help their classmates learn, 2) become near-peer role models (Murphey & Arao, 2001) for each other, and 3) co-construct a more socially sensitive learning environment within the language classroom.

PROCEDURE

1. In the beginning of the first or second lesson of the term, give students a question that promotes visualizing their ideal classmates. For example: *Please describe a group of classmates with whom you could learn English well. What would you all do to help each other learn better and more enjoyably?* The question can be given to the students on a handout or presented on a big screen in front of the classroom.

2. Students answer the question in words, phrases, or sentences, depending on their English language proficiency level.

3. Collect students' comments and put them on a handout, either through manually retyping their comments or copying them from an online platform. This concludes the first session.

4. In the second session, pass out (i.e., loop back) to the students the list of collected descriptions of their ideal classmates' images. Encourage them to think deeply about the ideas that they and their classmates had contributed, asking questions such as:

- Which descriptions are consistent with or different from your own?
- Which images do you think are important?
- Which ideas would you like to try in class today?
- What has helped you learn from your own classmates in the past?

5. Students form rotating pairs or small groups (three is good), and discuss their thoughts.

6. Ask students to summarize their discussions, asking them questions that might encourage them to apply what they have discussed to their subsequent participation in the classroom.

7. To continue fostering a supportive learning environment based on the students' own words, in the following lessons, encourage students to practice what they shared with each other (in earlier classes) as ways to learn better and more enjoyably together. Remind them from time to time that these ideas are their own.

CAVEATS AND OPTIONS

1. Students can describe their ideal second language classmate images through pictures, which they can share in rotating pairs or small groups. Also, students can lay out their pictures on a big table and take photographs of these using their smartphones. Additionally, you can collect these pictures and loop them back to the students, converting them into slideshow images and showing these on a big screen in front of the classroom.

2. Students can also make big posters of these ideas to hang in the classroom, or small prop-up posters to set on their tables. These posters can be made collaboratively in small groups that select the most important features of how to help each other learn better and more enjoyably. It is best if these posters are decorative and made with artistic creativity, furthering their ownership of and emphasizing the value of these ideas of ideal classmates.

REFERENCES AND FURTHER READING

Dörnyei, Z. (2009). The L2 motivational self system. In Z. Dörnyei & E. Ushioda (Eds.), *Motivation, language identity and the L2 self* (pp. 9–42). Bristol, England: Multilingual Matters.

Lockwood, P., & Kunda, Z. (1999). Increasing the salience of one's best selves can undermine inspiration by outstanding role models. *Journal of Personality and Social Psychology, 76*(2), 214–228.

Murphey, T., & Arao, H. (2001). Reported belief changes through near-peer role modeling. *TESL-EJ, 5*(3), 1–15.

Murphey, T., Falout, J., Fukuda, T., & Fukada, Y. (2014). Socio-dynamic motivating through idealizing classmates. *System*, *45*, 242–253.

Murphey, T., & Iswanti, S. (2014). Surprising humanity! Comparing ideal classmates in two countries. *ETAS Journal*, *31*(2), 33–35.

Five Points of Contact

Jason Hendryx

Levels	*Intermediate to advanced*
Aims	*Use past and future forms of language*
	Share and validate local cultures and customs
	Consider lifetime changes in value systems
Class Time	*Variable*
Preparation Time	*None*
Resources	*None*

Having students discuss a single concept from multiple points of contact across a lifetime allows them to use past and future forms of language. It provides students with the opportunity to consider the possible changes that could occur in one's value systems over time. This activity also makes it possible for local cultures and customs to be shared and validated in the target language, potentially making the target language more familiar.

PROCEDURE

1. On the board, draw a circle large enough to put a word in the center.
2. At the 2, 5, 7, 9, and 11 o'clock positions of this first circle, draw smaller circles (five in total). In a clockwise order starting at 2 o'clock, the smaller circles represent 1) just after birth, 2) entering high school, 3) starting a career, 4) retirement, and 5) a moment before death.
3. In the center of the larger circle, write a major theme/concept you would like students to explore. Examples include money, friendship, love, family, education, and success.
4. Divide students into five equal groups. Each group will discuss and report back to the class about the particular point of contact they are assigned. For example, the group assigned the first circle for the topic of money would discuss what money means to a newborn baby.

CAVEATS AND OPTIONS

1. Students at the intermediate level may find generating responses for the first (just after birth) and last (just before death) contact circles difficult to comment on. If that is the case, change those points of contact to 1) entering school/kindergarten and 5) going to a retirement home/starting assisted living.

2. For more advanced students, each group can be held responsible for reporting back on each of the five watershed moments.

3. This speaking activity could easily be employed as part of a weekly routine; it can link to and further support current subject matter, core content materials, or other topics.

REFERENCES AND FURTHER READING

Folse, K. S. (1996). *Discussion starters: Speaking fluency activities for advanced ESL/EFL students.* Ann Arbor, MI: University of Michigan.

Klippel, F. (1984). *Keep talking: Communicative fluency activities for language teaching.* Cambridge, United Kingdom: Cambridge University Press.

Ur, P. (1981). *Discussions that work: Task-centred fluency practice.* Cambridge, UK: Cambridge University Press.

Getting the Hang of Group Discussions

Melinda Sayavedra

Levels	*Intermediate to advanced*
Aims	*Practice various roles and useful phrases for group discussions*
Class Time	*Variable*
Preparation Time	*None*
Resources	*Handout (Appendixes A–C)*

Professors and instructors of mainstream content courses often express frustration that English language learners do not participate in group discussions effectively, if at all. It can be helpful to have our students practice discussions in our classes, using specific phrases and experimenting with various roles. By giving them this experience, they may become more comfortable participating in discussions in mainstream content courses.

PROCEDURE

1. Give each student a handout of "Useful Phrases for Group Discussion" (Appendix A).
2. Go over the phrases to clarify meaning as needed. Have students listen and repeat your words so they know where to put stress and use the appropriate pitch, intonation, and tone.
3. Put students into groups of four or five.
4. Hand each person in the group one strip of paper with a role/task (Appendix B). If working in groups of 4, omit a role or combine two roles so that one person will do both.
5. In each group, assign one person the role of group facilitator. Give the facilitator the list of discussion questions (Appendix C). The facilitator gets the task to start and end the conversation and decides which question will be discussed.
6. The facilitator reads the question, makes sure everyone understands it, and gives the group a little time to think about the language they will need to fulfill their task, as well as to get ideas about the topic for discussion.
7. When ready, the facilitator begins the conversation.
8. When the discussion winds down, the facilitator ends the conversation using a phrase to wrap it up. (A phrase may be selected from the handout, "Useful Phrases for Group Discussion.")

9. Students pass their role/task strip of paper clockwise so that each person has a new role. The new facilitator will choose a question for discussion, and proceed as before.

10. Continue to change roles until everyone has had a chance to try each role.

CAVEATS AND OPTIONS

1. Students can help one another fulfill their task as needed. With each new discussion, students get more comfortable in assuming their role without help.

2. Discussion topics can be about anything and written for lower or higher levels of language proficiency, as long as the questions are open ended with possibilities for a variety of ideas and opinions. Consider the needs and interests of your students when selecting topics.

3. Discussion phrases can be simplified, or fewer options presented, to differentiate for students with a lower level of proficiency.

4. Students can practice this at various times throughout the term.

5. When students feel comfortable participating in classroom discussions, native and/or fluent speakers of English can be invited in to participate. Roles/tasks would not be used, allowing the students the opportunity to assume these roles as needed.

6. Having students self-assess their skills at fulfilling these roles can help deepen their learning. Which ones are they comfortable with? Which ones do they need more practice with? How is discussion with their classmates different from discussion with native or fluent speakers of English? Did they pick up any new, useful expressions while having a discussion with native speakers?

Hot Air Balloon

Anna Forehand

Levels	*Intermediate to advanced*
Aims	*Develop fluency*
	Learn the strategy of preparation to improve fluency
Class Time	*30 minutes–1 hour*
Preparation Time	*None*
Resources	*None*

This is a fun group work activity that can be used within the topic of jobs/work or adapted for other topics. It allows students to practice fluency through the strategy of preparation. Students are motivated to speak because there is a true communicative purpose and they have more confidence owing to the preparation stage.

PROCEDURE

1. Tell students what your dream job is and discuss the meaning of *dream job*.

2. Ask your students what their dream jobs are.

3. Ask students to tell you why your dream job is useful/important. Write a list of responses on the board.

4. In pairs, students help each other make a list of reasons why their dream job is useful/important. Each student writes a list in their notebook.

5. Go around the classroom helping students as necessary.

6. Draw a hot air balloon on the board. Teach the meaning of *hot air balloon*.

7. Tell students they are all on a hot air balloon. There is enough room for all but one person. They have to choose one student to throw out of the balloon; otherwise, all will die.

8. Each student gives a speech about why their job is important. They may use their notes. Each student's goal is to convince his or her fellow travelers that he or she should stay on the balloon.

9. At the end, students have a discussion and then vote to choose one person with the least important job to throw out of the balloon.

CAVEATS AND OPTIONS

1. Students can be given a time limit for their talk.

2. In a large class, students can be divided into two or three groups, each having their own hot air balloon.

3. Students can do more formal and structured presentations as part of this activity.

4. Listen to students while they talk and note examples of correct and incorrect use of English. Provide feedback on accuracy at the end.

5. Have a reflection stage at the end and discuss whether the preparation stage helped students speak more fluently and confidently. Discuss how they can use this strategy in the future in other situations and contexts.

Instructional Conversation

Lynne Diaz-Rico

Levels	*High beginner to advanced; Grades 5–12 and adult*
Aims	*Practice impromptu speaking and active listening*
Class Time	*≈ 20 minutes per conversation*
Preparation Time	*5 minutes*
Resources	*Timer or clock*
	Handouts (Appendixes A and B)

The instructional conversation stimulates authentic oral interaction in the language classroom, featuring six to eight participants, who sit in a circle to discuss a shared prior reading, and a "thinker-leader," who facilitates the discussion. The classroom teacher is usually the thinker-leader. However, if the students are adults with at least intermediate English fluency, they may serve as thinker-leaders.

The instructional conversation contains five instructional elements (thematic focus, activation and use of background knowledge, direct teaching, promotion of more complex expression, and elicitation of bases for statements or positions) and five conversational elements (open-ended format; being responsive to participant contributions; promotion of rich discussion; use of connected discourse; and general participation, including self-selected turns). The prompt for discussion in this activity is "Should Lincoln Have Lied?" (based on Soto, 2003).

PROCEDURE

1. Students are seated in a circle, accompanied by the thinker-leader. Each receives a copy of the prompt (Appendix A) and the handout, "Get Your Turn" (Appendix B).

2. The thinker-leader states the following: "We will be discussing a situation in which there are no right or wrong answers. If you want to talk, use the ways that we'll go over from the 'Get Your Turn' sheet. We'll all read the prompt silently, and then I'll read the prompt aloud. If there are any unknown words, let me know."

3. The thinker-leader reviews "Get Your Turn." Students read the prompt silently. Then, the thinker-leader reads the story aloud; if there are any unknown words, the thinker-leader pronounces each word correctly and gives a brief definition.

4. The thinker-leader begins by asking, "So . . . what's your opinion about . . ." and paraphrases the question or dilemma at the end of the prompt.

5. Students discuss. The thinker-leader does not restate, rephrase, or comment unless it becomes evident that there is some misunderstanding on the part of other participants, but verbally or nonverbally encourages others to talk without calling on any one person.

6. Discussion on the same aspect of the topic continues until students' participation begins to wane. Then, rather than volunteering a new topic, the thinker-leader may return to a previous idea and ask the one who ventured the idea to elaborate.

7. Participants continue to discuss the topic; various themes may emerge that evince deeper thinking. It is not necessary that the prompt be "solved," but rather that the situation be thoroughly discussed.

8. To end the discussion (after about 20 minutes), the thinker-leader summarizes the various points that were made and thanks the participants.

CAVEATS AND OPTIONS

1. The circle of chairs should be small enough that everyone can be heard. The thinker-leader should resist "revoicing" anyone's input.

2. The thinker-leader should not introduce a new topic when members of the group fall silent. If necessary, a participant's prior idea may be reintroduced and explored.

3. For larger classes, classroom volunteers trained as thinker-leaders may hold other circles simultaneously.

4. The prompts are meant to build on prior class reading, but may also be built from "codes" (see Freire's critical pedagogy in Wink, 2004) that reflect class members' concerns.

REFERENCES AND FURTHER READING

Soto, G. (2003). *Pacific crossing*. New York, NY: Houghton Mifflin Harcourt.

Tharp, R. G., & Gallimore, R. (1991). *Teaching and learning in social activity*. Santa Cruz, CA: National Center for Research in Cultural Diversity and Second Language Learning.

Wink, J. (2004). *Critical pedagogy: Notes from the real world* (3rd ed.). Boston, MA: Allyn & Bacon.

APPENDIX A: *"Should Lincoln Have Lied?"*

(Prompt from *Pacific Crossing* [Soto, 2003, Ch. 9])

Should Lincoln Have Lied?

When Lincoln Mendoza was staying with a family in Japan during his 8th-grade study abroad visit, his mother wrote him a letter to fill him in on happenings at home and to tell him that she missed him. Seeing that his Japanese homestay parents, Mr. and Mrs. Ono, were curious about the contents of the letter, Lincoln lies and reads aloud sentences about home that aren't in the letter, including flattering comments about himself. The homestay parents were impressed with his mother's letter and her pride in, and affection for, her son. Should Lincoln have lied about what was in the letter?

APPENDIX B: *Get Your Turn*

Get Your Turn

Even when you have something to say, it is sometimes hard to get a turn in a conversation.

Two ways to get a turn: Non-verbal and Verbal

Non-verbal

> Make eye contact with the current speaker.
>
> Lean forward as if you will be next.
>
> Interrupt in a small way and then stop.
>
> Be ready to start your turn at the slightest pause.

Verbal

> When your idea is <u>connected</u> to the current speaker:
>
> > . . . I'd like to add to that . . .
> >
> > . . . Oh, yes, and besides . . .
> >
> > . . . Well, I see it like this . . .
>
> When your idea has <u>no connection</u> to the current one:
>
> > . . . Here's a different idea.
> >
> > . . . Going back to what _____ said,
> >
> > . . . Changing the topic somewhat, I'd like to mention . . .

News Groups

Frances A. Boyd

Levels	*Intermediate +*
Aims	*Build skills in giving an oral summary*
	Promote collaboration and learner autonomy
	Develop the practice of following and reflecting on the news
Class Time	*30–45 minutes per week (3–6 weeks)*
Preparation Time	*5–10 minutes*
Resources	*Handout (Appendix)*

In weekly news groups, groups of three students choose a newspaper article of mutual interest, read and take notes on it outside of class, and deliver oral summaries to each other in class, drawing a clear distinction between fact and opinion. This activity design frees the teacher to listen in and give feedback on speaking. Using at- or below-level news sources, students grow in confidence and fluency. They take responsibility for choosing interesting articles in the topic of their choice: in the arts, business, fashion, food, health, politics, science, sports, and so on. Also, they develop and enjoy the educated person's practice of following the news.

PROCEDURE

Before the First News Group Day

1. Lead a discussion on students' current news habits and sources and the value of following the news. Explain the aims of the News Group activity.

2. Divide the class into groups of three. Direct each group to scan a level-appropriate newspaper you provide to select an article of interest.

3. Pass out a set of role sheets to each group (Appendix). Have each student choose a role: Reporter, Commentator, or Language Maven. Explain that they will read and take notes on the role sheets at home. In addition, explain that they will deliver oral summaries in class, once a week, rotating roles each week.

On News Group Day

4. Have students use their completed role sheets to give an oral summary to their group. Sit in with one group at a time, listening without interrupting and taking feedback notes for whoever is speaking. When the speaker finishes, give feedback so that all in the group can hear, then move on to another group. Feedback can include oral error correction and commentary on language skills

(pronunciation, vocabulary, grammar) as well as oral summary skills (selection of main points, paraphrasing, eye contact, pacing/pausing).

5. Collect the role sheets at the end of the News Group activity. In the next class, pass them back with corrections and guidance.

6. After the third News Group session, regroup the students to create new interest. Continue rotation of roles each week.

CAVEATS AND OPTIONS

1. On News Group day, visually check role sheets to make sure students come to class fully prepared.

2. Choose newspapers that are *at* or *slightly below* the general reading level of the students. Here are some examples along with the level in the CEFR system: *News for You* for intermediate (B1.1); *USA Today* for high-intermediate (B1.2); *New York Times* for advanced/high-advanced (B2-C1).

3. Newspapers can be read online. However, there is more interaction when students spread them out all over the desks, scan for articles of interest, and offer suggestions within each group. Newspapers with multiple separate sections can serve several groups.

4. Add a second chance. After all speakers have given their oral summaries, ask the News Reporters to move clockwise to another group. If they have gotten feedback, remind them to apply it in this second oral summary. Encourage questions for clarification.

5. Add reflection. After several weeks of News Group, have students discuss and/or write down answers to such questions as: How is your oral summary skill? Why do you say that? What would you like to change about the News Group activity?

6. Add a culminating presentation. Assign either a prepared or impromptu presentation as an ending activity. In pairs, students select an article, take notes, and present their oral summaries to the class (News Reporter and News Commentator only). Audio or video record to give additional feedback and have students self-assess.

7. Once students have mastered the basic activity, you can experiment with many variations, such as moving Reporters to different groups, encouraging discussion in small or large groups, switching group members, and varying news sources.

Parody Talent Show

Phil Smith

Levels	**High intermediate to low advanced**
Aims	**Practice creativity with English**
	Develop proficiency with meter and rhyme
Class Time	**45 minutes–1 hour**
Preparation Time	**10 minutes**
Resources	**Example of a song and its parody**
	Lyrics handout (teacher created)
	YouTube videos

In this activity, students create a parody of a popular song, writing their own set of alternative lyrics. Parody is a fun and easy way to get students to flex their creative minds while also giving them practice with syllabic stress, meter, and rhyme. Because students use the original song as a framework to create their own lyrics, writing becomes a much easier process. Often, parodies have a silly or mocking tone, but this isn't necessary. Musical activities are engaging and parody is inherently humorous, so this activity should be light hearted.

PROCEDURE

1. Explain the meaning of *parody*.

2. Create a handout with the lyrics from both the original and the parody of a popular song, and provide this to students. One example is "Hello" by Adele and its parody "Hella Cravings" by Dustin & Genevieve (see References and Further Reading).

3. List three to five current popular songs and have the students vote on which one they want to parody as a class. Each song should be easy to stream on YouTube and should also have a karaoke (instrumental) version. Play snippets of the songs before initiating the voting process.

4. Brainstorm parody topics as a class, such as a date gone wrong or a fun summer day. Agree as a class on a topic to use as a theme for the parody.

5. Divide the students into groups of three or four and assign each group to a verse or chorus.

6. Listen to the full song. While students are listening, they should brainstorm lyrics individually.

7. Have the members of each group come together for 20–30 minutes and work on their lyric ideas until they complete a full section of the song.

8. Have all of the groups perform their parody sections in the order they appear in the song. For extra fun, put on the instrumental karaoke track!

CAVEATS AND OPTIONS

1. Shy students may work up some anxiety about performing in front of the class. Some students may also not want to sing. This could be resolved by not requiring the entire group to perform and/or allowing students to speak rather than sing their lyrics.

2. Students may disagree about which lines to use in the final draft. In this case, the teacher can facilitate an agreement.

3. A good resource for lesson materials is "Weird Al" Yankovic, who is famous for his parodies of popular songs.

4. For younger learners who might not be familiar with popular music, nursery rhymes provide great source material.

5. For less advanced learners, word banks can be provided to guide the students toward finishing the task.

6. If you want to integrate current class content, you can restrict the topic of the parody to the material being covered elsewhere. For example, if the class is currently doing a unit about a particular book, require the parody to be relevant to that topic.

REFERENCES AND FURTHER READING

"Hello," by Adele: www.youtube.com/watch?v=YQHsXMglC9A

"Hella Cravings," by Dustin & Genevieve: www.youtube.com/watch?v=lQ6-n CLeDsI

Survive

Alex Blumenstock

Levels	*Intermediate to advanced*
Aims	*Practicing agreement and disagreement*
Class Time	*40 minutes–1 hour*
Preparation Time	*None*
Resources	*Handout (Appendix)*
	List of example survival situations (optional)

Students need to practice agreeing and disagreeing in order to communicate effectively. This activity practices these skills by encouraging creativity in exciting hypothetical survival situations. Students should be encouraged to focus on fluency rather than accuracy, as this activity should reinforce agreement language from previous lessons.

PROCEDURE

1. Elicit interest and engage students with a question such as, "If I see a bear in the woods, what should I do?" Inform students that they will be discussing survival situations.

2. Brainstorm a list of survival situations on the board or provide a list for the students to choose from later. A few examples include being on a sinking ship, a zombie attack during class, being stranded on a desert island, being locked inside a store after closing, getting lost in the forest, and being at a restaurant without access to money.

3. Divide the class into groups of three to five students. Assign each group a different situation and provide them with the "Language for Expressing Opinions, Agreement, and Disagreement" handout (Appendix). Tell students to use this language during their discussion.

4. Tell students that each group will create a list of options and outcomes for their situation. On one sheet of paper, the group copies the situation and writes a list of at least four options. On a separate sheet of paper, the group writes a different outcome for each option they created. At least two outcomes should be negative, and one outcome should be very favorable or "correct."

5. If desired, model agreeing and disagreeing language for use during the process of creating options and outcomes.

6. After each group completes both sheets of paper (listing options and outcomes), collect the papers with the outcomes and keep these for later.

7. Direct the class to exchange their group's paper with the situations and options with another group's paper.

8. Each group must consider and debate the options the other group provided until the group can agree on one option as the best choice.

9. Record each group's selected one best option, but don't reveal the outcomes yet—the option that was decided to be the best by the original group. After a few minutes, rotate the papers containing the situation and options to new groups.

10. Continue this process until each group has read and discussed the work of all of the other groups and chosen an option for each situation.

11. Reveal the outcomes for each option. This determines which group chose the option with the best outcome as decided by the authoring group.

CAVEATS AND OPTIONS

1. A timer may simulate the urgency of action required in a survival situation, keep the progress of the groups synchronized, and promote greater fluency as students are thus required to speed up their discussions.

2. The activity is suitable for reinforcing conditional statements because each option requires a conditional statement to describe the outcome.

3. Encourage students to disagree with each other. It may be helpful to assign a role of "always disagrees" to a student from each group or require that students rotate the responsibility of disagreeing within their groups.

4. In some groups, it may be worthwhile to encourage them to attempt to create options to a given situation that seem like good options but actually lead to unexpected or poor outcomes. For example, when facing a bear, students could choose to fight the bear, and the outcome is that the bear is knocked unconscious because of a strong punch. The knowledge students have about each other can help them to guess when these sorts of outcomes are likely to occur, and discussing unexpected outcomes increases engagement.

5. This activity can be shortened or adapted into a warm-up activity if t you prepare situations, options, and outcomes without student input.

APPENDIX: *Language for Expressing Opinions, Agreement, and Disagreement*

Opinions

1. I think (that) _____   2. I feel (that) _____   3. In my opinion, _____

Agreement

1. I agree.   2. I completely agree.   3. Sure!   4. Exactly!

Disagreement

1. Good point, but . . .   2. Good idea, but . . .   3. True, but . . .

4. Sure, but . . .   5. I understand, but . . .   6. I agree, but . . .

7. But don't you think . . .   8. But maybe . . .   9. But perhaps . . .

10. But on the other hand . . .   11. But what about . . .

12. Shouldn't we consider that . . .   13. I disagree. We should . . .

14. I'm afraid I don't agree.

English or Englishes?

Andy Halvorsen

Levels	*Intermediate +*
Aims	*Raise awareness of the value and diversity of global Englishes*
Class Time	*50 minutes*
Preparation Time	*5–15 minutes to print/prepare the role cards plus time to review the activity's steps*
Resources	*Handout (Appendix)*
	Index cards (optional)
	Computer with projector (optional)

Many English as a second or foreign language students prefer studying the "correct" English of native speakers of certain preferred dialects. However, the vast majority of English in use around the world in the 21st century is between nonnative speakers of the language. This activity is designed to use small-group discussions and role-plays to help raise students' awareness of the various global Englishes in use today and to help break down possible negative associations students may have with the English of nonnative speakers.

PROCEDURE

1. As a warm-up, divide students into small groups of three to four. Ask each group to list on paper all the varieties of English they are aware of. A member from each group should go to the board and write at least two varieties of English from their list.

2. Review the list on the board, noting to students whether nonnative speaker varieties have been included. Put the following questions on the board for each group to discuss and guess the correct answer.

   a. How many native speakers of English are there in the world? ($\approx$ 350 million)

   b. Which country has the most native speakers of English? (United States)

   c. How many nonnative speakers of English are there in the world? ($\approx$ 1 billion)

3. Explain to students that today they will be role-playing in groups, and each group member will receive a role to play. They will have the experience of being a native or nonnative speaker of English or a person responding to those speakers.

4. Model the role-play with a group of two to three students. Hand out the appropriate roles (Appendix) for each student. While modeling, demonstrate by taking the role of either the native or nonnative speaker and have students play other roles. Enter the role-play and have students respond following their role cards.

5. Continue the role-play activity as modeled. In each student group there should be one student in the native-speaker role, one student in the nonnative speaker role, and one student in the responder role. In a group of four, use both responder cards.

6. Allow role-plays to continue for several minutes, and then ask students to switch role cards and continue. Make sure each student has a chance to play either the native speaker or nonnative-speaker role.

7. Conduct a small group discussion to debrief after the role-play is completed. Ask each group to discuss these questions and be prepared to share.

   a. How did you feel as the native or nonnative speaker?

   b. How does this role-play connect to the real world?

   c. Most English users in the world are nonnative speakers of the language. How can schools help students improve their ability to communicate with nonnative speakers of English?

8. Allow for class sharing and discussion. As a conclusion, remind students that all varieties of English should be equally valued and respected in society.

CAVEATS AND OPTIONS

1. This activity works in a low-resource context with only a chalkboard as a tool, but it can be enhanced through supplemental online materials, such as short video clips of various varieties of English and websites summarizing the number of native and nonnative speakers of English.

2. This is a fluency activity that is designed to also develop students' critical awareness of complex issues in sociolinguistics. Be prepared for students to have diverse opinions on the topic. Remind students to be sensitive when they are participating in the role-play activity and to avoid acting in a stereotypical way.

3. The roles listed in the Appendix can be adapted for different cultural circumstances. Use behaviors, words, and actions that make sense locally. Add other behaviors as needed.

4. The activity is primarily group focused, so it works with a class size of between four and approximately 40 (10 groups of four). For larger classes, you may need to limit the whole-class discussions and sharing.

APPENDIX

Native Speaker Card 1

Your Role: You are a native speaker of British English.

Your Task: Enter the group and introduce yourself as someone from London. Ask the group if they can give you some information about interesting local tourist sites.

Native Speaker Card 2

Your Role: You are a native speaker of Canadian English.

Your Task: Enter the group and introduce yourself as someone from Canada. Ask the group if they have any good recommendations for local restaurants.

Nonnative Speaker Card 1

Your Role: You are a nonnative speaker of English from Japan.

Your Task: Enter the group and introduce yourself as someone from Tokyo. Ask the group if they can give you some information about interesting local tourist sites.

Nonnative Speaker Card 2

Your Role: You are a nonnative speaker of English from Mexico.

Your Task: Enter the group and introduce yourself as someone from Mexico. Ask the group if they have any good recommendations for local restaurants.

Responder Card 1

Your Role:: You are going to respond to the speakers as described below.

Your Task: Participate in the conversation, following these guidelines.

If the speaker is a native speaker of English, then use very positive body language. Stand close, smile and laugh often, and encourage them to speak. Give them compliments. If the speaker is a nonnative speaker, then use uninterested body language. Do not make eye contact or smile. Generally show little interest.

Responder Card 2

Your Role: You are going to respond to the speakers as described below.

Your Task: Participate in the conversation, following these guidelines.

If the speaker is a native speaker of English, then act very interested and try to answer all of their questions. Ask lots of follow-up questions and encourage the conversation to continue. If the person is a nonnative speaker, then do the opposite. Respond with short answers and discourage real conversation.

Making Requests: Holiday Role-Play

Kimberly Flynn

Levels	*Intermediate*
Aims	*Practice making requests*
Class Time	*30–40 minutes*
Preparation Time	*10 minutes*
Resources	*Role-play cards (Appendix A)*
	Handout (optional; Appendix B)
	Photos of vocabulary items (online or printed)

This activity focuses on practicing requests during a holiday role-play. Students will be able to make requests to family members using correct grammar structures and vocabulary. The activity may focus on Thanksgiving or any other special day that brings people together in someone's home.

PROCEDURE

1. Begin with an introduction of common vocabulary, specifically concerning what people often do on that day and what they usually prepare to eat for dinner.

2. Practice new vocabulary by reviewing photos of each word and using it in a sentence.

3. Ask students how they can make requests if they want someone to do something for them.

4. Introduce the phrases "Can you . . . ," "Could you . . ." and "Please . . ." with examples. Direct students to use these expressions to make requests. Explain "Can you . . ." is the least formal and most commonly used for requests within families; however, "Could you . . ." or "Please . . ." are more polite and may be used when addressing older family members.

   • Can you . . . pick up the toys before dinner?

   • Could you . . . turn off the TV so we can get ready for dinner?

   • Please . . . help me set the table.

5. Tell students to make requests of one another using "Can you . . ." or "Please . . . ." After a classmate asks a question, they should respond with any of the following expressions or others they have previously learned:

   • Sure.

   • No problem.

   • Sorry, I can't right now because . . .

6. Model one or two example questions and responses with student volunteers.

7. Introduce the role-play by saying, "It is a special day and there is a lot to do! You will be in a group and everyone will be given a role. Student 1 will ask Student 2 (one of their family members) to do something for them. Student 2 will respond and ask Student 3 to do something. Student 3 will respond and make a request to Student 4, and finally Student 4 will respond and ask Student 1 to do something. Everyone must ask and answer at least one request. If there is still time after you have finished, everyone will choose a new role and make a different request. Remember to use the vocabulary we learned at the beginning of the class."

8. Break students into groups of four and let each one in the group choose a nametag assigning them a role (Appendix A). Allow them to act out their role-play for about 5 minutes before encouraging them to choose another role and try again.

CAVEATS AND OPTIONS

1. Some students may be reluctant to speak in a group, so monitor the groups as closely as possible to ensure all students are getting a chance to practice.

2. If students need more instruction or support, a handout can be provided (Appendix B).

3. More variety in grammar patterns could be taught, including a stronger emphasis on formality. The focus could also change from fluency to accuracy, by providing teacher-led review and practice at the activity's start and emphasizing that students should self-correct and help one another correctly make requests in their small groups.

4. Instead of only changing roles within a group, students could also change groups to get more practice with other students in the class.

5. If there is time after this activity, ask one or more groups to share their best or funniest role-play with the class.

6. Be aware of your students' emotional needs. For example, in a context where students are separated from their families, the characters in the role-play could be a group of friends.

Picture-Inspired Dialogues

Martha Raab

Levels	*Intermediate to advanced*
Aims	*Develop speaking fluency*
Class Time	*30–45 minutes*
Preparation Time	*0–10 minutes*
Resources	*Photographs of people*

This is a fun activity to encourage creativity and get students talking to one another. Using actual photographs helps students "set the scene," and including celebrities generates interest and inspires humor. The focus here is on the process rather than the product. Students need to speak with their partner to create their dialogue!

It's helpful to keep a stack of pictures on hand for various types of activities; these can be accumulated from magazines and other sources over time, or in a few minutes during prep time. Alternatively, if students have smartphones, they can choose one of their own pictures or do a quick internet image search of their favorite celebrity.

PROCEDURE

1. Direct students to get into groups of two or three. Have each group select two to three photographs (corresponding to the number of group members). These will be the characters in their dialogues.

2. Have each group decide on the following:
   - The names of the characters
   - The characters' relationship(s)
   - A problem the characters are having

3. Give students time to write a dialogue discussing the characters' problem and resolving it. When they finish their dialogue, each student will select a character and practice performing the scene.

4. When everyone is prepared, each group performs their dialogue for the rest of the class.

CAVEATS AND OPTIONS

1. Although the dialogues are typically quite entertaining and performing them has its benefits, in large classes, performing the scenes can be time consuming as well as detract from the primary goal of the activity—getting speaking practice

through negotiating the content of the dialogue. The dialogues can be presented to the class as time permits or until students begin to lose interest.

2. This activity can easily be adjusted to target a particular skill. For example, a situation/setting can be selected that would necessitate a particular grammar structure, target vocabulary words can be required, or students can be asked to focus on pronunciation or other areas.

3. For higher level learners or students who need more structure, a minimum number of turns per character can be required.

4. For an extra challenge or to add variety, students can trade pictures and papers with another group after Step 2 so that they are working with a scenario that the other group produced.

Talk Show Role-Play

Katherine Miller

Levels	*Intermediate to advanced*
Aims	*Practice impromptu speaking while responding to literature*
Class Time	*Variable*
Preparation Time	*None*
Resources	*Index cards*
	Prop for use as a microphone (e.g., ruler or marker)

Talk Show is a variation on the hot seat activity used as a reading strategy to encourage higher order thinking in response to a text. In this activity, students develop speaking fluency by performing an unscripted role-play assuming the identities of the characters from a story or novel they have read. Characters are introduced "to the stage" and audience members ask the group prewritten and impromptu questions. The students participating in the role-play answer these questions, demonstrating the characters' traits and motivations. They make inferences as to what the characters are thinking and feeling when asked about specific moments in the story. Besides checking students' literal comprehension of the text, this activity lets them evaluate what they've read and demonstrate their inferential understanding as it connects to literary elements including character, plot, conflict, and theme.

PROCEDURE

1. Write the names of the main characters from the story on the board. Give each student an index card and tell them, "On your index cards, write three questions that you would ask the characters in the story if you could speak to them." Circulate to make sure the questions are appropriate.

2. Arrange five desks in the front of the room.

3. Tell the students that they will complete a practice activity focusing on fluency and their understanding of what they have been reading. They will play the roles of the different characters.

4. Ask for a volunteer who wants to speak first in front of the class.

5. Announce the show: "Live from our studio, it's Talk Time! Today's topic is *Name of Story*, and we have some special guests waiting backstage to talk about their experiences!" Use a ruler or marker for a prop microphone.

6. Welcome the first volunteer to sit at the front ("Ladies and gentlemen, please welcome *Character's Name*!") and ask them a couple of warm-up questions to model for the students in "the audience."

7. Have audience members take turns asking the "character" their prewritten questions or others that come to mind based on the discussion. Circulate around the room to get to students who raise their hand with a question, and hold the prop microphone toward them to speak into.

8. Ask for another volunteer ("Who wants to be *Character's Mother*?") and then announce them: "We have another special guest waiting backstage who has been listening to the show. Please welcome *Character's Mother, New Character!*"

9. Performers stay "on stage" as you introduce successive characters and the audience continues to ask questions. Characters should also ask each other questions in addition to responding to the audience.

CAVEATS AND OPTIONS

1. Encourage audience interjections throughout the role-play. For example, have them boo when you introduce the villain to the stage, or have them say "Aww!" when a character declares their love.

2. As you host the show, encourage more elaborate answers from guests by asking follow-up questions such as, "Why?" Audience members can also ask follow-up questions as the discussion unfolds.

3. Have fun with the microphone prop. If you have a particularly capable student, have them take over the hosting duties.

4. If a character answers a question incorrectly or doesn't know an answer, ask the audience to clarify or help them out.

5. If students are shy to volunteer, they can usually playfully goad one another into taking the stage. Or you can ask or randomly choose a student, depending on how well you know your class. If a student is too uncomfortable with being at the front, you can jump in to play the character and have the student hold the microphone for the audience members.

6. You can choose one student to be the "camera operator" and mime filming the show with another prop. Students with cell phone cameras might start recording the activity if they are having fun. Be aware of your school district's policies concerning student privacy and digital recording. Do not allow students to record and share videos if the participants have not consented to this.

What Are You Going to Do?

Janine Berger

Levels	Beginner to intermediate
Aims	Develop fluency by performing without a script
	Practice making predictions based on present evidence using going to
Class Time	1 hour
Preparation Time	None
Resources	None

A key element of emotional intelligence is learning to interpret body language. In a class of learners of diverse nationalities and cultural backgrounds, the task becomes doubly challenging because often gestures or facial expressions that have one meaning in one place have a completely different meaning in another. This game allows players to explore those differences.

PROCEDURE

1. Students work in pairs to write two or three descriptions of different physical positions, such as:
   - Sit with your head in your hands.
   - Stand with both arms up.
   - Stand with one foot forward and your head down.

2. Collect these and randomly hand them out so that each student has a paper with a description of a position on it.

3. Students work in groups of two or three (either the same groups as before or different, as they wish). With their given positions as a starting point, the group prepares a short scene. They do not need to write anything or memorize a script. They simply plan more or less how the scene will go. The scene should not last longer than 1 minute.

4. The first group comes to the front of the class and assumes their positions.

5. The rest of the students predict what is going to happen in the scene, first by writing it down individually and then by volunteering their answers.

6. Say, "Go!" to allow the group to perform their scene.

7. The rest of the students watch the performance to see if their predictions were right, and if so, award themselves a point.

8. The next group performs, and so on until every group has had a turn.

9. For speaking, students act out their alternate endings for the class to spark discussion. For writing, students choose one of the scenes they watched and write an alternate ending.

CAVEATS AND OPTIONS

1. Students may need help in the first section with describing physical positions.

2. If students are struggling to use English while planning their scene, it might be preferable to ask them to focus on a specific theme that was recently studied in class. This supports them by giving them a topic with vocabulary words that they know.

3. When the audience writes down their predictions before the performing group begins, it might speed things along to have them write only notes, or limit them in some way, such as by allowing them to write a maximum of two sentences. This way, the group at the front won't have to hold their positions for too long.

4. If students act out the alternate endings, it may be helpful for the audience to write down a Venn diagram showing the similarities and differences between the original scene and the alternate ending. This allows them to check their comprehension before discussing the difference(s).

Bluff

Gordon Blaine West

Levels	High beginner to advanced
Aims	Increase fluency
	Practice making statements
Class Time	Variable
Preparation Time	5–10 minutes
Resources	Bluff cards (Appendix)

Many teachers are familiar with the "two truths and a lie" game, often used as an introductory activity wherein the teacher writes or says three statements about themselves and the students have to guess which two are true, and which is a lie.

This activity is an expansion of the concept behind that game. Bluff decenters the teacher from the activity and spreads the participation more evenly by shifting to a card game. Students then play in small groups where they may speak more and improve their fluency.

PROCEDURE

1. Break students into groups of five to six, depending on your class size.

2. Pass out the Bluff cards (Appendix). Give each player three "truth" cards and one "lie" card. The cards should be of exactly the same dimensions and not differentiated in any way.

3. The first player makes a statement and places one of their cards face down. The other players cannot see if it is a Truth or Lie card.

4. The game proceeds like this, with players taking turns around the table clockwise.

5. After someone makes their statement and places their card down, if another player feels that the statement was not true, they can call out "Bluff!" or "Lie!" and then the player who made the statement will have to turn over their card to show the table if it were true or not. If it was actually a Lie card and the statement was untrue, then that player will have to take back their own card and also all of the other cards on the table at that time.

6. After someone makes a statement that the others feel is true, they should not call out anything. The game just proceeds with the next player's turn. The card will remain on the table.

7. To win the game, the player must be the first person to get rid of all of their cards, both the Truth and Lie cards.

CAVEATS AND OPTIONS

1. Adjust the number of cards that each person starts with depending on how much time is allotted for the activity. If the game goes too long, declare that the winners will be those with the fewest remaining cards at the end of the current round.

2. This game may work better later in the term. After students know each other a bit more, they are better able to gauge which things might be true or not about their group members because they have had a chance to learn things about each other that might not have come up in earlier ice-breaker activities.

Countdown Timer Faceoff

Gordon Blaine West

Levels	*High beginner to advanced*
Aims	*Practice asking and answering questions*
Class Time	*Variable*
Preparation Time	*None*
Resources	*Timer (preferably one on which the time remaining can be hidden)*

Students often feel pressure when they are making English small talk outside of class settings. This game helps them to practice their fluency and adds urgency to help them deal better with pressure while asking and answering questions in English. The idea for this activity comes from a South Korean variety show, *Running Man*, where a contestant is able to play along despite having a fairly low level of Korean as a second language.

PROCEDURE

1. Break students into groups of five to six, depending on your class size.
2. Give students 5–10 minutes to brainstorm different questions that they can ask in English.
3. Have two teams face each other, standing in a line.
4. To start, one student will set the timer for any time between 30 seconds and 2 minutes. This should be a secret—only the one student who set the timer should know how long it is set for.
5. After setting the timer, the student should turn off the screen or cover the time so that no one can see the countdown.
6. The student asks a question to a person on a different team. After asking the question, the student hands the timer to the person they just asked the question to.
7. The student who was asked the question must answer as best as they can. They are not allowed to simply say, "I don't know." After answering, they can ask someone on a different team a new question. After asking the question, they hand the timer to the person they just asked the question to.
8. This continues; students pass the timer until it goes off. Whichever team is holding the timer when it goes off loses one point.

9. The first team to lose five points loses that round. The game continues in a round robin format, with the teams rotating until each has faced off against all of the other teams.

CAVEATS AND OPTIONS

1. The content should be chosen by the students, so that they are comfortable with the level of questions being asked and language being used. You may scaffold the questions by allowing them to have notecards with them while they play to help them think of questions quickly. You should also model the activity before playing.

2. To help ensure that all students are participating equally, you may need to establish rules so that each team member must ask and answer in sequence going down the line, so that each person must play.

3. You may also need to establish rules for teams so that they lose points if they do not make an honest attempt to answer the question. You may need to act as a referee for the first time they play.

Double or Nothing

Shantaya Ijya Rao

Levels	*All*
Aims	*Practice speaking and pronunciation*
Class Time	*20–35 minutes*
Preparation Time	*10–15 minutes*
Resources	*Game boards for each team (Appendixes A and B)*
	2 dice for each team
	10–15 place markers for each student
	Document camera (optional)

Double or Nothing is a versatile game that promotes dialogue, negotiation, discussion, recall, and fluency in pronunciation and speaking. It is designed to be an effective and fun review game for individual students to test their knowledge prior to an examination or just for fun in class. As students engage, they generally assist each other in answering the questions. Sometimes they play as a team, with all players assisting each other and no player ever missing a turn. Sometimes they play competitively, individually answering questions and missing a turn if the incorrect answer is given. Students build confidence in pronunciation and oral skills as they play.

PROCEDURE

1. Type questions into the boxes on the "Double or Nothing" game board template (Appendix A). Looking at the "Double or Nothing Sample Questions" may help in generating some ideas (Appendix B). Questions can be taken from one unit (as a review activity) or from several units (as a final exam review game) and can take many forms:

Examples

   a. True/False: The phonetic representation of "apple" is /ˈæpəl/. (pronunciation)

   b. Say the following word → /tʃɜˑtʃ/ (pronunciation)

   c. What is an appropriate response to the following statement? "My pet just died." (sociocultural competence)

   d. What is an appropriate response to the following statement? "I just won the lottery!" (sociocultural competence)

   e. Respond to the sentence, "I like apples," using agreement. (grammar)

2. Divide the class into teams of two, three, or four.

3. Give each team a game board (with questions), two dice, and place markers (10–15 place markers for each student). Give each student place markers that are the same color; this is important for scoring purposes. A team of four will receive place markers in four colors. All teams receive the same game board with the same questions.

4. Demonstrate the game with a document camera, if available. Roll both dice and find the dice roll on the game board. Explain the following rules/procedures.

    a. In the beginning, there will be two question options for each dice roll— except for when a student rolls a double, because doubles have only one question available.

    b. If the student does not roll a double, the student chooses one of the two question options they want to answer.

    c. If the student answers correctly, place their marker on the question.

    d. If another player rolls the same dice combination, but the questions have already been answered, that player must forfeit that turn. However, if one question is still available (of the two original options), they must answer it.

5. Continue the game until all questions have been answered correctly or until all questions have been attempted.

6. The winner is the student who answered the most questions (as shown by the highest number of place markers). Prizes for the winner of each game are optional.

CAVEATS AND OPTIONS

1. As more questions are answered and more boxes filled, the game becomes more challenging because the number of dice rolls/combinations becomes limited. Students can shift to rolling one dice as the rolls become more challenging.

2. Regarding game board options, each row of the game board can be a specific type of question, such as six pronunciation questions or six vocabulary questions. Another option is to have each board focus on a different skill area, such as a board with 36 pronunciation questions or 36 grammar questions.

3. If students help each other during the game, they may finish the game in less than 20 minutes.

4. To extend the game, make four to six different game boards for one class, with each game board focusing on a different skill area. Then, give each team a different game board. After they finish, have teams switch boards until all teams have played all of the games.

5. This game is adaptable to many skill areas such grammar, vocabulary, spelling, reading, and writing.

    Examples

    a. What are two symbols from the novel *The Giver*? (reading comprehension)

    b. Combine the sentences: The girl went to the cinema. The boy went to the cinema. (writing)

c. Add punctuation: Marks computer just crashed. (writing)

d. The sky _____ blue. (grammar)

e. Correct or incorrect? All of students in my class are adults. (grammar)

f. The sky is bl_____. (vocabulary)

g. The _____ is blue. a. skie   b. ski   c. sky   (spelling/vocabulary)

6. Some teams may finish before others. Prepare a short activity for these teams to do while they wait or answer any questions that they did not know during the wait time.

REFERENCES AND FURTHER READING

The game board is adapted from the chart by Jason Gorski, courtesy of the Exploratorium (Retrieved from https://www.sfsite.com/fsf/images/chart0205.jpg)

Rubbed Out: Discussion in Mafia Games

Michael Madson

Levels	*Advanced*
Aims	*Practice impromptu speaking and active listening*
	Develop fluency for in-class discussions
	Practice strategies for persuasion
Class Time	*30–45 minutes*
Preparation Time	*10 minutes*
Resources	*Notecards (Appendix)*
	A hat (or other object to pull notecards from, e.g., box, envelope)

Games can be useful for teaching speaking and engaging students through fantasy, challenge, competition, immediate feedback, and clearly-defined objectives (Wilson et al., 2009; Whitton, 2010). This activity focuses on Mafia, a classic party game adapted here for English language classrooms. In the game Mafia, accusations will fly, alliances will clash, and strategy will abound—providing valuable practice in discussion skills.

The storyline goes like this: The mafia are criminals who descend upon a town and its citizens. Each night, the mafia silently agree on one citizen to eliminate ("rub out"). If they eliminate enough citizens to become the majority, they overtake the town and win the game. However, if the citizens eliminate all of the mafia, the town is defended, and the game is theirs.

PROCEDURE

1. To prepare, gather one notecard for every student in your class. Write "mafia," along with a brief explanation of the role, on several notecards. Do the same for "citizen" on the remaining notecards (see Appendix). For a class of 15 students, you can start with 12 citizens and three mafia, but students often request more mafia when they play a second time.

2. Fold the notecards and place them in a hat or other object.

3. To begin the activity, explain the storyline of the game.

4. Ask each student to take one notecard from the hat. Explain that this is a secret identity, either mafia or a citizen. For the moment, nobody should know that identity.

5. Announce that night has come, and everyone has fallen asleep. All of the students should close their eyes and lay their heads on their desks. Ask the mafia to open their eyes. By using silent/nonverbal communication (such as pointing), the mafia should agree on one student to eliminate. When they have agreed, they fall back asleep.

6. Ask all students to wake up, and announce who has been eliminated. To ensure that everyone has a chance to speak, the eliminated student might venture a deathbed guess about who might be mafia.

7. Allow all students to discuss. When they have settled on two, or perhaps three mafia suspects, take a vote. Whoever the vote falls against is eliminated, and their secret identities (citizen or mafia) are revealed. Eliminated students continue to observe the game silently.

8. Repeat Steps 3 through 7. The game continues in this way until the mafia have overrun the town or the citizens have brought all of the mafia to justice.

CAVEATS AND OPTIONS

1. If possible, arrange the desks into a circle. A circle helps the mafia communicate with each other silently during the night. It also helps the citizens observe body language and decide on mafia suspects.

2. The discussion may lag at points, particularly when students are new to the game. To compensate, use a timer to maintain the game's pace during the day. If students cannot reach a vote within the allotted time, say 2 or 3 minutes, then night comes again, and it is the mafia's turn to eliminate someone.

3. As the game's moderator, listen closely and respond contingently, encouraging students to elaborate, consider different points of view, and ask substantive questions to their peers.

4. As an option, the game can focus on a target form for students to practice, such as expressions for agreeing and disagreeing, stating opinion, or supporting opinions with evidence. The target form can be introduced before the game and reinforced during the discussions that follow.

5. After a game finishes, consider prompting students to discuss differences they observed in body language, persuasion strategies, turn taking, or other areas. Such discussion can be rich, especially if students hail from different cultural backgrounds.

6. Some variations of Mafia include a doctor. After the mafia have chosen whom to eliminate and have fallen back asleep, the doctor wakes up and chooses someone to save. If the doctor makes the same choice as the mafia, then that student survives the night; the mafia's assassination attempt has been thwarted.

REFERENCES AND FURTHER READING

Whitton, N. (2010). Game engagement theory and adult learning. *Simulation & Gaming, 42*(5), 596–609.

Wilson, K. A., Bedwell, W. L., Lazzara, E. H., Salas, E., Burke, C. S., Estock, J. L., Orvis, K. L., Conkey, C. (2009). Relationships between game attributes and learning outcomes. *Simulation & Gaming*, *40*(2), 217–266.

APPENDIX: *Sample Notecards for Students*

You are a citizen. Eliminate all of the mafia to defend your town.

- Discuss who might be mafia.

- Vote on someone to eliminate.

You are a member of the mafia. Eliminate citizens until you take over the town.

- During the night, silently agree on someone to eliminate.

- During the day, avoid getting caught.

Say Something Interesting

Cameron Romney

Levels	All
Aims	Develop ability to engage in more interesting and effective small talk (phatic communication)
Class Time	10–15 minutes
Preparation Time	None
Resources	Tokens (e.g., poker chips, bottle caps, small pieces of colored paper)

Small talk, a kind of phatic communication, is a necessary communication skill for forming interpersonal relationships (Thornbury, 2006). Many teachers and textbooks cover basic advice, like asking questions and being a good listener; however, having something interesting to say is also an important part of small talk (Fine, 2005). One way to make small talk interesting is to include extra information. For example, if asked, "Where are you from?" the answer, "Tokyo," is fine, but not very interesting. A more interesting answer would be, "Tokyo, but to tell the truth, I don't like it very much." Another example is in answer to the question, "How long have you lived in San Francisco?" a factual answer of six years is not as interesting as, "Six years, and they've been the most exciting of my life." The more interesting the answer, the easier it is for the questioner to respond to it and for the conversation to continue (Garner, 1997).

PROCEDURE

1. Write several typical small talk questions on the board. These can be easy things like, "Where are you from?" or "What do you do?" or "How long have you lived here?" Give the students a few minutes to think about how they would answer the questions and specifically about how they can make their answers more interesting by including extra information.

2. Model giving factual answers versus more interesting answers with extra information. Discuss with the students which kind of response makes it easier for the conversation to continue.

3. Give the students a few tokens. Have the students stand up and move around and ask and answer the small talk questions. As each student answers, their partner should evaluate the level of interest they have in the answer and give their interlocutor one or more of their tokens.

4. The activity is over when the students have either given away all of their tokens or they have spoken to every student. The student with the most tokens at the end is the winner.

CAVEATS AND OPTIONS

1. Some students may realize that one way to win the game is to not give away any of their tokens, so you may want to give each student a unique color or number the tokens so that you can easily differentiate between the tokens that the students started with and the tokens they received.

2. Many students may feel obligated to give their speaking partner a token whether they found their response to the question interesting or not, and everyone will end the game with the same number of tokens. To avoid this, encourage the students to give more than one token for responses that they found interesting. Also, you as the teacher can participate but only give tokens for truly interesting responses.

REFERENCES AND FURTHER READING

Fine, D. (2005). *The fine art of small talk: How to start a conversation, keep it going, build networking skills—and leave a positive impression!* New York, NY: Hyperion.

Garner, A. (1997). *Conversationally speaking: Tested new ways to increase your personal and social effectiveness.* New York, NY: McGraw-Hill.

Thornbury, S. (2006). *An A–Z of ELT.* Oxford, England: Macmillan Education.

The Say 3 Challenge

Kevin McCaughey

Levels	*All*
Aims	*Engage in high-repetition speaking practice using student-generated content*
	Develop more complex language
Class Time	*20–30 minutes*
Preparation Time	*None*
Resources	*Paper or notecards*
	Handout (optional; Appendix)

T he Say 3 Challenge presents a speaking opportunity in which students express their own opinions in a game-like environment—which are two keys to successful speaking, according to Ur (2015). The fundamental design of the activity has learners creating content that asks for multiple responses and then mingling to achieve high-repetition speaking practice by talking to many other students. Learners create the content, so it should be at the appropriate level.

PROCEDURE

1. Write on the board, "Say 3 . . ." and then complete the sentence with an example, such as ". . . places you don't like to go."

2. Ask for some volunteers to each say three places they don't like to go.

3. Enlist the class's help in creating a few more Say 3 Challenges. Write prompts on the board, like so:

   - Say 3 **things** . . .
   - Say 3 **reasons** . . .
   - Say 3 **foods** . . .

   Let the class complete the prompts:

   - Say 3 **things** that you hate doing.
   - Say 3 **reasons** it's good to be alive.
   - Say 3 **foods** you can't live without.

4. Tell students it's their turn to make their own Say 3 Challenges. They can create these alone, in pairs, or in small groups. The ultimate goal is for each student to have one unique Say 3 Challenge written on a piece of paper or notecard. Rotate around the room helping students if they are stuck.

5. Begin the whole-class speaking task by telling the class to mingle. Each student, with their Say 3 Challenge written on a piece of paper, roams the classroom, presenting the challenge verbally to as many other students as possible during the time allotted (10–15 minutes). So, if Student Nat meets Student Yoko, Nat will read his challenge, "Say 3 things you do to pass the time on a long flight." Yoko replies, and then presents her challenge. Mingle groups are unfixed, so learners will be forming pairs or groups of three or more. Any size is fine, and flux is normal.

6. Tell the students that the owner of each Say 3 Challenge should write down on his paper the initials or name of each student who successfully answers. Set a benchmark, such as, "Get responses from 15 different students." (Note: This step encourages all students to seek more partners, and it increases the amount of speaking practice in the session.)

7. After the mingle, review the results as a class, eliciting the most fascinating Say 3 Challenges and the most intriguing responses.

CAVEATS AND OPTIONS

1. For lower level learners, make Say 3 Challenges that require simple answers, such as, "Say 3 things in your room," and answer, "Bed. Chair. Books."

2. For more advanced learners, offer more scaffolding in the content-creation phase, which will in turn lead to more complex Say 3 Challenges. Make a copy of a table to help kick-start student creativity (Appendix). Vary the number of responses asked, such as, "Say 2" or "Say 4." Also, offer subjects (e.g., things, events, and places) and relative clauses to elicit details.

REFERENCES AND FURTHER READING

Ur, P. (2015, 22 January). Getting them to talk in English (when they don't want to) [*Video webinar*]. Cambridge, England: Cambridge University Press ELT. Retrieved from http://www.cambridge.org/elt/blog/2015/01/23/penny-ur-get -talk-dont-want/

Un-Taboo: Modified Taboo

Ildiko Porter-Szucs

Levels	*Beginner to intermediate*
Aims	*Practice sentence structure and vocabulary*
	Increase spoken fluency
	Improve ability to describe and circumscribe
Class Time	*5 minutes +*
Preparation Time	*10–15 minutes*
Resources	*Un-Taboo cards (teacher created)*
	Sentence frames (Appendix)

Taboo is a popular word-guessing card game by Hasbro (Parker Brothers, 1989). Taboo cards consist of a head word and a list of taboo words underneath, which are closely associated in meaning to the head word. In the game, players take turns explaining the head word on their card without saying the head word, the taboo words, or any parts of the taboo words. Team members, in turn, attempt to guess the head word within a specified time.

Un-Taboo is the opposite of Taboo. It has been modified for students of low proficiency, who cannot yet describe a word by avoiding its most commonly associated collocates, but who can only use words they have been taught.

PROCEDURE

1. Prepare for the activity. First, look at an example of a regular Taboo card in case students are familiar with that game. For example:

```
┌─────────────────────┐
│      YEARBOOK       │
│                     │
│       PHOTOS        │
│                     │
│        CLASS        │
│                     │
│        SIGN         │
│                     │
│      MEMORIES       │
│                     │
│       SCHOOL        │
│                     │
└─────────────────────┘
```

2. Then, create your own set of Un-Taboo cards. You should create three or more cards per student. Here are examples of Un-Taboo cards:

ANIMAL	PLAY THE GUITAR
DOG	MAKE MUSIC
CAT	INSTRUMENT
(not) HUMAN	STRINGS
WILD	CLASSICAL
PET	ELECTRIC

3. Write sentence frames on the board for students to use during the activity (Appendix).

4. Students pair up. If there is an odd number of students, create a group of three.

5. Each pair receives a pack of Un-Taboo cards and puts them face down.

6. In pairs, students take turns drawing an Un-Taboo card and explaining the head word to their partner. Unlike Taboo, in Un-Taboo speakers must use all of the associated words listed on the card rather than avoid mentioning them. Using the sentence frames on the board, students create sentences with the words. Students add sentences of their own as needed.

7. While the speakers speak, the listeners keep guessing the head word out loud until they say the right answer.

8. Students switch roles and repeat for as many rounds as time permits.

9. Walk around, listen in on pairs, help out as needed, and take notes on areas for improvement.

CAVEATS AND OPTIONS

1. At all levels of proficiency, it is important to discourage gesturing and pointing. Otherwise, this speaking game will turn into a nonverbal game such as charades.

2. Absolute beginners may find it difficult to say complete sentences even with the help of sentence frames. At the teacher's discretion, it may be acceptable for such students just to read the list of associated words and to add a few words of their own.

3. High-intermediate and advanced students should be able to play the unmodified Taboo game.

4. For less proficient students, play without a per-turn time limit.

REFERENCES AND FURTHER READING

Parker Brothers. (1989). *Taboo: The game of unspeakable fun!* Beverly, MA: Author.

Part II

Developing Accuracy

- **Grammatical Task-Based Speaking**
- **Vocabulary**

II

ABC Conversation

Magali Arteaga

Levels	*Beginner*
Aims	*Practice accuracy when using simple present tense*
Class Time	*10 minutes +*
Preparation Time	*Minimal*
Resources	*None*

T his activity enhances accuracy when speaking. It does not require much preparation, except for some key questions that the teacher needs to practice. Many variations can be applied to the activity to practice other grammar points at different accuracy levels. The activity is carried out in groups of three students, which encourages class participation and student involvement.

PROCEDURE

1. Depending on the size of the class, divide the students into groups of three. If there is a pair of students or one student working alone, a student from another group can help.

2. On the board, write some topics to be used in writing questions. Allow some time for students to prepare to ask the questions. Examples of topics are *name*, *job*, and *favorite hobby*.

3. Remind the students that this activity's purpose is to improve accuracy.

4. Ask students to choose a role: A, B, or C.

5. Explain that Student A will ask Student B the questions; the questions will be about Student C. Student B listens to the question (in third person) and asks the same question in second person, but to Student C. Student C listens to the question (in second person) and answers it.

   Example (The topic is *name* and student C is a woman.)

   Student A (asks B): What is her name?

   Student B (asks C): What is your name?

   Student C (answers): My name is . . .

6. After two rounds are finished, ask the students to switch roles: Student A becomes Student B, Student B becomes Student C, and Student C becomes Student A.

7. Call on some groups to share their responses. Check for accuracy and give feedback as needed.

CAVEATS AND OPTIONS

1. Remind students to speak loudly, so their partners can hear them. Be aware that Student B has the hardest role, because this person listens to the question in third person and asks the same question in second person.

2. More topics can be given to students and they can choose which to discuss. Instead of writing the topics on the board, the prompts may be written on paper and given to the groups.

Conditionals Creation: Expected to Absurd

Elena Shvidko

Levels	Intermediate to advanced
Aims	Practice developing correct sentences with second conditionals
Class Time	30 minutes
Preparation Time	20 minutes
Resources	Handout and premade cards with if-clauses (Appendix)
	Small blank cards

Second conditionals (e.g., *If I knew, I would . . .*) can be challenging even for advanced language learners. In this activity, students practice this structure by participating in an interactive speaking task.

PROCEDURE

1. Prepare cards with if-clauses (see Appendix). These cards comprise Pack 1. Put aside these cards to use later in the activity.

2. Divide the students into small groups of three to six. Depending on the size of your class, the number of students per group can differ.

3. Give each group the handout and a set of blank cards; the number of the cards should correspond with the number of the if-clauses on the handout.

4. Direct the students to read each if-clause from the handout, think of an ending for the sentence, and write only that ending on a blank card. For example, if the clause says, "If my pet were hungry," the student writes on the blank card, "I would give my pet something to eat." Encourage the students to be creative.

5. When the students have finished writing each sentence, ask them to shuffle the cards and put them face down on the desk in front of them. Tell them that this is called Pack 2.

6. Distribute the premade cards (Pack 1). Direct the students to shuffle the pack and put it in front of them. Tell them that this stack is called Pack 1 and the cards have the same clauses that are on the handout.

7. On the board, write the question, "What would you do if . . . ?"

8. One person from the group will randomly pick a premade card from Pack 1 and finish the question on the board with the participation of others. For example, if the student picked the card that says, "If my pet were hungry," he or she would say, "What would you do if your pet were hungry?" Another group member

will pick any card from Pack 2 and read the end of the if-clause, such as, "If my pet were hungry, I would wear my best outfit." Because it was probably written for a different if-clause, the result will most likely be funny, bizarre, and even nonsensical, causing laughter from the students.

9. Explain that other students can create follow-up questions for their group member to answer.

CAVEATS AND OPTIONS

1. Challenge students by adding a competitive aspect. Assign categories for their sentences (e.g., the most realistic, the most bizarre, the most nonsensical) and give points or a prize to the winner of each category.

2. Modify this activity to practice first conditionals or third conditionals by revising the clauses in the Appendix.

3. As a follow-up activity, the students can write their own original sentences to practice using correct grammar and punctuation.

APPENDIX: *If-Clauses*

Use these examples or create your own.

If my pet were hungry

If a cashier accidently gave me too much change

If my friend wrongly accused me of lying

If I lived in a desert

If I lost the ability to speak

If I owned an airplane

If my best friend crashed my car

If I were to fly to Antarctica

If I knew how to speak the language of animals

If I had dinner with the President of the United States

If I found a wallet full of money in the street

If I happened to be on a deserted island all by myself

If I saw someone stealing from a store

Confirming or Denying Truths and Lies With Tag Endings

Cathrine-Mette Mork

Levels	*Beginner to intermediate*
Aims	*Practice use of tag endings*
Class Time	*Variable*
Preparation Time	*0–5 minutes*
Resources	*Handout (Appendix)*

This activity is aimed at Japanese learners or other native speakers of a language that does not use *yes* or *no* to confirm or deny in the same way as they are used in English. Encouraging learner use of tag endings to confirm or deny statements not only helps learners use English the way proficient speakers in the target language do, but also forces students to think critically about the accuracy of their responses just before (or during) speech.

Typically, confusion results for many Japanese learners of English because truths formulated in the negative are usually confirmed with a *yes* or a *that's right* in Japanese. Similarly, falsehoods in the negative are negated with, *Yes, that's right*, in Japanese. Direct translation of agreement or disagreement, typically without the use of tag endings, can result in major miscommunication, so getting used to the English pattern is essential.

PROCEDURE

1. Write the following chart on the board, leaving space under the example sentences.

	+ Positive	− Negative
True	Blueberries are blue.	Blueberries aren't red.
False	Blueberries are red.	Blueberries aren't blue.

2. Tell students to write a large grid on a piece of paper and write down as many example sentences that match the example patterns in each of the four quadrants as they can in an allotted time frame. (At least five examples is ideal.) Depending on the proficiency level of students, they can use verbs other than *be* and different tenses. Encourage learners to write statements that everyone will be able to identify as either true or false. Circulate to check the accuracy of statements as they are being written. If class time is limited, this could be done for homework, and the remainder of the activity continued in the next class.

3. Add to the chart on the board the following information. Be sure to change the tone of voice to indicate disagreement (shown with exclamation marks) when modeling.

	+ Positive	– Negative
True (agree)	Blueberries are blue. *Yes, they are.* OR *Yes, that's right.*	Blueberries aren't red. *No, they're not. They're blue.*
False (disagree)	Blueberries are red. *No, they're not! They're blue!* OR *No, they aren't! They're blue!*	Blueberries aren't blue. *Yes, they are!*

4. Optional, but highly recommended for beginning students: Tell the students to put aside their own examples for the moment and get into pairs for practice. Distribute a pair work handout (Appendix) with Partner A on one side and Partner B on the other. Students can decide who is A and who is B. Read the top of the page (same for both partners) together, or have students read alone, and do the activity. Circulate the room to monitor and assist students. As they finish the activity, invite students to switch A and B roles. When all (or most if there is a large speed gap) students have finished their initial role, stop the activity and answer any questions.

5. Perhaps with a new partner, students can now practice the same activity, but this time randomly selecting from the example sentences they created earlier. There are now no example appropriate responses, so students must listen more carefully to their partners' confirmation or rejection and give appropriate feedback to each other.

6. Students can continue to practice the activity with different partners for allotted periods of time, or they can circulate freely to other partners when they have exhausted their examples.

CAVEATS AND OPTIONS

1. Remind students to change their tone when they disagree and to correct false statements.

2. At any point, you can engage the whole class and solicit responses from individual students with impromptu or prepared true or false (positive or negative) statements to assess or gauge students' general understanding. Two specific times where this smoothly fits into the activity may be at the beginning, between the handout activity and the student example activity, or between the switching of pairs.

3. The student example sentence activity can be gamified by putting students into groups of three or more. Students take turns reading their statements. The fastest student to respond satisfactorily (as judged by the group) gets a point.

Crowdsourced Conversation

Sherry Schafer

Levels	*High-beginner to advanced*
Aims	*Practice forming grammatically correct questions*
Class Time	*15 minutes +*
Preparation Time	*None*
Resources	*Small pieces of paper (optional)*

Although many conversation activities involve predetermined questions, this activity pushes students to generate their own questions on a particular topic. After working in pairs to form questions, students go to the board and write down a question they have formed. Student-generated questions on the board can be used by all students as the basis for conversation.

PROCEDURE

Place the students into pairs. If there is an odd number of students, having a group of three students is fine.

1. Announce a broad conversation theme, such as family, jobs/careers, or school life. Then direct students to work with their partner to create as many questions as possible related to the theme and to write all of the questions they have created on a sheet of paper.

2. Distribute one whiteboard marker or piece of chalk to each pair. Tell one student per pair to write down one of their questions on the board. It must be different from all of the other questions on the board.

3. Discuss the grammar of each question, providing corrections as necessary.

4. After all of the questions have been corrected, give each pair 5–10 minutes to use any of the questions on the board as the basis for conversation. Encourage students to ask their partner any other questions they can think of beyond what is written on the board.

CAVEATS AND OPTIONS

1. Error correction of the student-formed questions can occur at various points in the activity. For example, look at the students' questions before they are written on the board and guide the correction of any ungrammatical question. Other options are to correct the questions after they have been put on the board, so that the entire class can learn from the mistakes, or to collect the papers, correct all of the questions, and return the papers in the next class.

2. Instead of telling students to write down as many questions as they can think of, require each pair to come up with a certain number of questions. This may push some students to generate more questions than they would have otherwise.

3. Hand out a small piece of paper to each student. Each student generates a question and writes it on the paper. Collect all of the questions and quickly look through them, searching for the most interesting, thought-provoking questions. Write the selected questions on the board for all students to see.

4. This activity can also be used to practice pronunciation. For instance, read the questions aloud and have the class repeat them.

5. An optional conclusion is to debrief the activity as a class. For example, ask the pairs which question they discussed and compare/contrast responses.

Devil's Advocate: Teaching Students How to Disagree Politely

Sara Okello

Levels	Intermediate to advanced
Aims	*Develop accuracy performing the speech act of disagreeing politely*
	Develop fluency continuing a conversation
	Develop critical thinking skills to defend one's position
Class Time	30 minutes
Preparation Time	10 minutes
Resources	Handouts (Appendixes A and B)

Often, students agree with one another for the sake of maintaining classroom harmony. They are sometimes afraid to disagree with one another to avoid the risk of offending others or being viewed in a negative light. However, it is important for students to learn how to express their opinions and support them with clear, cogent reasons. The term *devil's advocate* refers to someone who does not agree with another person simply for the sake of disagreement and to make the conversation more interesting. This interactive activity enables students to practice disagreeing politely with a partner.

PROCEDURE

1. In a previous class, discuss the speech act of how to disagree politely. To introduce this activity, review the phrases for disagreeing politely (Appendix A). Remind students that it is okay to disagree as long as you do so politely and respectfully and listen to the other side's point of view.

2. Divide students into pairs (or one group of three if there is an odd number).

3. Give one person in each pair a slip of paper with a controversial statement on it (Appendix B) and ask him or her to read it quietly and think about his or her opinion and three reasons to support that opinion.

4. Choose the person in each pair who does not have the paper and ask those students to go out in the hallway with you.

5. Explain to the students in the hallway that they have to disagree with their partner's opinion about the statement on the slip of paper, but make it seem natural. (Tell them not to tell their partner they were told to disagree.) Remind the students to use the phrases they learned to disagree politely.

6. When the partners return to the room, have the partner with the slip of paper read the statement aloud and then give their opinion. Then, the partner who was in the hallway will respond and disagree. Encourage the partners to listen to each other, continue the conversation, ask questions, and provide reasons for their opinions.

7. After 5–10 minutes or once the conversations have died down, ask the class if their partners agreed or disagreed with them and how they felt when their partners disagreed with them. Then, explain the purpose of this activity was to teach the students how to express and defend their opinions in a polite manner when someone disagrees with them. Discuss that the disagreeing partner was acting as a *devil's advocate*, a person who disagrees with another for the sake of disagreement and to stimulate a more interesting conversation.

CAVEATS AND OPTIONS

1. Explain that the students should not take their partner's disagreement as a personal attack. Disagreement can develop critical thinking skills. This activity was conducted in class for instructional purposes.

2. Remind students to listen to the other side and disagree politely and respectfully. There is no place for personal attacks or offensive comments in the classroom.

3. An extension for this activity is to have the pairs of students perform their conversations in front of the class as role-plays to demonstrate how to disagree politely.

4. Adapt this activity and make controversial statements to fit the topic being discussed in class that day.

REFERENCES AND FURTHER READING

Phrases for disagreeing politely (used in Appendix A):
- www.espressoenglish.net/practical-english-speaking-how-to-disagree -politely/
- www.englishclub.com/speaking/agreeing-disagreeing-expressions.htm

"Teaching Students How to Disagree Without Being Disagreeable," by Dr. Allen Mendler: www.talktocanada.com/blog/teaching-students-how-to -disagree-without-being-disagreeable-2/

"Five Ways to (Respectfully) Disagree": kidshealth.org/en/teens/tips-disagree.html

Following Up With Follow-Up Questions

Kurtis McDonald

Levels	*High beginner to advanced*
Aims	*Develop attention to accuracy, fluency, and pragmatics*
Class Time	*Variable*
Preparation Time	*5 minutes*
Resources	*Timer*
	Document camera (or board space for each group)

Asking good follow-up questions can be difficult because doing so requires language learners to comprehend what others are saying and quickly respond with questions that are 1) connected to the topic at hand, 2) pragmatically appropriate and interesting, and 3) grammatically correct. This activity provides focused practice with asking follow-up questions in a way that is very manageable for the learners and the teacher: a class-based game conducted with groups. The game strives to compel learners to go beyond the initial, most obvious question by encouraging them to work together to create lists of potential follow-up questions to a comment. Giving learners time to brainstorm questions and write down their ideas slows down the conversational interaction so that students have the chance to more fully dedicate their cognitive resources to attending to form, meaning, and use. It also allows students to get feedback on their proposed questions from their peers as well as the teacher. The group aspect also takes the pressure of potential embarrassment off of any individual student, allowing learners of all abilities to participate and have fun.

PROCEDURE

1. Put students into two to four groups, each composed of two to six members. Tell the students that each group needs a rotating recorder; "rock, paper, scissors" could be used to quickly decide the order. Distribute one piece of paper to each group. Also, each student needs either a notebook or a piece of paper for note-taking.

2. Go over the following *Directions* and *Example*, giving students time with their group to check that they understand the game.

    Directions: Listen carefully to each comment your teacher says and write it down on the **Comment** line. Then, as a group, list as many good follow-up questions as possible in the time given. After time is up, one member will share your group's questions with the class for a score. To get the most points, your follow-up questions should be *closely connected to the topic*, *appropriate for the situation*, and *grammatically correct*.

Example

"Yesterday was my best friend's birthday."

Q1. Did you have a party for your friend?

Q2. How old is your friend now?

Q3. What did you give to your friend present?

Q4. Do you like your friend?

Q5. Do you like pizza?

Q	Connected	Appropriate	Grammatical	Score
1	+1	+1	+1	3
2	+1	+1	+1	3
3	+1	+1	X	2
4	+1	X	+1	2
5	X	X	+1	1
			Total	11

3. Start the first round of the game by reciting Comment 1 several times to be sure all groups can copy it to their group paper correctly. Give the students 2 minutes to list potential follow-up questions to the comment on their group paper. Announce when time is up.

4. Collect each group recorder's paper and show it on the document camera.

5. Check all of the questions along the three dimensions (connectedness, appropriateness, and grammaticality), giving a point for each only when that dimension is completely correct and offering brief explanations as to why any dimensions are incorrect. Keep a running total of each group's points.

6. After all of the questions in a round have been checked, have the students copy down the best questions (in their notebooks or on individual papers) so that they can remember them.

7. Repeat Steps 3–6 for the remaining comments prepared or the time allotted.

8. When finished, compare total scores and congratulate the winning group. Summarize the importance of asking good follow-up questions to wrap up the activity.

CAVEATS AND OPTIONS

1. It is advisable to prepare the comments in advance and considering the particular topics, situations, and/or grammar point/tenses to be targeted. Note that this activity could be repeated with the same or different aspects targeted each time.

2. Preparing a handout with the directions, example, and formatted areas for each comment and questions to be filled in could help students more quickly grasp how the game is to be played.

3. More (or less) time could be given to listing the potential questions in groups (Step 3) depending on student proficiency levels or time available.

4. Some matters of appropriateness may be open to interpretation. In such cases, groups may need to be called on to explain what they had imagined or assumed before deciding whether a certain question is actually appropriate to the situation or not.

5. Teachers without a document camera could have each group's recorder copy their questions to their group's part of the board.

Follow the Leader

Patricia Hart

Levels	Beginner
Aims	Practice and improve language functions for following directions
	Use transitions to indicate order
	Use imperatives
Class Time	20–30 minutes
Preparation Time	10 minutes
Resources	Set of cards (teacher created)

Experiential learning and taking the class outside of the classroom is often refreshing and invigorating for students. So too is being able to apply language learned inside class to the students' immediate environment. This activity engages students in using language for giving and following directions in a creative manner, relevant to their real-world needs.

PROCEDURE

1. Prepare a set of cards, with one card per student. Write the names or numbers of rooms or physical structures/fixed objects (e.g., bathrooms, fire extinguishers, utility closets) in the building. If the activity is extended to include your school grounds or campus, prepare the cards with the names of buildings or structures (e.g., fountains, fire hydrants, statues, snack bar).

2. Review language for giving directions. Then review transitions to indicate order (e.g., *first, next, after*). Ask students to stand up and give a series of commands directing them to move around the classroom, such as, "First, everyone stand up. Next, everyone walk to the right. Now, stop and turn left. Next, turn right."

3. Explain to the class that they will be playing a game that involves leaving the classroom. Give each student a card, and instruct them to keep it a secret.

4. Explain that students will take turns giving directions to one other student in the class. The person giving directions will walk behind the student and tell them how to get to the secret destination without telling them the destination. The rest of the class will follow behind.

5. After the first student takes their turn, ask them to show everyone their card. Discuss what directions were helpful and/or clear (or less clear). Elicit class feedback about what language they used to give/follow directions. If the leader

and the follower wound up lost, elicit feedback about why. (E.g., did they take a right instead of a left? Did they say to go straight when they should have gone up some stairs?)

CAVEATS AND OPTIONS

1. This activity can be done inside a classroom with a map of a campus or city. In this case, photocopy the map so each student has their own copy. Simply write names of places from the map on the cards. Give one map to each student. The student must give directions to their secret place while the rest of the class tries to follow with their maps. It is beneficial for the students to use a pencil and try to trace the route as the directions are given. When the instructing student's secret place is revealed, the class gives feedback about why they could or couldn't follow with their maps.

2. Depending on the class, each student can complete the activity independently with their partner or the entire class can walk along to observe how the pair does.

Let Me Ask: Yes/No Questions

Phoebe Daurio

Levels	*Beginner*
Aims	*Develop accuracy in yes/no questions and answers*
Class Time	*10–15 minutes*
Preparation Time	*5 minutes*
Resources	*Index cards*
	Model/image of the activity (Appendix)

R

This activity works well as a follow-up oral practice activity after students have been introduced to the grammar of yes/no questions and answers. It is also helpful if students have been studying adjectives as vocabulary.

PROCEDURE

1. Prepare index cards by writing one adjective on each card. Adjectives that work well are ones that don't contain judgment but that might contain humorous elements (e.g., *happy, tired, bored, excited, talkative, friendly, hardworking, generous, silly*).

2. Write example yes/no questions and answers on the board. Review them with the class and leave the questions and answers on the board as a reference.

3. Write the following on the board, "I'm not sure. Hold on. Let me ask." Explain that this is a good response when a person asks a question and you are not completely sure/certain of how to answer. (I.e., More information is needed before answering.)

4. Ask for three volunteers from the class who will play the roles of Students A, B, and C. You may want to play Student B in the initial presentation (modeling) of the activity.

5. Model the activity, including with the image of the dialogue (Appendix). Model the activity again, but, this time, include your index cards. Have Student C pick an index card and ask Student B about Student A. Use the sample questions and answers on the board if students need help.

6. The students rotate roles. A new student moves into the C position, C moves to B, and B moves to A. C picks a different index card and asks Student B about Student A. The students rotate again.

7. Continue until everyone has had a chance to practice all three roles. Provide correction and guidance as needed.

CAVEATS AND OPTIONS

1. Incorporate pronunciation practice by showing students how *Let me ask* becomes *lemmeask* in connected speech.

2. Once students understand the activity, they could practice in groups of three.

3. This activity can be used as a warm-up or review in subsequent class periods.

Tag Question Collection

Jesse Giacomini

Levels	*High beginner to advanced*
Aims	*Learn about classmates*
	Practice tag questions
	Develop fluency
Class Time	*20–40 minutes*
Preparation Time	*2 minutes*
Resources	*None*

This activity is good for developing speaking confidence and encouraging inter-action. Students use deductive reasoning to ask personal questions while practicing the grammar needed for tag questions. This activity is most effective as a review or reinforcement to be used after students have studied tag questions and understand their function and construction. It can be helpful to remind students that speakers often use tag questions to involve a listener in a conversation and to confirm infor-mation believed to be correct.

PROCEDURE

1. Hand out 5–10 blank strips of paper to each student.

2. Ask students to write one true statement about themselves on each strip. Encourage students to use a variety of grammatical structures and tenses, including negative and positive statements. Provide some examples on the board, such as:

   • I went to Panama last year.

   • I don't have a driver's license.

   • My sister-in-law is pregnant.

   • I can speak Turkish.

   • I have been to Barcelona.

   • I don't know how to ski.

   • Next week is my birthday.

3. Move around the room to check grammar and spelling while collecting the stu-dents' completed strips. Check that they are legible and grammatically correct.

4. When everyone is finished, shuffle the strips and put them face down on a table in the centre of the class.

5. Review the rules for creating tag questions. Use the example statements on the board and demonstrate how to identify the verb, change the subjects, and create a tag after the comma by changing a positive verb to a negative and vice versa, and then adding the subject pronoun.

Examples

- "My sister-in-law is pregnant" changes to "Your sister-in-law is pregnant, isn't she?"
- "I don't know how to ski" changes to "You don't know how to ski, do you?"

6. Elicit responses to these questions by asking students. Encourage students to use the verbs in their answers, for clarity.

Examples

- "You can speak Turkish, can't you?" can be answered as, "Yes, I can."/"No, I can't."
- "You don't have a driver's license, do you?" can be answered as, "No, I don't."/Yes, I do."

7. Tell students that they will stand, take a strip from the pile, and change the statement into a tag question. They should move around the room asking their classmates until they find someone for whom the statement is true. They should write the name of that person on the strip, keep it, and take another strip to start again.

8. The activity continues until all of the strips are completed. Then, ask for volunteers to share some surprising or interesting things that they learned about their friends.

9. There may be more than one student for whom a statement is true, and they can share this at the end of the activity. This can be done by changing statements into another question form.

Examples

- "Next week is my birthday" is used to create the question "Does anyone else have a birthday next week?"
- "I have been to Barcelona" is used to create the question "Has anyone else been to Barcelona?"

CAVEATS AND OPTIONS

1. This activity can be useful as an icebreaker at the beginning of a course for higher level students who may just need a quick reminder of how to structure a tag question.

2. The game can take more or less time depending on the number of statements students are asked to write.

3. As an extension activity, encourage students to ask follow-up questions about interesting information they heard and continue/extend a conversation.

I Don't Believe It!

Amy Crofford

Levels	*All*
Aims	*Develop vocabulary through interaction*
Class Time	*Variable*
Preparation Time	*5 minutes*
Resources	*None*

For decades, *Ripley's Believe It or Not!* was a popular feature on cartoon pages in several countries because people enjoy learning bizarre facts from around the world.

In this activity, students are presented a statement. They vote on whether they believe it. Beginners can make a simple statement about the topic, and intermediate and advanced learners can persuade or debate. After hearing their classmates' opinions and possibly sharing their own, they vote again.

PROCEDURE

1. The activity leader reads a statement and clarifies vocabulary as necessary. For example, "You can buy green-bean-flavoured ice pops in China!" (This is true according to the National Geographic Kids website; see References and Further Reading.)

2. Students vote on whether they believe it.

3. The leader asks for volunteers to say why they believe it or not.

4. Students vote again.

5. After the second vote, the leader reveals whether the statement is true or false.

CAVEATS AND OPTIONS

1. Because this activity could be repeated often, remember to have some false statements.

2. Any level of student can find a fact or falsehood to present. The fun of knowing what no one else in the class, even the teacher, knows can be a confidence builder. If students are not able or comfortable lead the discussion, you can step in. The student would only be required to write the statement out and reveal its veracity at the end.

3. The activity can be used to fill time at the end of class or as an opening activity if students tend to straggle in.

4. If several statements are used in succession, vocabulary can be introduced or reviewed. For example, if you were to teach vocabulary about the human body, many interesting facts could be used or distorted. For example, you could say, "The average person has 100 different species of bacteria in their belly button." (This is false, because the actual number is 67. See the National Geographic Kids website in References and Further Reading.)

5. As an option for advanced students, after the initial vote, the class can be divided into groups based on their responses. Groups with the same responses can build their cases to persuade the other group of the truth or falseness of the statement. If you divide groups randomly, students in groups can discuss why they believe what they believe.

REFERENCES AND FURTHER READING

A search for "fascinating facts" will garner many possibilities. National Geographic Kids is an excellent resource. The language is easily accessible, and the topics are inoffensive.

- National Geographic Kids: www.natgeokids.com/za/category/discover
- National Geographic Kids "30 Cool Facts About China!": www.natgeokids .com/za/discover/geography/countries/30-cool-facts-about-china
- National Geographic Kids "15 Facts About the Human Body!": www .natgeokids.com/za/discover/science/general-science/15-facts-about-the -human-body

I'm Proud to Be . . .

Melissa Quasunella and Jenna Bollinger

Levels	*High beginner to low intermediate*
Aims	*Identify cultural differences*
	Transition into a new cultural environment
	Engage in discussion about identity
Class Time	*90 minutes*
Preparation Time	*10–15 minutes*
Resources	*Computer with speakers and access to YouTube*
	Handouts (Appendixes A–D)

R

Though some adult English as a second language classes focus on teaching "survival English," it is also important to engage students on a deeper human level and to teach to their intellect rather than their language proficiency level (Carr & Snell, 2012). Pursuing identity work with English language learners is critical for their language development. Students should have opportunities to develop a definition of self-identity by examining their identity in their home country and their identity in the target culture, while developing their English oral proficiency skills (Cummins, Hu, Markus, & Montero, 2015). Kramsch (1993) also asserts that it is important for learners to use their own experiences in the classroom and reflect on their "associations, feelings, attitudes, and ideas that these words and their referents arouse within them" (p. 123, as cited in Carr & Snell, 2012). This activity offers students an opportunity to talk about identity.

PROCEDURE

1. Ask students to think of a famous song from their culture/country or from the culture/country of their families or ancestors and fill in a chart on the board with the country/culture and song names (Appendix A).

2. Pass out "Wavin' Flag" vocabulary handouts (Appendix B) to students with keywords and corresponding pictures. Practice saying these words aloud as a whole group. Direct students to find the meanings of these words and match them to the correct picture. (E.g., draw a line from the word *freedom* to the picture of a bird). Encourage students to work together and assist them as needed.

3. Distribute the "Wavin' Flag" song lyrics (Appendix C). Read the handout together. Practice saying these words aloud as a group: *proud*, *flag*, *game*, *nation*, and *freedom*. Tell students that they will watch a video of the song and should focus on the words that they just practiced pronouncing. Also tell students that they should work with partners to fill in the blanks on their song lyric handout.

4. Play the "Wavin' Flag" video (www.youtube.com/watch?v=WTJSt4wP2ME). Replay it two to three times.

5. After listening, distribute the "Guided Discussion" handout (Appendix D). For the first question, ask students to circle the emotion that best captures their feelings about the song and the lyrics. Guide discussion by asking students to respond to each question aloud.

CAVEATS AND OPTIONS

1. Before starting the activity, introduce students to popular songs from the target culture to activate their schema and to get them thinking about music.

2. An option during the guided discussion is to utilize the pair-share technique until all discussion questions are answered. After students talk to their partners, students could volunteer to share their answers with the class.

3. After watching the "Wavin' Flag" video, which primarily shows males, provide some additional speaking practice. Show a video with more female representation and lead a class discussion about gender imbalance in sports and media, especially related to the concepts of bravery and freedom. Clips of the FIFA Women's World Cup could work well.

   Another practice activity is a categorizing task. Show the class some pictures of female athletes, world leaders, astronauts, and so on. Tell students to write down words they associate with these pictures and have them explain their word choices to the class. Listen for vocabulary words, such as *proud*, and if they aren't used follow up by saying each vocabulary word and asking students which picture matches the word and why. For additional activities for class discussion about gender roles, go to the Edutopia website at www .edutopia.org/blog/womens-history-month-lesson-plans-matt-davis

   To prompt additional discussion regarding inclusivity in sports, introduce students to the Paralympic Games, Special Olympics, and/or Gay Games and have students talk about why these different events were developed. Show the video from ESPN, "Inspirational interview after winning 100M freestyle gold at Special Olympics," at www.youtube.com/watch?v=radnpFrdW4Q. Watch the entire video or only the interview from 4:15–5:45. Then, discuss the video with the class, reinforcing vocabulary from the handout used earlier in the activity. Ask students to name the emotion that best describes the athlete's reaction to the victory and the emotion that best describes their feelings about the person's win.

4. Introduce students to the book *When I Get Older: The Story Behind Wavin' Flag* (Warsame & Sol, 2012). This book would serve as a guide for students to write their own story of their transition to the target culture from their home country. Develop a highly scaffolded model story template for students to complete. Pages of the story could include a map of their home country, picture of its flag, what students are proud of from their country, and so on. This activity would allow students to practice writing and then could be material used to support them in presenting or reading it to their peers.

REFERENCES AND FURTHER READING

Carr, C., & Snell, A. (2012). Beyond proficiency: Engaging adult 'beginners' at the level of their intellect and the depth of their humanity. *Indiana Teachers of English to Speakers of Other Languages Journal, 9*(1), 67–77. Retrieved from https://journals.iupui.edu/index.php/intesol/article/download/15540/15589/

Cummins, J., Hu, S., Markus, P., & Montero, M. K. (2015). Identity texts and academic achievement: Connecting the dots in multilingual school contexts. *TESOL Quarterly, 49*, 555–581.

Kramsch, C. (1993). *Context and culture in language teaching.* Oxford, England: Oxford University Press.

Warsame, K. (2010, March 5). *Wavin' Flag (Coca-Cola Celebration Mix)* [Video file]. Retrieved from https://www.youtube.com/watch?v=WTJSt4wP2ME

Warsame, K., & Sol, S. (2012). *When I get older: The story behind "wavin' flag."* Toronto, Ontario, Canada: Tundra Books.

Name It and Claim It Game

Janet Pierce

Levels	All
Aims	*Develop accuracy in use of new vocabulary words*
	Develop fluency
	Show knowledge of specific content vocabulary used in class
Class Time	*45 minutes*
Preparation Time	*Variable; 10 minutes + for each unit of new vocabulary*
Resources	*27 envelopes and many notecards*
	Bulletin board and tacks

Remembering new vocabulary can be challenging, especially after the focus on a particular unit and set of target words ends. This game, Name It and Claim It, focuses on reviewing vocabulary. At the beginning of a new unit, the students read and go over new vocabulary. Students copy each new word onto an index card and write its definition on the other side. The cards are added to envelopes and used in the game. As they learn new words throughout the year, those words are added to the envelopes so that the students are continually learning new vocabulary and reviewing previous vocabulary they have studied. This activity can be adapted to all grade levels and all levels of English proficiency.

PROCEDURE

1. To prepare for this activity, select a bulletin board to use for the academic year. Label envelopes with each letter of the alphabet and attach those to the board with tacks. Then, take one more envelope, label it "Alphabet Letters," and attach that to the board. For placement in the Alphabet Letters envelope, write each letter of the alphabet on a separate index card.

2. Hand out notecards whenever students are learning new vocabulary. Students will create cards with the new word on one side and the definition on the other side. Parts of speech of the words may be noted and the words used in sentences can also be practiced.

3. Collect one card per word and put it in the correct envelope according to the first letter of the word.

4. Play the game:
   a. Choose who will be the score keeper (you or a student).
   b. Have one student reach into the Alphabet Letters envelope and select a letter card. You will use the corresponding letter envelope.

c. Take the selected letter envelope with words down from the board. Reach into the envelope, pull out a card, and start by saying the word.

d. Students raise their hand to answer with either the definition of the word or use of the word in a sentence.

e. The definition can be checked by looking at the back of the card. If the student gives the correct definition, they are given a point. If they do not, another student is given a chance to answer. Remember that students choose to define or use it in a sentence.

f. When students give a sentence, the score keeper or students in the group can decide if the sentence uses the word correctly according to its meaning.

g. The person with the most points at the end of the time period is the winner.

CAVEATS AND OPTIONS

1. Remind students to speak loudly and clearly when they answer.

2. Consider giving out a reward, decided in advance by you or the class, to the winner.

3. This game helps you see which vocabulary words need more work, how well students can pronounce the words, and how well they can use the words they are learning in a fun way that can be nonthreatening to beginners.

4. Students who have higher English proficiency can be told to give both the definition and use the word in a sentence. Additionally, those more proficient students may also be chosen to be the score keeper.

Spell, Write, Speak

Smoky Kelly

Levels	*All*
Aims	*Practice fluency in speaking*
	Develop accuracy in pronunciation and spelling
	Engage in a team-based activity
Class Time	*10–15 minutes*
Preparation Time	*1–5 minutes*
Resources	*Timer*

Focused on vocabulary review and accuracy, this fast-paced activity could be used with any skill and level being taught by modifying the target words, possibly from students' vocabulary cards or a wordlist. It works well with a class size of 10–15 students. The objective of the activity is to be the fastest team to spell and pronounce the vocabulary words correctly and use the same words accurately and coherently in sentences. Students work on word recognition, accuracy, fluency, and spelling when the teacher calls out a vocabulary word, and the students simultaneously write the vocabulary word(s) on the board in their team's area. Then, the students turn around to face the teacher and create a sentence using the same word accurately in context. The quickest and most accurate student in each turn earns the most points for their team.

PROCEDURE

1. Explain the purpose of the activity—to review vocabulary and develop fluency and accuracy using the target vocabulary. Give an overview of how the activity is played. Teams can earn points by demonstrating fluency and accuracy in three areas: spelling the vocabulary word accurately, creating a coherent and accurate sentence using the vocabulary word, and using clear pronunciation. The team at the end with the most points wins the activity.

2. Divide the class into teams of three or four and let teams decide team names. Then, invite the students to come up to the board and stand together with their teams.

3. Divide the board into sections and let the students write their team names on the board.

4. Have each team select a person to go first, second, third, and so on (so that each student gets a turn in order). For each turn, the new student will get a different vocabulary word.

5. While you explain how the activity is played, do a trial run. Have the first group of students stand in front of their areas of the board. Say the first vocabulary word and tell the students to try and accurately spell the word on the board the fastest. Next, tell the students to face you and correctly use the vocabulary word in a sentence with their best pronunciation.

6. Explain to the students how the scoring works. If desired, show them this chart.

Speed of Student	Correct Spelling	Clear Pronunciation	Accurately Uses the Vocabulary Word in Context	Points Awarded
Fastest	x	x	x	3
2nd fastest	x	x	x	2
3rd fastest	x	x	x	1

7. Explain and demonstrate two simple rules:
   a. Rule 1: Points are not awarded within a category if a student makes a mistake in that category.
      • Misspelling a word (do not receive 1 point)
      • Inaccurately using the vocabulary word in a sentence (do not receive 1 point)
      • Mispronouncing the word or other words in a sentence (do not receive 1 point)
   b. Rule 2: Team members on each team can help the student whose turn it is (e.g., correct spelling, correct pronunciation)

8. After everyone understands the activity, set the timer for 10–15 minutes and begin when ready. You can use the board to keep track of the score. (Seeing the board gives students immediate feedback on their answer.)

9. Continue rotating students after each vocabulary word (turn) until the timer goes off. The team with the most points at the end wins.

CAVEATS AND OPTIONS

1. Add a competitive component by having one or two students on each team point out the errors of students' spelling and speech on other teams.

2. Encourage and emphasize that writing must be legible and the sentences must be comprehensible each time. Obviously with unfamiliar words, you are the final judge.

3. A great follow-up activity can be a reading passage in a textbook or article, which you can do as a class or in groups (depending on the class size). Using the same target vocabulary, let the students know they are working on word articulation and summarizing skills. Select the first student to read the first paragraph out

loud. The other students will need to follow along to be ready to summarize the passage that was read by the first student. Call on a different student to ask them to summarize what was read. Then, the second student will read the next paragraph and another student will be asked to summarize what was read. This continues until everyone has had a chance to read a paragraph and summarize what another student has read.

Vocabulary Scattergories

Michele Kim

Levels	High beginner to advanced
Aims	Reinforce meaning and use of new vocabulary
Class Time	10–30 minutes
Preparation Time	15 minutes
Resources	Handouts (teacher created)
	Examples of the handout and the board (Appendixes A and B)

R

Textbooks often introduce 5–10 new vocabulary words in a section but may include only a couple of activities to practice using the new words. With this low-prep activity, students can get repeated practice of how to appropriately use three to six new words or phrases in a fun and competitive group game that encourages creativity.

PROCEDURE

1. Before class, create three to five categories using new vocabulary words.

   Examples

   Something that might **chase** you

   Something that an **energetic** person might do

   Something that is **illegal**

   Then, make a simple handout for your class, including the categories with vocabulary words in bold. Under each category, include a sentence form using the vocabulary word (see Appendix A).

2. Put students into groups of three to four. Tell them that the class will play a vocabulary game. Write the categories on the board. Then, introduce the categories and elicit possible answers for each category from students. Write answers on the board under each category.

3. Tell the students you will give them one letter of the alphabet. Explain that the first team to think of one answer that begins with that letter for each category will get a point. You can play until one team reaches a certain number of points or as many rounds as time allows.

4. To confirm that students understand what to do, play a sample round together. Put a letter on the board and elicit answers for each category that begins with that letter. (See Appendix B for an example.)

5. After the sample round, give another letter and have teams work together to create their own answers. One person may write or they all may write. Have the first team that finishes read their answers aloud in the sentence form provided. Write their answers on the board. If an answer does not make sense or doesn't work grammatically, you can deem their attempt unsuccessful and have teams continue to work until another team finishes.

6. Continue to play, giving a new letter of the alphabet for each round until time is up or one team reaches a certain number of points.

CAVEATS AND OPTIONS

1. The first time a class plays will require more time as you explain how to play the game. Subsequent games will require less explanation—just a review of the categories.

2. If lower level students do not have enough vocabulary to generate answers easily, or if students are getting stumped, you may allow the use of dictionaries.

3. Require teams of students to take turns reading their answers, and make sure they read their answers in the context of the sentence provided. If a student reads an answer in an incorrect form but the meaning is clear and makes sense, correct the form but accept the answer (e.g., "An energetic person might boxing.")

REFERENCES AND FURTHER READING

This game is loosely based on the board game "The Game of Scattergories," produced in 1988 by Milton Bradley.

Part III

Developing Pronunciation

- **Segmental Phonemes**
- **Suprasegmental Phonemes**
- **Game-Based Learning**
- **Miscellaneous**

III

Favorite Things: Learning the Pronunciation of the Final –S Sound

Jolene Jaquays and Sara Okello

Levels	All
Aims	*Develop accuracy of the pronunciation of the final –s sound*
Class Time	*30 minutes*
Preparation Time	*10 minutes*
Resources	*Computer*
	Video projector
	Handouts (Appendixes A and B)

According to Longfellow, "Music is the universal language of mankind" (Notable Quotes, 2018). It can motivate students to learn English. Songs have been shown to provide a relaxing environment and enhance students' skills in speaking, pronunciation, and rhythm (Lo & Fai Li, 1998). One study showed that music helped improve English pronunciation in Chinese students (Wu & McMahon, 2013). In this activity, students learn the popular song *My Favorite Things* to practice pronouncing the final –*s* sound, which can be pronounced \s\, \z\, or \iz\.

PROCEDURE

1. For homework, prior to this in-class activity, have students make a list of their favorite things to share in class. In class, have students read their lists aloud and check their pronunciation of the final –*s* sound.

2. Explain the rule for pronouncing the final –*s*. It is pronounced \s\ when the word ends in a voiceless sound, \z\ when it ends in a voiced sound, and \iz\ when it ends in the \s\, \z\, \j\, \x\, or \ch\ sounds.

3. Make a chart with three columns on the board. Label each column with one of the headings: \s\, \z\, and \iz\

4. Lead the students as they take turns reading their lists out loud. Repeat with correct pronunciation according to the rule.

5. Tell the students to write their lists of favorite things under the appropriate heading on the chart (Appendix A) and share their answers with the class. Check the students' charts to make sure the words are in the correct columns.

6. Show the video of the song *Favorite Things* from *The Sound of Music* movie and have students watch during the first listening. During the second listening, have the students read the vocabulary from *Favorite Things* (Appendix B) while

they're watching and write the sound the final –*s* makes for each word. Explain any vocabulary that students do not understand.

CAVEATS AND OPTIONS

1. The first time the students watch the video, tell them to make a list of the favorite things from the song and then give them the vocabulary from *Favorite Things* (Appendix B) for the second listening.

2. Show the students a video of the song that includes images of the vocabulary (see References and Further Reading).

3. Give the students the song lyrics and tell them to highlight the words ending with the final –*s*. Then, provide pronunciation practice by directing students to read the highlighted words out loud. Give feedback on their pronunciation.

4. When the activity is completed, lead the class in singing the karaoke version of the song to practice the pronunciation of the final –*s* sound.

REFERENCES AND FURTHER READING

Lo, R., & Fai Li, H. C. (1998). Songs enhance learner involvement. *English Teaching Forum, 36*(3), 8–11.

Notable Quotes. (2018). Henry Wadsworth Longfellow quotes. Retrieved from www.notable-quotes.com/l/longfellow_henry_wadsworth.html

Wu, L., & McMahon, M. (2013). Adopting a musical intelligence and e-learning approach to improve the English language pronunciation of Chinese students. *AI & Society, 29*(2), 231–240.

Online Materials

- Scene from *The Sound of Music* movie: www.youtube.com/watch?v=0Iag RZBvLtw
- Song with images of vocabulary: www.youtube.com/watch?v=K7uISBk0tcw
- *Favorite Things* Song lyrics: www.songlyrics.com/the-sound-of-music/my -favorite-things-lyrics/
- Karaoke version of song: www.youtube.com/watch?v=iSUyD1I9OoU
- Viewpure.com can be used to remove advertisements surrounding videos.
- Explanation of final –*s* sounds with practice:
  — English-Zone.com: www.english-zone.com/convo/pron-s1.html
  — "Pronunciation and Music," by Susan Bergman Miyake: http:// teachingpronunciation.pbworks.com/w/file/fetch/48227890/miyake .pdf
  — EnglishClub.com: www.englishclub.com/teaching-tips/music-class room.htm

Pronunciation Practice: \v\ and \f\ Sounds

Bernadette M. López-Fitzsimmons and Amanda D'Alto

Levels	Intermediate
Aims	Practice pronunciation sounds \v\ and \f\
Class Time	Variable
Preparation Time	Variable
Resources	Diagram of Articulatory System and Features (optional; Appendix A)
	PowerPoint with pictures (Appendix A) or cards with pictures
	Handouts (Appendix B)

Practicing differentiating between \v\ and \f\ sounds is important in the development of listening and speaking skills in American English. This activity presents enjoyable and engaging ways to learn how to distinguish between the two sounds. The activity includes several exceptions and modeling and repeating the phonemes when they appear in different environments—in initial, medial, and final positions. The activity can be used to teach pronunciation in the transitional stages of learners' acquisition of English as well as a way to tweak pronunciation at more advanced levels.

PROCEDURE

1. Explain the purpose of the activity and review the articulatory system (e.g., lips, teeth, tongue). Explain articulatory features with the aid of a visual (e.g., PowerPoint [Appendix A], picture on poster board, illustration drawn on the board).

2. Instruct students to practice the place of articulation: for the \v\ sound—*turn your voice on*; for the \f\ sound—*turn your voice off*.

3. Model pronouncing words with the phonemes in different environments—in initial, medial, and final positions.

4. Tell students to repeat pronouncing sample words for each sound, using their hands to feel the vibration on their throats in the \v\ sound and the absence of the vibration in the \f\ sound.

5. Present different spellings for the \f\ sound with pictures or other visuals representing \f\, \ph\, and \gh\ spellings, and tell students to practice pronouncing the words.

6. Give students time to work in pairs or small groups to repeat pronouncing words using total physical response (TPR).

7. Present the exception to the \v\ sound in the word *of*. The \f\ in the word *of* sounds like a \v\. Tell students to feel the vibration by placing their hands on their throat and lips (TPR).

8. Distribute the handout (Appendix B) with different pictures of words with the \v\ and \f\ sounds that might cause confusion in listening.

9. Say one word aloud for each pair of pictures. Direct students to circle the picture of the word they hear.

10. Tell students to work with a partner and underline the \v\ and \f\ sounds in the words with pictures.

11. Start the next part of the activity, providing additional practice by having fun with tongue twisters. Read the tongue twisters aloud. Tell students to work with a partner and practice saying each of the tongue twisters.

12. Ask for volunteers from each pair to read the tongue twisters aloud.

13. Continue with the entire class sharing. Invite everyone to read tongue twisters aloud.

14. Assign writing original tongue twisters using the \v\ and \f\ sounds as a follow-up activity.

CAVEATS AND OPTIONS

1. The unit plan is appropriate for intermediate (transitioning) level. This may be used in its entirety as a pronunciation lesson. However, when pronunciation issues occur, parts of the activity can be modified to facilitate the improvement of the listening and speaking skills focusing on the sounds of \f\ and \v\.

2. The explanation of the articulatory system is optional, depending on the group's chemistry and age range. When it is used, a visual should be displayed with an explanation of "turning one's voice on and off."

3. When PowerPoint is unavailable, teachers may substitute pictures on cards made from poster board or cardboard. They can show each picture individually and post them—individually and together—on the wall or board.

4. The activity can be cotaught by two individuals (e.g., two cooperating teachers, mentor-teacher and mentee) or as part of a teaching practicum/supervised teaching, and in other scenarios.

REFERENCES AND FURTHER READING

Celce-Murcia, M., Brinton, D., & Goodwin, J. (2010). *Teaching pronunciation paperback with audio CDs (2): A course book and reference guide* (2nd ed.). Cambridge, England: Cambridge University Press.

Gillette, N. (2011, March 21). Understanding and teaching the /f/ and /v/ sounds to deaf and hard of hearing children. In *Exploring the /f/ and /v/ sounds*. Retrieved from https://prezi.com/m0eyf15lxyly/exploring-the-f-and-v-sounds/

Kraut. (2010, December 10). Some tongue twisters with /v/ and /w/. In *Kraut's English phonetic blog: Occasional observations of English pronunciation features, phonetics, teaching, and learning*. Retrieved from http://matters-phonetic.blogspot.com/2010/12/some-tongue-twisters-with-v-and-w.html

Kravchenko, D. (2016, September 30). 8 tongue twisters to improve English pronunciation. In *Kaplan International: K Blog*. Retrieved from https://www.kaplan international.com/blog/8-tongue-twisters-to-improve-english-pronunciation

Language Avenue. (2017). Sound F. In *Language Avenue: Your place for studying languages*. Retrieved from https://languageavenue.com/teachers/teaching-ideas/english -tongue-twisters/item/sound-f

III

Vowel Walk

Eileen Boswell

Levels	*All*
Aims	*Improve skills in listening and pronunciation of English vowel sounds*
Class Time	*25–30 minutes*
Preparation Time	*10–15 minutes*
Resources	*PowerPoint with "Vowel Walk" Animation—Sample Slides (Appendix)*
	International Phonetic Alphabet flashcards (teacher created)
	Computer with projector

Ⓡ

The Vowel Walk activity is designed to help students identify English vowel sounds that are the same or different in their first language and to begin producing them. Additionally, it establishes a physical movement to help them practice the physical differences among English monophthongs.

PROCEDURE

1. Prepare a slide that shows the English vowel distribution on a standard vowel chart, such as that of the International Phonetic Association (IPA). Label the vowel sounds with numbers, and add an animated arrow that shows the movement from one vowel sound to the next (e.g., \I\→\i\→\ɛ\→\æ\, and so forth). Use the sample slides as a guide (Appendix).

2. Prepare large IPA flashcards. Design them in the same general shape of the chart/ mouth with the symbol and keyword(s) for each vowel sound. Laminate them or place them in plastic sheet protector sleeves. Place them around the room.

3. Have students stand on or near one vowel to start. As you advance the slide through the animations, the students move from one vowel sound to the next, repeating the sound and its keyword.

4. As they move, students should be reminded of the relative height, backness and roundness of each vowel. The height and backness correspond to students' physical position in the room.

CAVEATS AND OPTIONS

1. Students can use flashcards of the vowel sounds that they have created earlier in the course as they move through the life-size vowel chart. They can use their own keywords or those you assign.

2. If their first language has a vowel sound that is not on the chart, such as the Spanish \o\ or the Japanese \ɯ\, students can approximate where it would fit relative to the English sounds they are learning.

3. Students could also put something down on the floor or move back and forth between their two most difficult sounds, or two they cannot distinguish. Note that sometimes a learner can hear the difference, but not produce the difference, between two vowel sounds.

REFERENCES AND FURTHER READING

These resources will help prepare students in advance of the Vowel Walk activity:

Clickable IPA chart with sounds: www.internationalphoneticalphabet.org/ipa-sounds /ipa-chart-with-sounds/

Interactive color vowel charts from English Language Training Solutions: http://elts .solutions/color-vowel-chart/explore/

Clickable chart with minimal pairs for vowel sounds between \b\ and \t\ (*bit*, *bet*, *bat*, etc.) from the University of Kansas: http://cmed.faculty.ku.edu/ipafolder /vowels.html

III

Focused Pronunciation Practice for Presentations

DJ Kaiser

Levels	*Intermediate to advanced*
Aims	*Focus on pronouncing keywords and difficult words in presentation preparation*
Class Time	*1–2 hours (across class periods)*
Preparation Time	*5–10 minutes*
Resources	*Handouts (Appendixes A and B)*

ocused pronunciation practice for presentations promotes stronger awareness for learners about the importance of preparing and practicing keywords and phrases or words they know they have difficulty pronouncing. Prior preparation through phonetic transcription of words that learners select based on their presentation topic allows instructors to assess prediction skills and production skills separately. This activity consists of three presentations that are ordered to start with learners focusing on fewer words until they work up to preparing and practicing more words for presentations.

PROCEDURE

Preparation

1. Provide learners with a copy of the transcription system to be used for the class (e.g., International Phonetic Alphabet [IPA] or a modified IPA system).

2. Take adequate class time (based on level and prior instruction) to teach the consonant and vowels sounds of English along with the IPA symbols and transcription.

Introduce Focused Pronunciation Practice

3. In preparation for the assigned presentations, take learners through the "Focused Pronunciation Practice Presentation Assignment" sheet (Appendix A). Then review the "Sample Focused Pronunciation Practice Preparation" sheet (Appendix B), so learners can see an example of a word list with transcriptions.

4. Assign learners to prepare their word list with transcriptions and their presentation as homework (with an assigned presentation day).

Presentations

5. On presentation day, learners give you a copy of their focused word list with transcriptions before their presentation.

6. Before the presentation, briefly review the words the learner has selected to be able to listen for these words during the presentation.

7. Make notations on word-level pronunciation errors during the presentation for the words that the learner selected. Outside of class, grade the phonetic transcriptions.

Feedback

8. In the next class, provide feedback on both the transcriptions (prediction) and the pronunciation of those words during the presentation (production).

CAVEATS AND OPTIONS

1. After Step 2, assign learners to go to the board to transcribe various words as practice. Suggested word groups for transcription practice are numbers; days of the week; months of the year; country names; and names of states, provinces, or regions.

2. For lower level learners, you may lower the number of words to start with (for example, only start with five words and work up from there). For learners in academic programs or in English for specific purposes classes, you may require that their final presentation focus on their academic or work field.

3. Additional feedback on speaking skills, presentation skills, and other pronunciation features may be given; however, this focused approach draws learners' attention to word-level preparation.

III

Presenting Poetry and Prose

John Schmidt

Levels	*High beginner to advanced*
Aims	*Orally interpret poetry or prose*
	Experience a new work of literature and its author
	Enhance use of vocal variety and clear pronunciation when reciting a literary passage
Class Time	*40–45 minutes*
Preparation Time	*30 minutes*
Resources	*Copies of a poem or prose (excerpt)*

Reciting poetry and telling stories is one of the oldest forms of public speaking. Students often have limited familiarity with literature written in English. This activity introduces a short poem, a folktale, a lively children's story, or an excerpt of a longer work of prose. In addition to appreciating the literary work, its author, and the genre, students have an opportunity to express the ideas, emotions, and attitudes of the author. While employing vocal variety, students can also focus on clear pronunciation in their presentations.

PROCEDURE

1. Following a short introduction of the work and its author, demonstrate an interpretive reading of a literary passage.
2. Give students copies of the passage and clarify vocabulary, as needed.
3. Introduce and provide practice of selected segmental phonemes and/or suprasegmental phonemes in the text.
4. Review aspects of vocal variety, including volume, pitch, rate and quality, as well as appropriate pauses. For poetry, rhythm is an additional feature to cover. Students should consider the ideas, emotions, and attitudes of the author and any character.
5. Give the students an opportunity to practice the excerpts alone and with a partner.
6. Students present the passage to classmates. Passages might be recorded, if the students want to share them with others or if they or you plan to further work on pronunciation or other aspects of delivery of the passage.
7. After this introductory activity in presenting poetry or prose, consider ways to follow up on or expand the procedures. Individually or in groups, students could select literary works or passages to study, practice, and present.

CAVEATS AND OPTIONS

1. Although there are innumerable literary works to choose from, children's literature, particularly whimsical works, can be a good starting point, even for adults. In addition to having fun with the passages, which tend to be limited in length and vocabulary, students can focus on pronunciation, vocal variety, and rhythmic patterns. They can also become familiar with the author and other works by the author or within the genre.

2. English as a second language/English as a foreign language students enjoy the stories and illustrations of Dr. Seuss (Theodor Seuss Geisel), and some students are familiar with his stories that have been made into movies. However, given the challenge of translating much of his work into other languages, most of his stories will likely be new to them. *Green Eggs and Ham* (1960) is popular with students, with its two expressive characters, rhyme, and 50-word simplicity (49 monosyllabic words and one polysyllabic word); it is useful for focusing on clear pronunciation of the 10 different vowel sounds.

   Another whimsical children's writer, popular with young and old, is Shel Silverstein, whose poetry is accompanied by his drawings. "Every Thing On It" and many of Silverstein's other poems range from four to 20 lines and can be readily used in class.

3. Additional literary sources include fables, folk tales and fairy tales, short stories, novels, and memoirs. Excerpts of most literature can be used for presentation. Passage selection can be a good challenge for students, as well as the students' development of an introduction to the passage to provide listeners with background and context.

4. Following this introduction to presenting poetry and prose, subsequent activities could involve student research and selection of works and authors to present. English as a second language/English as a foreign language students are proud to present poetry and prose from their own culture and language that has been translated into English. Some choose to first read their excerpt in their native language and then in English. Popular with Spanish speakers is Pablo Neruda's *Odes to Common Things* (1994). The 225 odes include poems to a dog, a guitar, a bed, socks, and an apple. A student favorite is often "Ode to French Fries." Students in some classes follow up by writing their own odes to underappreciated objects.

REFERENCES AND FURTHER READING

Geisel, T. S. (1960). *Green eggs and ham*. New York, NY: Random House.

Neruda, P. (1994). *Odes to common things* (K. Krabbenhoft, Trans.). New York, NY: Bulfinch.

Silverstein, S. (2011). *Every thing on it*. New York, NY: Harper.

Syllable Stones

Marla Yoshida

Levels	*Beginner to high intermediate*
Aims	*Build awareness of counting syllables and word stress patterns*
Class Time	*10 minutes +*
Preparation Time	*None*
Resources	*Objects in variable sizes (5–6 larger objects, 10–12 smaller ones per student or pair)*

Pronouncing words with the right number of syllables and appropriate word stress is very important in making learners' pronunciation intelligible, yet many students find it difficult to count syllables or to recognize where the stress falls. This is especially true if the students' first language has a very different syllable structure than English. This activity builds awareness of syllables and stress patterns by having learners build models of syllable patterns for words; this is similar to the common practice of drawing large and small circles to represent the syllables of words, but more tactile and memorable. This activity can be done individually, but it is more effective if done in pairs.

PROCEDURE

1. Tell students about the importance of producing syllables and word stress correctly in being understood, and give an example. (E.g., "If I say *conversation*, it's easy to understand. If I say *conVERsation* or *conversaTION*, people might not understand.")

2. Have the class brainstorm some words they've learned or take some from class materials. Write the chosen words on the board. Try to include some types of words that might cause confusion about syllables:

   • Past tense forms of regular verbs (Do they add an extra syllable or not?)

   • Words with consonant clusters that are perceived by speakers of some languages as having more syllables than they actually have (*school*, *strong*, *spring*)

   • Words that are usually pronounced with fewer syllables than the spelling would suggest (*restaurant*, *vegetable*, *chocolate*)

   • Longer words with four or more syllables. Students sometimes get lost while counting syllables in these.

3. Divide the class into pairs and give each pair five to six large objects and a handful of small ones. These objects can include stones, balls, or pieces of pasta; Cuisenaire rods; or other types of objects in variable sizes. For the smaller objects, glass vase fillers sold in craft stores work well.

4. Explain that the larger objects represent stressed syllables. Point out how they're bigger, heavier, and more detailed, just as stressed syllables are longer, louder, higher in pitch, and have clearer vowel sounds than unstressed ones. The smaller objects represent unstressed syllables—small and plain.

5. Show how to make a syllable model of a word using an example like *banana*. Have the students say the word, count the syllables, and determine which one is stressed. Show that we need three syllable shapes, one big and two small, to depict this word and elicit how we should arrange them: small, big, small. Discuss another syllable model using the example of *conversation* and show the students an illustration of the four syllable shapes (Appendix). To make this demonstration easier for the class to see, use objects on a larger scale: a basketball and two baseballs, large and small boxes, or large and small magnets stuck on the board.

6. Ask students to follow the same procedure for the remaining words, discussing how many syllables each has and where the stress should fall, and then making syllable models.

7. Call the class together and check their syllable patterns. Discuss any words that they found difficult, clap the syllables, and talk about what made those words tricky.

CAVEATS AND OPTIONS

1. To reinforce the contrast between stressed and unstressed syllables, choose larger objects that are more detailed or interesting-looking, and smaller ones that are plainer and less significant-looking.

2. With very young students, don't use objects that are breakable or small enough to swallow.

3. If you'd like to include secondary stress in your practice, add middle-sized objects to represent them.

4. Instead of using physical objects, draw shapes in a document projected on a screen and have students drag them into position. Draw large and small circles or other shapes to represent syllables, making sure that the shape can be moved around the document. (If using Microsoft Word, change the "Wrap Text" setting in the "Format" menu if the shape can't be moved.) Copy and paste to create a supply of large and small "syllables" and have students drag the shapes they need into position to form syllable patterns.

APPENDIX: *Illustration of Syllable Stones Model for Conversation*

The Inner-Outer Circle: A Platform to Integrate Pronunciation Into Speaking

Ivanne Deneroff

Levels	*All*
Aims	*Incorporate stress and intonation into speaking and listening*
Class Time	*20 minutes +*
Preparation Time	*10–15 minutes (optional)*
Resources	*Index cards or paper with teacher-created questions/topics written on them*
	Timer

Inner-outer circle activities have been successfully employed in language learning in varied forms as a simple way to get learners on their feet while using conversation questions on any topic to promote fluency. Many variations center around this basic format: Learners form two concentric circles where those in the inner circle are paired with those in the outer one. What differentiates this version is what occurs before and after the activity itself. In the preactivities, schema is activated by providing any source of input to preteach target vocabulary, including specific pronunciation features used contextually in the conversation questions.

Postactivities raise awareness by eliciting patterns of error that occurred during the activity and providing corrective feedback.

This version of the inner-outer circle activity is a practical application with a broader, theory-driven movement: to integrate pronunciation, speaking, and listening as subsets of oral communication. It also more pointedly addresses teaching the skill of speaking versus talking for talking's sake. The activity promotes both accuracy (preactivities) and fluency (uninterrupted speech) across planned and more spontaneous discourse.

In this version, the pairs in each circle (inner and outer) are provided with a different set of questions (an information-gap task) promoting the genuine negotiation of meaning, which occurs in naturalistic discourse.

Many variations of this activity are possible, as long as some source of input is provided prior to the activity itself so that it can serve as practice or reinforcement of the preestablished linguistic or content objectives.

PROCEDURE

Preactivity

1. Before class, prepare two questions (one for Group 1, one for Group 2) on any topic, copied as needed so each student has one question (either for Group 1 or Group 2).

2. Activate schema by introducing or reviewing specific vocabulary.

3. Review syllable stress at the word, sentence, and discourse level (i.e., model asking and answering a sample conversation question).

4. Explicitly address articulation on the segmental level if necessary.

Activity

1. Divide the group in half, Group 1 (inner circle) and Group 2 (outer circle).

2. Guide Group 1 to form a shoulder-to-shoulder circle facing outward.

3. Direct each member in Group 2 to face a member of the inner circle.

4. Explain that pairs will have a time limit (1–3 minutes) to ask and answer only one question. Speakers in Group 1 ask their question first. Students that finish early (before 3 minutes) should continue to the Group 2 question. After 3 minutes, pairs discuss the Group 2 question if they have not already started doing so. The timer stops at 6 minutes.

5. Explain that when you call out "switch," members of Group 2 move one person to the right.

6. Model the exercise with a volunteer if necessary. Set the timer and begin.

Postactivities

1. As a class, raise awareness by reproducing patterns of error in pitch, stress, and intonation.

2. Ask learners to physically mark the stress (e.g., clap and have the loudest, longest clap on the stressed syllable) or draw patterns of intonation on paper and share it with the class.

3. Check comprehension.

CAVEATS AND OPTIONS

1. For classes with an odd number of learners, place the extra member in Group 2 (outer circle); two students in the outer circle rotate as a pair. Alternatively, you can participate in the activity; however, monitoring for students' fluency in their ability to extend, cope with silence, and accurately pronounce words is opportune for formative assessment.

2. Take students outside or to another location with ample space for movement if possible. The change in environment coupled with a kinesthetic activity can often energize learners.

3. Project questions for a paperless version of the activity.

4. Consider these variations for higher levels.

   - Provide less scaffolding with more open-ended questions (i.e., "describe a time when . . .") and longer uninterrupted stretches of discourse.

   - Increase the time to extend discourse: 1 minute uninterrupted to 2 minutes to 3 minutes, and so on.

   - Cut questions into strips, challenging learners to find relevant ways to fill silence.

   - Ask students to generate at least one spontaneous question related to the topic.

5. Consider these variations on conversation questions.

   - The content of conversation questions/topics can be shaped by any linguistic or content objectives, such as "Have you ever" questions on the present perfect or a common greeting, such as "How're you?," to address contractions that are routinely difficult for learners to pronounce.

   - Input sources can vary widely, from a brief introduction of a collocation to inductive listening to authentic speech where learners identify new vocabulary.

6. Use this activity at any phase to promote acquisition.

REFERENCES AND FURTHER READING

Derwing, T. M., & Munro, M. J. (2015). *Pronunciation fundamentals: Evidence-based perspectives for L2 teaching and research.* Philadelphia, PA: John Benjamins.

III

Fishing for Pronunciation

Patricia Hart

Levels	**Beginning**
Aims	**Practice and improve pronunciation focusing on consonant clusters**
Class Time	**15–20 minutes**
Preparation Time	**15 minutes (first time only)**
Resources	**Flashcards (30–40 per each group of 3 students)**

Most students enjoy learning when games are involved. Card games like "Go Fish" have international appeal. Fishing for Pronunciation follows some of the basic fun elements of "Go Fish" while motivating students to practice key areas of pronunciation. If the words on the flashcards are changed, this game can also focus on minimal pairs, phonemes, and rhyming words.

PROCEDURE

1. Prepare four sets (or more) of 30–40 flashcards. As a timesaver, make one set of cards and then copy it as many times as needed. On the card, write one word. On the next card, write one word with a similar sound that has a consonant cluster. For example, write "trick" on one card and write "trees" on the next card. Make an even number of cards with the same consonant cluster because the students will match the cards. Other examples of words are *try, trip, train, cheese, chick, chain,* and *chew*. (See References and Further Reading for a resource that lists more words.)

2. Introduce the activity with a pronunciation review of the words on the flashcards. Write each word on the board, say it to the class, and tell them to repeat it.

3. Divide the class into groups with three students in each.

4. Distribute six flashcards to each student. Instruct them not to show the rest of the group their cards. Put the remaining flashcards face down in the middle of each group.

5. Explain that students must take turns and ask only one other student in their group if they have a word that sounds like their word. For example, the first student would say, "Ali, do you have a word that sounds like *tr-trees?*"

6. If the student being asked does have a matching card, such as the word *trick*, he would give it to that student. If not, the student must take a card from the pile in the center.

7. If the student who asked for the matching card finds it, he keeps it with his card and puts the pair to the side.

8. Walk around, listen, and tell students if they make an error, such as thinking they don't have a matching card because they don't pronounce it correctly.

9. The student with the most pairs when the card pile runs out wins.

CAVEATS AND OPTIONS

Remind students to clearly pronounce the consonant cluster sound they are asking another student for.

REFERENCES AND FURTHER READING

Speech-language-therapy.com: This website provides word lists, including consonant clusters, minimal pairs, vowels, and consonants, that focus on common pronunciation problems:

Bowen, C. (2012, February 18). Speech-language-therapy dot com. Retrieved from http://www.speech-language-therapy.com/index.php?option=com_content &view=article&id=134:mp2&catid=9:resources&Itemid=108

III

Minimal Pair Memory

Patricia Hart

Levels	*Beginning*
Aims	*Practice and improve pronunciation focusing on minimal pairs*
Class Time	*15–20 minutes*
Preparation Time	*15 minutes (first time only)*
Resources	*Flashcards (30–40 per each group of 4 students)*

Instead of a dreary lesson spent memorizing language elements, this game is a fun, motivating activity for students to remember how to pronounce difficult sounds. Students practice pronouncing minimal pairs, words that are exactly the same except for one sound, such as *ship/sheep* or *better/butter*. The flashcards can be changed to practice consonant clusters, phonemes, and rhyming words.

PROCEDURE

1. Prepare four sets (or more) of 30–40 flashcards. As a timesaver, make one set of cards and then copy it as many times as needed. Write one word on one card and write one word with a similar sound on the next, so that together the two cards form a minimal pair. For example, write "ship" on one card and write "sheep" on the other card. Make an even number of cards with the same minimal pair because the students will match the cards. (See References and Further Reading for a resource that lists more words.)

2. Divide the class into groups with four students in each.

3. Spread out cards face down in a square pattern, so that no two cards overlap.

4. Explain that students must take turns flipping any two cards over. Each student must read the pair of cards out loud.

5. Explain that the goal is to find a minimal pair. Describe the meaning of "minimal pair." Give examples as needed.

6. If the two cards form a minimal pair, the student takes the pair and sets it in front of them.

7. If the two cards do not form a matching minimal pair, the student must replace the cards, face down.

8. The next student flips over two flashcards of their choice. Monitor students to ensure they are pronouncing the words out loud (and doing so properly) as much as possible.

9. The student with the most pairs when the card pile runs out wins.

CAVEATS AND OPTIONS

Remind students to clearly pronounce the words on the cards.

REFERENCES AND FURTHER READING

Speech-language-therapy.com: This website provides word lists, including minimal pairs, consonant clusters, vowels, and consonants, that focus on common pronunciation problems.

Bowen, C. (2012, February 18). Speech-language-therapy dot com. Retrieved from http://www.speech-language-therapy.com/index.php?option=com_content &view=article&id=134:mp2&catid=9:resources&Itemid=108

III

Pronunciation Basketball

Melinda Cuyul-Gordon

Levels	*All*
Aims	*Increase motivation*
	Improve pronunciation accuracy
	Review vocabulary
Class Time	*10–15 minutes (per round)*
Preparation Time	*5 minutes*
Resources	*Trash can or other receptacle*
	Small ball, rock, or crumpled piece of paper in the shape of a ball

What makes students jump to their feet and roar in excitement? Pronunciation Basketball! This competitive team game wildly increases motivation, encourages accurate pronunciation development, and reinforces vocabulary. Pronunciation Basketball combines aural and kinesthetic learning styles to help students increase pronunciation accuracy. Don't worry about breaking a sweat in this basketball game, though—this game only calls for quick thinking and a steady hand. Any skill level—language skill or physical skill—is appropriate for this activity; participants do not need to be athletic to be successful in this game. Both young learners and adults love this game. When the teams start cheering and the ball starts flying, students won't even remember they are studying.

PROCEDURE

1. Make two teams and have each team sit together.

2. Have all students take out their vocabulary lists.

3. Put the trash can in the front of the classroom. Tell students that the trash can is the "basket" and show them the ball. Let students know they will be playing basketball with these.

4. Go to the rear of the classroom and shoot a few baskets to demonstrate.

5. Tell students they will be playing a competitive team game. One person from each team will stand up in the rear of the classroom. You will read the definition of a vocabulary word, and both students will try to pronounce the correct vocabulary word accurately. For example, you say, "This is a sport that involves an orange ball, a wooden floor, and a hoop." The students say, "Basketball!"

6. Tell students that the first student to pronounce the correct vocabulary word accurately is the winner. You can decide to check accuracy in terms of word stress, phoneme production, or both.

7. The winner gets to shoot a basket two times. The student who did not win gets to shoot a basket one time. Explain to students that the benefit of this is that students who are not strong in pronunciation can still help their team to win by making baskets.

8. Tell the teams that they can help their teammate by whispering the vocabulary word. For classes with strong students, or for an easy vocabulary set, teams can help their teammate by offering just the first letter of the vocabulary word.

9. Now, begin the game! Invite two students to stand up in the rear of the classroom. Read one vocabulary definition. Both students compete to pronounce the correct vocabulary word accurately.

10. The first student who pronounces the vocabulary word accurately is the winner.

11. The winning student shoots two baskets. The other student shoots one basket.

12. Award one point for each basket made.

13. Invite two new students to stand up. Continue playing until everyone on each team has had one or more turns.

CAVEATS AND OPTIONS

1. This game can get rather loud. You may want to make sure you are not playing this game if other nearby classes need quiet.

2. If students become overly competitive, try not keeping score, or try mixing up the teams after each round.

3. The scoring method may be adjusted to have the student who correctly pronounces the word earn a point before attempting to earn more points by shooting a basket twice. The benefit is that students who miss the basket can still earn points for their team by getting the answer correct first.

4. Use gap-fill sentences: You say a sentence that has the correct vocabulary word missing instead of a definition. For example, you say, "I love to play the sport of _____ with my orange ball because I love to shoot hoops."

5. If you want to work on pronunciation accuracy for multiple words at a time, ask students to read out a complete sentence. In this case, you should prepare sentences in advance by writing the same sentence on two slips of paper. Hand the identical sentences to the two students who are standing up. Each student reads out the sentence. The student who has more accurate pronunciation of the entire sentence is declared the winner.

6. Call out synonyms or antonyms instead of definitions. The aim of the game is still pronunciation accuracy, but you can check vocabulary comprehension in a different way.

REFERENCES AND FURTHER READING

Here are two websites that offer different approaches to playing this game:

- *Vocabulary Toss* from Education World: www.educationworld.com/a_lesson/04/lp328-05.shtml
- *Vocab Shot* from Flocabulary: www.flocabulary.com/vocabulary-mini-games/

Peer Dictation

Jean L. Arnold

Levels	*Beginner to advanced*
Aims	*Practice pronunciation while dictating text to a peer*
	Use repair strategies to complete the task
Class Time	*10–15 minutes*
Preparation Time	*5–10 minutes*
Resources	*Handout (Appendix)*

P eer Dictation can be a very eye-opening exercise for students, helping them become aware of sounds that they are not producing comprehensibly. Students take turns dictating sentences to each other, which keeps them both engaged and aware of the difficulties of each role—speaker and writer. This activity works best to highlight pronunciation difficulties if students can be paired with someone who speaks a different native language, but the dictation is a valuable listening/speaking/spelling practice, regardless.

PROCEDURE

1. Before class, prepare a text that you want students to read and separate the text into lines. Number the lines if desired. Copy the text and give them distinctive names, such as Text A and Text B (see Appendix for a sample "Peer Dictation: Quotations about Service"). If you're working in Microsoft Word, go to View > Zoom > Multiple pages. You can now easily see the texts side by side and take out alternate lines. Text A will have blank lines for lines 1, 3, 5, etc., and Text B will have blank lines for the even numbers.

2. Put the students in pairs and explain the activity. Each student has sentences that they dictate to their partner for the partner to write them down correctly. The person dictating can see what the partner is writing, but the partner who is writing cannot look at the text that is being dictated. If the speaker notices that something has not been transcribed correctly, the speaker can clarify. If the writer cannot understand something that the person dictating has said, he or she must ask for clarification. Encourage students to use the helpful expressions at the top of the handout (Appendix). Tell students to begin the activity, taking turns dictating and writing sentences.

3. Observe the class and assist as needed. As pairs finish, tell them to read the sentences back to check and then look at the other student's paper to check for accuracy.

4. In pairs or as a class, students may discuss the content of what they have just dictated and written.

5. As a final step, lead a class discussion about the challenges and benefits of the activity.

CAVEATS AND OPTIONS

1. The texts used for the peer dictation can be anything you want the students to spend a little extra time with—a recipe, key points of a lecture or reading, a list of vocabulary words and their definitions, or a list of inspirational quotes.

2. You can have students include the punctuation marks in their dictation. In this way, they become familiar with the words for the marks and the marks themselves, as well as noticing when they are used in context.

3. This is a good way to introduce the importance of using quotation marks to denote that you are recording exactly what another person has said or written.

Pronunciation Workouts With Print or Online Resources

William Haselton

Levels	*Low intermediate to advanced*
Aims	*Create tools for self-guided pronunciation practice and reflection*
Class Time	*15–20 minutes*
Preparation Time	*10 minutes*
Resources	*Handout (Appendix)*

Ⓡ

One way to help students improve their pronunciation is to guide them in designing a regular plan for practicing. Just as working out in the gym can make our bodies stronger and healthier, students can do "pronunciation workouts" to improve their pronunciation. These workouts, conducted in class or outside of class, involve students in designing their own plan for pronunciation practice. The specific exercises that compose the workouts are based on instructor feedback from pronunciation diagnostics or class presentations. This feedback highlights specific phonemes or pronunciation patterns that need attention. Students not only design their own plan for pronunciation practice, but they also engage in regular self-reflection to help them monitor their progress. Teachers can use students' self-reflection to refine pronunciation instruction in class and to offer students further constructive feedback. These pronunciation workouts enable students to take charge of their own learning.

PROCEDURE

1. Provide students with a menu of resources (Appendix) that they can use for the pronunciation workouts.
2. As a whole-class activity, demonstrate how to use the resources.
3. Give students 10–15 minutes to work on their pronunciation, focusing on specific skills. You may allow students to choose their own pronunciation focus for the workouts, or you could have the whole class work together on a particular aspect of pronunciation.
4. Students should do at least two or three brief workouts per week to focus on specific areas where their pronunciation needs improvement.
5. Following the workouts, either in class or outside of class, have students write a short paragraph to reflect on their pronunciation progress.
6. Read the students' reflections to gain insight into areas where they need more focused instruction or practice. Offer them feedback that they can use in future pronunciation workouts.

CAVEATS AND OPTIONS

1. You may choose to have the students record their pronunciation workouts and submit them for your review. However, this will add considerable grading time to the activity.

2. If you choose not to have students record and submit their workouts, some students may offer reflections on practices they have not done. Remind the students that if they choose not to do the workouts, they are only hurting themselves. Generally, you can tell from the reflection paragraph whether the students have properly done the workouts.

3. Evaluate the students' reflections using a simple 4-point rubric:

   4—Very Thorough: Excellent insights and personal reflection. Clear comments about areas that need improvement.

   3—Generally Good: Some personal reflection, but general and superficial at times. May be lacking comments about areas that need improvement.

   2—Somewhat Lacking: Very little personal reflection. No comments about areas that need improvement.

   1—Poor: Extremely weak reflection on this week's practices.

REFERENCES AND FURTHER READING

Chau, J., & Cheng, G. (2012). Developing Chinese students' reflective second language learning skills in higher education. *The Journal of Language Teaching and Learning, 2*(1), 15–32.

Lear, E. (2015). Using guided reflective journals in large classes: Motivating students to independently improve pronunciation. *The Asian EFL Journal, 15*(3), 113–137.

Long, N., & Huang, J. (2015). Out-of-class pronunciation learning: Are EFL learners ready in China? In D. Nunan & J. C. Richards (Eds.), *Language learning beyond the classroom*, (pp. 43–52). New York, NY: Routledge.

Suwartono, S. (2014). Enhancing the pronunciation of English suprasegmental features through reflective learning method. *TEFLIN Journal, 25*(1), 80–93. Retrieved from http://www.teflin.org/journal/index.php/journal/article/viewFile/184/161

Quote of the Day

Eileen Boswell

Levels	*Intermediate*
Aims	*Practice intonation, word stress, and pronunciation*
	Increase confidence
Class Time	*15–20 minutes*
Preparation Time	*2 minutes*
Resources	*Example images of this exercise's progression (Appendix A)*
	Handouts (Appendixes B and C)

Ⓡ

The Quote of the Day exercise guides students through a regular, rigorous practice in improving their intonation in spoken English. Its direct application is to presentational English, but it has benefits in spoken conversation, too, as well as benefits for students' listening comprehension in presentations, lectures, videos, classroom interactions, and personal conversations. The specific skills targeted are 1) pacing, 2) pausing, 3) pronunciation, and 4) "power" (sentence focus), which can conveniently be referred to as The Four Ps when presenting this exercise. Quote of the Day works best when implemented as a regular practice near the beginning of each class.

III

PROCEDURE

1. To prepare for this activity, choose a quotation that has an appropriate topic, message, and vocabulary level. Review the following steps, including "Images of this Exercise's Progression" (Appendix A) to see an example of how to mark a quote with your class.

2. Write the quote and the attribution of the person who said it (if known) on the whiteboard with a dark color marker.

3. Have students read the quote silently.

4. To one side of the quote, make a list of the 4 Ps: Pacing, Pausing, Pronunciation, Power.

5. Say the quote one or two times, asking students to listen for your rhythm and intonation.

6. Say the quote again. Above the 4 Ps, draw a line and write "Grammar/ Vocabulary" above that line. Ask if any of the grammar or vocabulary needs clarification before students can focus on the way you are saying the quote. The third P, pronunciation, can be written Pronunciation/linking, once linking has been taught as a listening skill, even if it has not been taught as a speaking skill.

7. Say the quote again. Ask students, "What do you hear?" Over time, establish during this activity that we do not communicate in English solely with words; we use our voices to communicate in English. Ask them what they hear that you are doing with your voice to say this quote naturally. If you need to prompt them, ask if they hear where you paused, went up or down, fast or slow, or loud or soft; if they notice any linking; or if there are any strange consonant or vowel sounds they heard or couldn't hear (such as a schwa sound).

8. Repeat the quote several times as students listen for various aspects of your intonation. Keep asking them, "What do you hear in my voice?" As this becomes an established activity, they will not need so much prompting, but they will still need the quote repeated.

9. As they point out various aspects of your intonation, mark the quote with a contrasting color marker.

   - Mark linking with a curved line between the end of one word and the beginning of the following word.

   - Mark faster pacing with a jagged line beneath the words said quickly together, or a circle around words said as a chunk or phrase.

   - Mark word stress however you would during a lesson on word stress (perhaps with an accent mark over the stressed syllable or stressed vowel).

   - Mark rising pitch with an up arrow, especially in lists or sequences; mark falling pitch with a down arrow, especially at the end of a list or sequence, and at the end of the sentence.

   - Mark pauses with parentheses around empty space between words where students heard a pause. You can also mark pauses that correspond to punctuation by putting the parentheses around the comma or semicolon that indicates a pause.

   - Mark sentence focus or power by drawing a rectangle around the words that have the most vocal force.

10. Repeat and mark the quote as students identify more intonational features. Have students stand and say the quote with the appropriate intonation, one at a time, while focusing on the contrasting color marks for cues.

11. Beneath the Four Ps list, draw a line. Write "Meaning/Message" below that line. Time permitting, paraphrase what the quote means so students understand it as they are saying it. This step can happen before or after the previous step, depending on the level of the group/complexity of the quote.

CAVEATS AND OPTIONS

1. Choose the quote carefully. Ideally, it will be thematically linked to some content the students are studying. If not, perhaps it contains particular sounds or stress patterns they have been studying. Be wary of including idioms or other figurative language that would draw attention away from the way the quote is said. It should not be so abstract that it becomes a reading comprehension lesson.

2. After several weeks, students can lead the exercise themselves or choose the quotes. The exercise can be included in listening homework by having students choose their favorite quotation from an audio/video sample and mark the way the speaker said it. (See Appendix B for a handout of the listening homework. See Appendix C for a sample of the listening homework.)

See It Right

Charles Hall

Levels	*High beginner to advanced*
Aims	*Receive visual, immediate correction of significant phonemic mistakes*
Class Time	*5–10 minutes first time, 30 seconds afterward*
Preparation Time	*30 minutes per phonemic contrast*
Resources	*None*

Teachers and students are interested in efficient, effective learning. This activity describes a simple visual correction technique that provides individualized feedback and corrects important pronunciation errors in little instructional time. Use this immediately as students make a meaningful mistake and concentrate only on significant phonemic contrasts matched to each group's need. For example, Czech students prototypically have problems distinguishing \ε\ as in *bed* from \æ\ as in *bad*. On the other hand, many Arabs confuse \p\ and \b\ in speech.

After determining the one or two most significant contrasts that cause problems for a class, create simple, highly visual hand signs that can be "flashed" at students when immediate mistake correction is appropriate while the student is speaking.

For example, in the Czech case, use an "alligator or snake mouth" that opens up toward the student to indicate the student should have said \æ\ instead of \ε\ as in "This is a really *bed* [*sic*] decision." Should the opposite happen, put your index finger and thumb together in the "just a pinch" sign and slowly move the hand parallel to your body to indicate that \ε\ as in *bed* should have been used, for example, to correct "I want a *rad* [*sic*] car!"

For the Arabic example, put two fingers in a salute on your lips and use a quick motion like blowing a kiss, but much sharper and quicker, to remind the student of the aspiration necessary to distinguish \p\ from the student's mistaken use of \b\ as in "Kathy *bushed* [*sic*] the fire alarm." Should the Arabic student hypercorrect, and say, "I like these tennis *palls* [*sic*]," (noiselessly) smack your lips while clutching your throat to remind the student of the voicing necessary for the correct \b\ sound.

PROCEDURE

One-Time Preparation Before Class

1. Determine one or two phonemic contrasts that are problematic for each group, such as initial \b\ and \v\ for most Spanish speakers.

2. Create simple, clear minimal pairs and blatantly different example sentences. Here are some examples for Spanish \b\ and \v\:
   a. base/vase
   b. Let's play baseball. Put the flowers in the vase.
3. Devise a simple, clear, and very visual sign for each sound.
   a. For \b\, firmly close your lips together and run your finger quickly across your lips as in the "don't breathe a word" sign.
   b. For \v\, bite your lower lip with your upper teeth so that the upper teeth are visible while tapping your index finger sharply against the visible upper teeth to show how the sound \v\ is made.

One-Time Activity in Class

1. In class, help the students elicit the sound contrasts you have prepared.
2. If the group is high beginner, you may need to just present or demonstrate the problematic contrasts. For example, say, "Remember we had some problem with the b/v in *boat* and *vote*?"
3. Explain that you will give them a sign to help them correct themselves sometimes when they are speaking. The sign will help them remember to use the right sound.
4. Demonstrate the signs with the minimal pair and then in the example sentences.
5. Do a lightning quiz (a very quick quiz) by writing the words on the board and labeling them 1 and 2. As you give the sign, ask them for the number of the word you are signing. Do not ask which word, because you need to be able to know if they get it right.
6. Now have them produce the sign and the sounds.

In Class When a Student Produces a Mistake

1. Depending on the context and the individual student, you can now flash the appropriate sign. For example, flash the "v" sign (biting lower lip with upper teeth) if the student says, "I liked that movie *berry* [*sic*] much."
2. Do not say the correct form.
3. Do not repeat the sign.
4. If the student doesn't self-correct, just continue as though nothing occurred.
5. If the student self-corrects, smile, nod, and continue as though nothing occurred.

CAVEATS AND OPTIONS

1. This procedure is used only for mistakes that students can self-correct, not errors that would need explanation.
2. Speed is of the essence. Do not linger on the correction; it should not interfere with the communicative nature of any task.

3. Once the signs are learned, they can also be used for quick in-class listening discrimination tasks that might be appropriate for a specific class.

4. For example, after writing band \æ\ and bend \ɛ\ and a couple of other \æ\ and \ɛ\ minimal pairs on the board, say, "Show me with the right sound which word I'm saying." This should be done only a few times and very quickly. Do not spend more than 5 minutes total, or the exercise becomes counterproductive. Be creative!

Part IV

Speaking in Specific Contexts

- **Interviews and Questioning**
- **Oral Presentation Skills**
- **Oral Presentations**
- **Spoken English for Academic and Professional Purposes**
- **Young Speakers**

IV

Class Statistics

Jesse Giacomini

Levels	*Intermediate to advanced*
Aims	*Learn about class demographics*
	Participate in surveying, asking follow-up questions, organizing data into graphs, and presenting statistics
	Improve critical thinking skills
Class Time	*1–2 hours*
Preparation Time	*15 minutes*
Resources	*Projector or handout (Appendix)*
	Examples of graphs

Class Statistics works well on the first day or in the first week of class. It is especially appropriate in an academic setting where students may be working with data or graphs and could use practice creating and presenting them. In the initial data gathering stage, students ask each other a simple question and follow-up questions, recording all responses. Students organize the data into a visual graph and present their results to the class using academic language.

Questions can be adapted to focus on specific topics connected to the curriculum of the course and to address or avoid more personal or political topics.

PROCEDURE

1. Prepare a list of hypotheses/guesses about the class, or adapt the one provided (Appendix). Provide more hypotheses than students.

2. Project the list or distribute copies of it and ask students to read it (individually/ in partners/as a class) and decide if they agree with the percentages. Check for vocabulary comprehension.

3. Explain that students will be responsible for surveying and collecting data from classmates to check the hypotheses.

4. Ask each student to choose one hypothesis. Keep a list of who chooses each hypothesis.

5. Give students some time to prepare. First, they should change their hypothesis statements into questions for surveying an individual. Then they should think of follow-up questions. Finally, they should create a chart to record the responses.

   - Example from the handout: "I bet that 70% of us take public transit to school."

IV

- Example follow-up questions: Do you walk to school? How do you get to school? How long does it take you to get to school?

6. Begin the data collection. Students move around the room and conduct the survey, recording responses on their charts.

7. When the data collection is complete, ask for a volunteer to explain how to turn the data into percentages.

8. Show examples of a bar graph, pie graph, and line graph and talk about the best way to represent different data. Give students some time to create a visual representation of their data, either on the board or using paper/poster board and markers, or on a computer using the chart function in Microsoft Word or PowerPoint.

9. Students present their data and comment on the accuracy of the teacher's hypothesis (typed on the handout) or their own hypotheses that they created.

- Example: "According to my research, only 25% of us walk to school, while 30% drive and the remaining 45% take public transit."

CAVEATS AND OPTIONS

1. There are many ways to adapt the handout, making it more or less academic, personal, political, and so on. Also, students could make their own original statements and bring those to class.

2. To save time, the hypothesis portion of the activity can be omitted, although it can be good to demonstrate your impressions/beliefs about the class.

3. The graph-making portion of this activity can be omitted if time is tight, or if it isn't relevant to the course, but students often appreciate the opportunity to be creative in this way.

4. This activity can also be used to encourage students to do research outside of class, such as to survey other students on campus or their neighbours.

5. Participate as part of the survey sample; participating gives you a chance to speak to each student and can help you to situate yourself as part of the class community.

Job Interviews in Pairs: Talk and Evaluate

Feifei Han

Levels	*Intermediate to advanced*
Aims	*Practice spoken English in a job interview context*
	Offer and receive feedback on interview performance
	Give job interview tips
Class Time	*30 minutes*
Preparation Time	*15–30 minutes*
Resources	*2 job advertisements (as handouts)*
	Handout (Appendixes A and B)

For adult English language learners, job interview skills in English are essential to master, as these students are likely to work in English-speaking countries or in professional contexts where the working language is English. This activity provides an opportunity for students to practice their spoken English by using formal language, including appropriate word choice and accurate usage of expressions. It also hones their job interview skills in terms of maintaining eye contact, appearing confident, and using effective body language. Students learn through the evaluation of their performance in a mock job interview that concentrates on two broad aspects. The first aspect focuses on students' job interview performance in general, whereas the second aspect specifically targets students' spoken English, including pronunciation; stress and intonation; grammatical accuracy; and appropriateness of pragmatics, coherence, and fluency. Students can use the feedback in the evaluation form to improve their answers to job interview questions. At the end of the activity, the class creates a list of tips for successful job interview skills in English.

PROCEDURE

1. To prepare for the activity, select two job advertisements. Make one copy for each pair of students. Then make one copy for each student of the handouts, "Sample Interview Questions" (Appendix A) and "Sample Job Interview Evaluation Form" (Appendix B).

2. Begin the activity by dividing students into pairs. Students can be randomly divided or they can be divided by the similarity of their majors or job interests.

3. Ask students in each pair to take turns playing the role of an interviewer and an interviewee.

4. Hand out two job advertisements, two copies of "Sample Interview Questions," and two copies of the "Sample Job Interview Evaluation Form" to each pair.

5. Allow students to have sufficient time to read the job advertisements and sample interview questions and to prepare for a role-play interview—either asking or answering the questions.

6. Students start to conduct job interviews in the role-play. After each round of an interview, the student who plays the role of the interviewer completes the evaluation form to offer feedback to the other student, who plays the role of the interviewee.

7. Within the pair, students change their roles and conduct the interview again. The interviewer becomes the interviewee.

8. After the role-play activity, organize a class discussion to lead the class in creating a list of tips for successful job interviews in English.

CAVEATS AND OPTIONS

1. Before selecting the job advertisements, conduct a needs analysis to find out students' majors and job interests and then select job advertisements in accordance with students' responses.

2. Alternatively, ask students to prepare job advertisements in advance and to bring them to the class. This would result in additional copies of the advertisements, which could be circulated from pair to pair.

3. If time allows, select a few pairs of students to perform their role-plays at the front of the classroom. After the role-play, ask the whole class to evaluate the students' job interview performance using the evaluation form.

REFERENCES AND FURTHER READING

"Useful Vocabulary for a Résumé and Interview": This article lists useful vocabulary for job interviews (www.thoughtco.com/useful-vocabulary-resume-and -interview-1210231)

Job Interviews in Trios

Vander Viana

Levels	*High intermediate to advanced*
Aims	*Design a person specification for a post*
	Create and ask relevant job-related questions
	Develop fluency in answering job interview questions
	Evaluate and provide feedback on candidates' spoken performances
	Prepare for a job interview
Class Time	*50 minutes*
Preparation Time	*None*
Resources	*Timer*

ob interviews are one of the experiences that most (if not all) students will have to go through at some point in their lives. This is a high-stakes genre in which both parties involved—interviewers and interviewees—are looking for a perfect match. They also have their own agendas: The former are trying to identify who the best candidate for the job is while the latter are seeking to be employed. Practicing speaking in this environment allows students to rehearse asking/answering questions in a formal and meaningful environment. The provision of peer feedback in this activity, Job Interviews in Trios, means that students can profit from useful suggestions from third-party observers. In addition to English language proficiency gains, the activity has clear advantages for students' professional lives. The more they practice this genre in English, the better prepared they will be for real job interviews in the future.

PROCEDURE

1. Brainstorm all the details of the dream job that the students would want to have.

2. Write the details of the job post—including the essential and desired criteria for the person specification—on the board. Explain that a person specification is more detailed than a job description. In addition to skills and experience, it describes the personality of the ideal candidate for the job.

3. Explain the roles. The interviewer should ask questions to assess the candidate's suitability for the job post, the interviewee should answer the interviewer's questions in the best way possible, and the human resources (HR) representative should collect evidence of the candidate's preparedness (or lack of it).

4. Organize students in trios.

IV

5. Assign a role (interviewer, interviewee, HR representative) to each student in the trio.

6. Give students 3 minutes to prepare for the interview.

7. Set the timer and tell students that they will have 10 minutes for the interview.

8. Ask students to swap their roles when the time is up, and repeat Step 7. This should be done twice so that the students have a chance to perform all three of the roles.

9. Invite students to provide feedback to the peers in their trios about the performance that they evaluated as the HR representatives.

10. Hold a class discussion on what the students learned about each of the posts (i.e., what should and should not be done).

CAVEATS AND OPTIONS

1. Steps 1 and 2 may be omitted if students are not fully familiarized with this genre and/or with the relevant language items. Instead, students can be provided with a previously prepared job description. This will require some prep time to either write or find it.

2. If students have different interests, they can be grouped into smaller groups for Steps 1 and 2. Each group should then work on a job description that suits their needs and wants. Alternatively, students can be asked to bring a job ad of their dreams to the class. This could be a real job post that has been advertised in the local newspaper, for instance.

3. The role of HR representative may be omitted if having pairs is a better option in the local class environment. The interviewer should then be in charge of providing feedback.

4. The activity can be tailored to different class contexts by increasing or reducing the time assigned to Steps 6, 7, 9 and 10.

REFERENCES AND FURTHER READING

Kern, F. (2002). Culture, genres and the problem of sequentiality: An attempt to describe local organization and global structures in talk-in-situation. In A. Fetzer, & C. Meierkord (Eds.), *Rethinking sequentiality: Linguistics meets conversational interaction* (pp. 207–229). Amsterdam, The Netherlands: John Benjamins.

Lipovsky, C. (2010). *Negotiating solidarity: A social-linguistic approach to job interviews.* Newcastle upon Tyne, England: Cambridge Scholars.

Thornbury, S., & Slade, D. (2006). *Conversation: From description to pedagogy.* Cambridge, England: Cambridge University Press.

Wawra, D. (2014) *Job interview corpus: Data transcription and major topics in corpus linguistics.* Frankfurt, Germany: Peter Lang.

On Your Feet

John Schmidt

Levels	High beginner to advanced
Aims	Develop the ability to think "on one's feet"
	Respond substantively and with ease to questions
	Enhance fluency and extemporaneous speaking skills
Class Time	5–20 minutes
Preparation Time	5–10 minutes
Resources	5+ question prompts
	Strips of paper
	3 timing "lights" (green, yellow, and red cards or sheets of paper)
	Timer

On Your Feet is a classroom variation of "Table Topics," conducted in club meetings of Toastmasters International around the world. Being able to respond substantively to questions is relevant to everyone on a daily basis—at home, at school, at work, and in the community. Similar to Toastmasters, students who practice responding to questions using this technique show remarkable progress as they enhance their comfort, fluency, and eloquence in giving short, impromptu speeches.

This activity is effective as a class warm-up. Given the flexible time frame, it also works well during the last minutes of class to end with an engaging, participatory oral activity.

PROCEDURE

1. Prepare five or more short question prompts related to a single topic or theme and strips of paper each labeled with one student's name; there should be one strip for each student in class.

2. Introduce the system of "timing lights": green at 60 seconds (speaker has reached the minimum amount of time and may conclude or continue); yellow at 90 seconds (speaker should begin to finish); and red (speaker can continue through the red light but must stop within 30 seconds).

3. Solicit a student volunteer to serve as timekeeper.

4. Choose and read a question.

5. Draw the name of a student.

IV

6. As the student is coming up to the front of the class, repeat the question.

7. The speaker gives a 1- to 2-minute response in the form of a short extemporaneous speech, noting the time cards displayed by the timekeeper.

8. Lead applause, as the student concludes and sits down.

9. The activity continues with additional questions and student speakers.

CAVEATS AND OPTIONS

1. Initially, some students may have difficulty speaking for 60 seconds, but they expand their fluency through practice. Although coming up to the front of the room provides speakers with time to think of an answer, students may be eased into giving short speeches by speaking from where they are. In some classrooms (and in Toastmasters meetings), speakers might be invited to volunteer after they hear the question. Balanced participation is ideal in the classroom.

2. The series of short questions may be developed about everyday topics (food, hobbies, movies, vacation, friends) or academic/professional topics (environment, culture, current events, careers, jobs). Short, "Wh–" questions work well, corresponding to the students' familiarity of grammar and vocabulary. This activity prepares students to confidently answer questions at school and at job interviews.

3. Questions may vary in verb tense, complexity, and type from broad, basic prompts ("What is your favorite . . . ?," "Tell us about . . .") to hypothetical ones ("If you could . . . ?"). Questions for a given class session might be sequenced or asked randomly.

4. Beyond directly answering questions, many students develop the ability to give a 1- to 2-minute extemporaneous speech with a beginning, body, and conclusion. Some speakers employ humor, and some answer as a politician might, intentionally pivoting to a different topic or unasked question.

5. Once the procedure is familiar to the class, the activity can be conducted in student groups, each led by a group member.

6. In advance of class, students can be assigned to select topics and write questions that you check for clarity and grammaticality. You would then have sets of prepared questions ready for use in future classes.

7. Individually or as a class, students could visit community Toastmasters club meetings to observe Table Topics sessions, and some students may be invited to volunteer as speakers. Students might also attend Toastmasters Table Topics contests. Videos of both Table Topic sessions and contests are plentiful on YouTube, and Table Topics questions and tips are innumerable on the internet.

8. On Your Feet can be adapted to class contests and/or to instructor assessment of extemporaneous oral English.

REFERENCES AND FURTHER READING

Toastmasters International

- To find clubs to visit or more information: www.toastmasters.org
- Table Topics segment of meetings: www.toastmasters.org/membership/club-meeting-roles/table-topics-speaker
- Contests: www.toastmasters.org/leadership-central/speech-contests

IV

Reported Speech With Famous Quotations

Amber Scroggs

Levels	*Intermediate to advanced*
Aims	*Practice accuracy with orally reported speech*
Class Time	*Variable*
Preparation Time	*10–15 minutes*
Resources	*Strips of paper that each contain one short quote (1 per student)*

Through initially reporting the words of well-known people, students gain confidence to orally report the words of those around them in their everyday speech. In this activity, students practice saying what other people say by discussing it in small groups and then by passing information as in a game of telephone. This activity should follow explicit instruction or review of reported speech that highlights the function of noun clauses.

PROCEDURE

1. In preparation for the activity, write a short quotation on a strip of paper from a well-known author, businessperson, politician, celebrity, and so on. Make one per student. Quotes can be selected according to topic, to a specific trait/characteristic of the speaker, or at random.

2. Give each student a strip of paper. Tell the students to read the quote and to think about its meaning. If a student does not understand a quote, swap out the strip for an extra or discuss the quote's meaning with the student.

3. Place students in pairs or small groups. As a warm-up to the activity, encourage students to discuss their feelings about the quotes (e.g., if they agree or disagree with the message, if it makes them feel inspired or hopeful). Tell students to share their ideas about what the author of their quote is communicating. Check in with the groups to confirm the students' comprehension of their quotes.

4. Ask students to form one group and direct them to form either a circle or a line.

5. As in a game of telephone where a message is passed from person to person, have the first student turn the strip of paper face down and tell the student beside them the information using reported speech. Students will continue to pass the information using reported speech until it gets to the last student.

6. Ask the final student to repeat the information using reported speech. Invite the students to evaluate the form of the final message (i.e., choice of reporting verb, tense, and changes of person). Discuss any errors or other possible answers.

7. Finally, ask the first student to turn the strip of paper face up and to read the quote as printed. Listen for disparity between what is read and what is written on the paper.

8. Continue rotating students through the line or circle until everyone has had an opportunity to be in the first and final positions.

CAVEATS AND OPTIONS

1. Depending on the level of the students and the class size, students can be divided into two or more groups as they pass information. If students are competitive, the groups can race to determine who can pass the information more accurately.

2. Instead of supplying quotes to students, students can be asked to find and bring one to two quotes to class for the activity.

IV

Who's Who in My Community

Zuzana Tomaš

Levels	*Intermediate to advanced*
Aims	*Develop interview and presentation skills*
	Foster a sense of community belonging
Class Time	*90 minutes–2 hours*
Preparation Time	*5 minutes*
Resources	*Interview guide (optional; Appendix A)*
	Presentation checklist/rubrics (Appendix B)

For various reasons, our learners can feel isolated from the communities in which they live. In English as a second language academic contexts, they may be unsure about leaving campus, while those in community contexts may face pressing employment and family-related obligations that prevent them from investing time and effort into getting to know their communities. Others still may feel like they do not have sufficient language skills to reach out to other community members in meaningful ways. In English as a foreign language contexts, learners may struggle to view their communities as asset-based and worthy of exploring, especially as a way of learning English. This speaking activity has been designed to help learners view their communities as possessing "funds of knowledge" (González, Moll, & Amanti, 2006) and to foster a sense of belonging and pride while improving interview and presentation skills in English.

PROCEDURE

1. Challenge students, working in small groups, to come up with a definition of "community" and brainstorm together what they value about their immediate communities (i.e., the street, neighborhood, or town in which they live). Have groups compare ideas, carefully guiding them to consider their community's assets.

2. Model a short presentation about someone from the community you appreciate. Share their picture, explain who they are, and share information about what makes this person valuable to your community.

3. Challenge students to come up with a list of people in the community they value or would like to know more about. These people can be community elders, nursing home residents, people in socially oriented professions (e.g., nursing, law enforcement, firefighting, social work), local librarians, local school staff, business owners, business employees, or others.

4. Tell students that they will identify one person and set up a brief interview with them to find out more about their life and value to the community. Students can get support by working in pairs.

5. Help students brainstorm appropriate interview questions that would enable them to collect responses that can inform them about the person's life and contribution to the community. Students can also collect personal stories or anecdotes about their interviewee's work and life. (See Appendix A for an interview guide that can be used as a springboard.)

6. If the person agrees, students may audio record their interviews. If they do not, students should take brief notes.

7. After students collect the interview data, help them organize the gathered information and explain how you expect them to present it to their peers. Depending on the number of students and the time allocated to this activity, students can prepare short PowerPoint or poster presentations. (A good length is 2–5 minutes.) To scaffold this part of the task, remind students of the presentation you modeled early in the process, give them sufficient time to prepare, and be explicit about your expectations. (See Appendix B for a checklist that can be used to guide students in preparing for their presentations and, if needed, can be turned into an assessment rubric.)

8. Encourage students listening to the presentations to ask follow-up questions or otherwise keep them active during peer presentations.

CAVEATS AND OPTIONS

1. If needed, scaffold the interview development process with a separate lesson on interview questions, etiquette, and logistics on how to get to the interview location.

2. To support hesitant students even further, prepare a list of community members willing to be interviewed and have your students choose from that list.

3. To integrate other skills, have your students prepare a newsletter about the interviewed community members. Alternatively, they could design a bulletin board in the classroom or a hallway at your institution and share their work.

REFERENCES AND FURTHER READING

González, N., Moll, L. C., & Amanti, C. (Eds.). (2006). *Funds of knowledge: Theorizing practices in households, communities, and classrooms*. Abingdon, United Kingdom: Routledge.

IV

Binary Feature Assessment for Presentations

DJ Kaiser

Levels	*All*
Aims	*Understand expectations of in-class presentations*
	Use a drafting process to approach presentations
	Track progress in presentation skills
Class Time	*≈ 2–4 hours (initially)*
	Numerous hours (throughout the class term)
Preparation Time	*5–10 minutes*
R *Resources*	*Handout (Appendix)*

Too often, presentations are treated as one-time (often culminating) activities or assessments. The Binary Feature Assessment (BFA) tool was designed to be used as part of a drafting process for presentations, thus treating the instruction of presentation as a developmental process (often the process used for teaching writing skills). The BFA tool makes transparent the features of presentation that may be viewed positively or negatively by audience members. This promotes a wider array of skills and saves instructors time in providing feedback during graded presentations. More importantly, the BFA tool sets an initial benchmark for each learner at their own level and then allows the tracking of progress between presentation drafts and over the length of the course.

PROCEDURE

Preparation

1. Provide learners with a copy of the Binary Feature Assessment tool (Appendix). Explain that this same rubric will be used for all presentations.

2. Cover presentation features assessed using the BFA tool (e.g., articulation, use of gestures, organization of presentations). Point out that each category has groups of features in shaded and unshaded blocks. This organization is simply to group together related features (e.g., putting all features related to eye contact together.)

Assigning Presentations

3. Make clear that the same presentation will be given two times. Learners will present, receive feedback on the first presentation, incorporate that feedback, and present for the second time.

4. Explain to learners that their improvement in the features on the BFA tool will be tracked and compared between the first and second presentations. Also explain that the same tool will be used to assess subsequent presentations.

Use of the Binary Feature Assessment Tool the First Time

5. While each learner gives their presentation, circle any negative or positive features observed during the presentation using prewritten binary features on the BFA tool. You may also add additional comments and feedback to the BFA tool.

6. Add up the number of negative features circled and the number of positive features circled. Then, subtract the total sum of negative features circled from the total sum of positive features circled. Note that learners may end up with a negative number.

7. If learners have a negative score, instruct them to pay attention to addressing the circled negative comments and try to remove as many of those negative features as possible during the next presentation. If learners have a lower positive score (or a score of zero), instruct them to pay attention to focusing on adding uncircled positive features in their next presentation. Note that this is a way of differentiating assessment and follow-up instruction.

Use of the Binary Feature Assessment Tool the Second Time

8. Ask learners to give the same presentation after reviewing their feedback, especially with a focus on decreasing negative features and exhibiting more positive features. Note that it is important for learners to do a second draft of the *same* presentation so that they can focus on their presentation skills more than addressing new content.

9. While each learner gives the second draft of their presentation, use a copy of the first rated BFA tool for that learner. Cross out any negative features that have successfully been addressed. Circle any new negative features that may be observed. Also cross out any positive features previously circled that may be absent during the second draft and circle newly observed positive features.

10. Repeat Step 6 of adding up negative and positive features for a new composite score. The goal is for learners to increase their composite score (e.g., $-12 \rightarrow -6$, $-2 \rightarrow +3$, $+9 \rightarrow +11$).

Subsequent Use of the Binary Feature Assessment Tool

11. For new presentation topics, use a blank copy of the BFA tool for each first draft. New composite scores may be compared to older scores. To track progress, it is best to compare first-draft composite scores to previous first-draft composite scores and second-draft composite scores to second-draft composite scores.

12. At the end of the course, you may show learners their progress from the beginning of the course to the end based on their composite scores. The total increase in score may be used as part of their final grade.

IV

CAVEATS AND OPTIONS

1. Video record learners' presentations and assign them to watch their own presentation at home and fill out the BFA tool while watching it. Then have the learners compare their ratings to those of the instructor. This can help raise learners' awareness of their own presentation skills.

2. It's a good idea to provide a brief overview of all presentation features on the BFA and then revisit presentation features in more detail throughout the course.

Special Notes on Using the BFA Tool

3. The BFA tool is divided into categories (vocal delivery, nonverbals, organization, and miscellaneous). These categories may be adapted for your class and your learners' goals. Adaptation may be necessary for classes with an English for specific purposes approach or when being used with international teaching assistants.

4. A different BFA tool may be developed to assess other aspects of English (for example, a BFA tool was developed to track the progress of cover letter writing for learners working on their business English).

5. During the assessment process, it is not necessary to circle a negative or positive feature in each category or for each binary pair. It is completely possible for there to be no identifiably negative or positive features in a category. This simply means that there were no negative features observed and there are opportunities for the learner to strengthen their presentation skills by adding positive features or making those features more obvious to the audience. In other words, you may circle few features (negative or positive) during a first presentation for a learner with intermediate presentation skills.

Compelling Conclusions to Speeches

Lisa Leopold

Levels	*Intermediate to advanced*
Aims	*Learn discourse strategies TED presenters use in speech conclusions*
	Apply that knowledge to deliver compelling conclusions
Class Time	*≈ 45 minutes*
Preparation Time	*10 minutes*
Resources	*TED.com transcripts and videos (Appendix)*

To deliver successful presentations, students must learn how to engage the audience and use an appropriate opening and closing (Richards, 2006). One way students can hone their public speaking skills is by critiquing authentic video-recorded presentations (Barrett & Liu, 2016). This activity helps students create memorable speech conclusions by analyzing the conclusions from dynamic presentations posted on the TED website (www.ted.com).

PROCEDURE

1. Ask students the strategies they might use to conclude a speech memorably (e.g., pose a provocative question, recite a memorable quotation, or deliver a persuasive call to action). Write the students' responses on the board.

2. Play memorable conclusions such as those in the Appendix from professional TED speeches. Have students identify the strategies the presenters used to conclude the speech and the qualities that made their conclusions compelling. For example, perhaps a call to action was memorable because the speaker used an object to symbolize action; perhaps a question was provocative because the speaker piqued the audience's curiosity or instilled hope.

3. Return to the original list of concluding strategies (written on the board) and ask students what makes a question provocative, a quotation memorable, or a call to action persuasive. Explain that their goal is to create that type of engaging conclusion.

4. Instruct students, in teams of two or three, to develop and deliver the most compelling conclusion about any speech topic. Provide topics if needed (e.g., a persuasive speech to end poverty or improve literacy) and ensure every student speaks. Ten minutes of preparation usually suffices.

5. Invite teams to deliver their conclusion to the class and solicit peer feedback: Was their conclusion powerful? What could have made it more compelling?

CAVEATS AND OPTIONS

1. Turn the last step into a competition for the "most" compelling conclusion (as voted on by peers) and award the winning team a prize.

2. Gloss vocabulary terms on the transcript for less proficient students to read before class.

REFERENCES AND FURTHER READING

Barrett, N. E., & Liu, G. (2016). Global trends and research aims for English academic oral presentations: Changes, challenges, and opportunities for learning technology. *Review of Educational Research, 86*(4), 1227–1271.

Richards, J. (2006). Developing classroom speaking activities; From theory to practice. *Guidelines, 28*(2), 3–9.

Confronting Challenging Sentences: Station Rotation and Panel of Experts

Eileen Boswell

Levels	Intermediate to advanced
Aims	Practice speaking with presentational English
	Improve fluency, including pronunciation of vowels and consonants, word stress, sentence focus, pacing, pausing
	Increase confidence
Class Time	Station Rotation: 25–45 minutes (adaptable)
	Panel of Experts: 5–10 minutes (per student)
Preparation Time	5 minutes
Resources	Index cards
	Tape
	Timer
	Handouts (Appendixes A and B)
	PowerPoint

These activities are ideal for intermediate or advanced students who are in the final stages of preparing a presentation. As students near their presentation day, have them identify the sentences that are still the most difficult for them to produce confidently. You may have them think about the parts of their upcoming speech that are difficult or that they "don't like," which could indicate a weak point in their speaking. It does not matter why that specific part is difficult; these activities will give them targeted practice in all aspects of their speaking for their trickiest sentences.

The Station Rotation activity and Panel of Experts activity are designed to be completed on subsequent class days, or teachers may choose just one of these two similar activities, based on time constraints.

PROCEDURE

Either for homework or in class, have students write down their three most difficult sentences from an upcoming presentation on an index card.

Station Rotation

Before class

1. Prepare signs for each station of the room that have the skill(s) to focus on at that station clearly explained. See Appendix A for a five-station rotation with full descriptions for each station.

2. Create a schedule for the stations so each student knows where to begin. (Every student will visit every station; the order of stations does not matter.)

3. Decide how time will be used in your class. Decide (based on time available) how long students should spend at each station; 3–5 minutes is recommended. Also include 5 minutes before the activity starts to explain the stations and 5 minutes to debrief the activity.

The Activity

4. Briefly tour the stations with students so they know which skill(s) they will be practicing in each location. Remind them that when they visit a new station, they must read the instructions at that station.

5. Have students (individually, or in pairs or small groups, depending on class size) bring their index cards to one station as their first location. Set a timer and say "Go!" The students should be practicing their difficult sentences with a focus on that particular station's skill(s). They can practice the sentences there as many times as necessary within the allotted time. After the time is up, say "Rotate!" Students move to the next station in a clockwise fashion and practice their sentences again—this time, with a new focus. The rotation continues until every student or group has visited each station. By the end, their difficult sentences should be much improved.

6. For larger classes, use stations that include a role for a listener as well as the speaker so students can work with a partner. Distribute printed instructions at each station. (See "Sample Listener Roles," Appendix B.) Begin the activity. During the rotation, speakers rotate, but listeners stay at a station to give feedback on the skill(s) targeted at that station. After the speakers visit each station, reverse the roles so listeners get a chance to rotate with their sentences and speakers become listeners.

Panel of Experts

Before Class

1. If possible, collect the student sentences a day or two before you plan to do Panel of Experts.

2. Create PowerPoint slides that display students' difficult sentences for the entire class. Make one slide per student with all three sentences. It is important to type the students' sentences so that everyone will be able to read them on the screen during the activity.

3. Create "Expert" cards, one per student, for various aspects of pronunciation and public speaking that you would like students to practice. Following is a sample set of "Expert" roles for a small class:

   a. "You are an expert on . . . consonant sounds and linking."

   b. "You are an expert on . . . pacing."

   c. "You are an expert on . . . sentence focus and volume."

   d. "You are an expert on . . . pausing."

   e. "You are an expert on . . . eye contact, gestures, and movement."

   f. "You are an expert on . . . vowel sounds."

The Activity

4. One by one, students will present their difficult sentences. They can repeat their sentences as many times as they want, depending on how much time is available.

5. When the speaker is finished, the "Experts" should clap, and then offer feedback based on the specific speaking skill(s) each of them was listening for.

6. The speaker can try each sentence again and improve it based on classmates' feedback.

7. Students can hand their Expert cards to you when speaking so that you can listen for whatever aspect is listed on the card (so they do not miss out on feedback for that specific aspect of their speaking).

CAVEATS AND OPTIONS

1. If the "feedback sandwich" model has been used in class, encourage students to use this format when offering feedback to their classmates so that they include positive reinforcement in their comments to each other.

2. Because this activity resembles "American Idol" and several other competition shows, you may want to reference those shows when demonstrating the activity and/or create a fun theme or title for the activity that is more locally relevant (such as including the name of a local sports team, mascot, or community competition).

IV

Dynamic Transitions

Raquel M. Rojas

Levels	*Intermediate to advanced*
Aims	*Practice appropriate pacing and transitions in academic presentations*
Class Time	*15–20 minutes*
Preparation Time	*30–40 minutes*
Resources	*Handouts (Appendixes A and B)*
	Presentation script
	Soft ball that can be easily thrown and caught

Presentations are a required component of many academic courses. Presentation skills include appropriate pacing and clear, well-chosen transition words to help students with lower levels of English proficiency deliver an easy-to-follow presentation. By giving students access only to their part of the presentation and requiring them to pass the turn to the next student, the natural breaks in presentations, which facilitate comprehension, are highlighted by the literal time taken to pass and receive the new information from the next student.

PROCEDURE

Before Class

1. Prepare folded papers that can stand on the students' desks, like a name plaque. On each folded paper, write one part of a presentation on it. For example, write "greeting" on one and write "thesis" on another. Write in large, clear letters so that everyone in the class can easily read the names of the parts. Additional examples of parts include Background, Reason 1, Reason 1 Evidence, Reason 2, and so on (Appendix A). The number of parts should equal the number of students in class. If there is an additional student without a part, they can take on the role of note-taker. Their job is to record the transitions that the other students use when presenting their parts and moving from one student to the next.

2. Prepare the presentation script. Cut it into the parts that match the folded papers (e.g., Thesis and outline, Background, Reason 1; Appendix B). Do not include transitions, just content.

3. Arrange the desks in the room so that everyone can see each other and pass the ball easily to each other.

In Class

4. Pass out student "parts" (folded paper with part clearly labeled and script of part) randomly. Tell students to make the folded papers stand on their desks so they are visible to everyone.

5. The student who has Part 1 of the presentation gets the ball first. They complete their part with an appropriate transition, and then pass the ball to the student who has the next part. The student passing the ball decides who is coming next based on their knowledge of presentation structure.

6. The student who receives the ball uses an appropriate transition, and then reads their given part before passing it on to the student who has the following part. This continues until the presentation is completed.

7. At the end, go over the transitions used for each part (possibly recorded by a student note-taker or by you) and discuss with the class whether they were appropriate.

8. The activity can be completed a second time by having students switch their parts. You would provide the script for a new part to the appropriate students.

CAVEATS AND OPTIONS

1. Before the day of the activity, either teach or review the different parts of a presentation.

2. On the day of the activity, have a list of the parts of the presentation divided on the board or projector with possible transitions under each part (see ideas in Appendix A). To increase difficulty, this reference sheet could be hidden.

3. When creating scripts for your students, make sure to use language that is appropriate for their reading level. A class could also be spent creating the script together.

4. Parts can be combined if there are a fewer number of students than parts.

5. Keep scripts short. The purpose of the activity is to elicit appropriate transitions and move through a presentation logically. If students are practicing citing sources, this could also be included.

6. Some parts do not require a script. The part of "greeting" just requires the student to introduce themselves. For a lower level of proficiency, a fill-in-the-blank statement can be included.

IV

Moving Beyond Body Language Basics

Lisa Leopold

Levels	*Advanced*
Aims	*Raise awareness of culturally appropriate nonverbal communication*
	Enhance eye contact, facial expressions, movement, hand gestures, and posture in public speeches
Class Time	*50 minutes*
Preparation Time	*30 minutes*
Resources	*Handout (teacher created; see also Appendix)*
	A list of 5–7 extemporaneous speech topics

Differences in nonverbal communication across cultures may cause misunderstanding or even a breakdown in communication (Robinson, Strong, Whittle, & Nobe, 2001). Thus, training in culturally appropriate forms of nonverbal communication is essential, and this activity helps students polish their nonverbal communication skills when delivering public speeches for a U.S. audience.

PROCEDURE

Before Class

1. Prepare the materials. First, develop a written summary of tips for "good" and "poor" performance by adapting information from online sources (see some sources in References and Further Reading). Focus on the five delivery skills of eye contact, posture, facial expressions, movement, and gestures. Prepare one summary/chart for each of the five areas. (See the Appendix for an example about gestures.)

2. Prepare a list of five to seven extemporaneous speech topics, such as "Tell me about your favorite childhood memory" or "Tell me about a global issue which concerns you."

In Class

3. Introduce nonverbal delivery skills, such as eye contact, posture, facial expressions, gestures, movement, and more.

4. Separate students into teams of three members. Assign each team one of the five delivery skills. Distribute the tips for "good" and "poor" performance prepared before class.

5. Explain that one student will demonstrate to the class the "poor" performance and another student will demonstrate the "good" performance for their assigned nonverbal delivery skill. They cannot tell the class which delivery skill they are modeling, though the class will guess from the students' performance. When the class has correctly identified this nonverbal skill, the third student will orally summarize the tips.

6. Give students 5–8 minutes to review the tips on their handout, discuss their respective roles, and plan a 1-minute extemporaneous speech about any topic of their choice in which they will demonstrate "good" or "poor" performance with respect to their assigned nonverbal skill.

7. Invite each team to deliver their 1-minute speeches to the class.

8. Debrief with students about which delivery skill was modeled and the ways in which nonverbal delivery enhanced or detracted from the speakers' verbal message.

9. Transition to the next phase of this activity. Give each student a new slip of paper with tips for one of the five nonverbal delivery skills. Tell students to keep that paper throughout all rounds and do not tell anyone which skill they have. Students disclose the delivery skill only after they have listened to their partner's extemporaneous speech.

10. Provide students a list of extemporaneous speech topics and give them 5–8 minutes to prepare a 3-minute extemporaneous speech about any topic on the list.

11. Invite students to stand up and find a partner so that they can deliver their 3-minute extemporaneous speech face-to-face. (The entire class completes the activity simultaneously in pairs.) While a student is speaking, the partner should attentively observe his or her assigned delivery skill.

12. After 3 minutes, signal all groups to stop. Invite the listener to provide constructive feedback on the one feature of the speaker's nonverbal delivery, according to the expert tips on his or her handout.

13. Invite students to switch roles and repeat Steps 11 and 12.

14. Announce that everyone should find a new partner. Students are to deliver their speech again, but this time in only 2 minutes. Students repeat Step 11, this time receiving feedback from a new partner on a different aspect of their nonverbal delivery (according to that partner's handout).

15. Announce that students should switch partners again. Students are to deliver their speech a third time, but this time in only 1 minute. Students repeat Step 11, this time receiving feedback from a new partner on a different aspect of their delivery.

16. Facilitate a debriefing session about what students have learned from this exercise. How did their delivery skills change throughout the exercise?

IV

CAVEATS AND OPTIONS

Consider videotaping your class during this activity. Because all of the delivery skills can be seen, watching the video will help students to better understand how their skills can improve. Many students are inspired seeing their improvement when watching video clips from the beginning, middle, and end of a course.

REFERENCES AND FURTHER READING

Kapoor, H. (2017, April 18). 7 dos and don'ts of body language to enhance public speaking. [Web log comment]. Retrieved from https://www.slideteam.net /blog/7-dos-and-donts-of-body-language-to-enhance-public-speaking/

Robinson, P., Strong, G., Whittle, J., & Nobe, S. (2001). The development of EAP oral discussion ability. In J. Flowerdew & M. Peacock (Eds.), *Research perspectives on English for academic purposes* (pp. 347–359). Cambridge: Cambridge University Press.

University of Pittsburgh. (2008, August 21). *Nonverbal delivery tips.* Retrieved from http://www.speaking.pitt.edu/student/public-speaking/suggestions-nonverbal .html

APPENDIX: *Tips for Gestures*

Gestures*

DO	DON'T
Move your hands naturally to complement your words and ideas	Fidget with an object in your hand
Keep your arms and palms open	Fold your arms across your chest or fold your hands
When a gesture is not necessary, hold your arms in a resting position with the elbows slightly bent and away from your body in preparation for your next gesture	Hold objects in front of your body
	Hang your arms by your side
	Keep both hands in your pockets
	Clasp your hands in front of or behind your body
	Grasp or lean on the lectern

*Adapted from www.slideteam.net/blog/7-dos-and-donts-of-body-language-to-enhance-public -speaking/ and www.speaking.pitt.edu/student/public-speaking/suggestions-nonverbal.html

Movie Magic Collages

Katherine Rhodes Fields and Tamara Warhol

Levels	*Intermediate to advanced*
Aims	*Practice fluently and accurately describing a shared experience*
	Constructively critique peers' descriptions
Class Time	*3 (50-minute) class periods*
Preparation Time	*Variable*
Resources	*4–5 movie clips*
	Bristol board for each student
	A large variety and quantity of paint chips
	Glue sticks/rubber cement/white glue, scissors or X-acto knives, rulers
	Handout (Appendix A)
	Example collage (Appendix B)

U nderstanding is always interactionally achieved. Everyone participating in an interaction needs to be able to figure out what specifically is being talked about. Adjectives are an important tool in creating this understanding. People need to be able to accurately describe what they are talking about as well as respond to others' descriptions. This entails the ability to use adjectives to provide detail and differentiate among similar events, objects, and/or topics.

This activity uses movies and art as discussion prompts to encourage detailed description. Students watch movie clips and create small collages representing the colors in the clips. They then discuss their collages with the class and listen to their peers critique their creations. The collages serve both as objects of discussion and visual aids for students' presentations.

PROCEDURE

Before Class

1. Choose four to five video clips to show the class.
2. Add the movie titles to the Movie Magic Reflection Chart (Appendix A). Make one copy per student.

Part 1: Watching and Describing Movie Clips

3. Distribute the Movie Magic Reflection Chart (Appendix A).

4. Read over the handout and check that the directions are clear.

5. Tell the students to watch the video clips and complete the chart, describing the colors found in each clip.

6. Show the class four to five 5-minute video clips from popular movies.

7. Lead the class in a discussion about the colors in the various clips.

Part 2 : Creating Collages

8. Tell students to read over their handouts and choose two movie clips about which to create color collages. Explain the word "collage" if needed and/or show an example (Appendix B).

9. Pass out paint chips and other supplies to the class. Tell students to select paint chips of colors that reflect the emotions or activities found in the movie clips.

10. On the Bristol board, students create designs that mimic the feel of the movie clips and matches the students' written descriptions. Students cut or tear and then paste the chips onto their Bristol board.

Part 3: Peer Critique

11. In turn, students present their collages, explaining why they chose the colors and what they believe the colors to mean.

12. Similar to a critique session in a studio art class, after each presentation, the class discusses the strengths and weaknesses of each collage.

CAVEATS AND OPTIONS

1. Materials for collages and their size may vary based on context. A 3" × 3" square or larger works well.

2. In lieu of completing the reflection chart, students may describe the colors from each movie clip in a journal or notebook.

3. To prepare for their presentations, the students may write a paragraph or essay about their collage. While this writing may be useful to organize their thoughts, they should not read it for their presentations.

4. Scans of the collages, with accompanying descriptions—either written or oral—may be uploaded to a social network site (e.g., a blog or wiki) for a wider audience.

REFERENCES AND FURTHER READING

Warhol, T. (2013, September). TC quick tip: Using movie trailers to teach adjectives. *TESOL Connections.* Retrieved from http://newsmanager.commpartners.com/tesolc/issues/2013-09-01/index.html

Presenting on Public Squares as Symbols of Culture and Identity

Irene Wan

Levels	Intermediate to advanced
Aims	Practice impromptu speaking and presentation skills
Class Time	≈ 2 (75-minute) class periods
Preparation Time	Variable
Resources	List of public squares (Appendix)
	Cards with the photograph and name of one public square

This activity gives students the opportunity to practice their skills while presenting about public squares. Because there are so many public squares around the world, students can relate to the topic and are motivated to learn more about it.

PROCEDURE

Activity 1

1. Depending on the number of students in the class, this can be an individual, pair, or group work activity. Prepare cards, each with a photograph and name of one public square. (Do not include the country where the square is located. See the Appendix for a list of public squares.) Give each student/pair/group one card. In a full class discussion, ask the students to list the functions of public squares. Then guide the students to make the connection between public squares and the culture and identity of a place.

2. Explain to the class that they will do some research about their public square and present their findings to the class. They should find its exact location, its history, and one interesting fact about it.

3. Get the students together as a class to present on their assigned public squares. After the presentations, lead a class discussion. Connect the historical information with the culture and identity of each public square.

4. Assign each student/pair/group to a public square that is different from the one on which they presented and give them at least one photograph of the place. Ask the students to find the symbols around the squares. Tell the students to think about how the symbols represent the culture and identity of a place and to write down their thoughts about that. Then, get the class together and ask students to share their thoughts.

IV

5. Ask the students to think about how the spaces appeal to the older, present, and future generations. Provide students time to sit and think about the question and write down their ideas. Ask students to share with a friend and ask for volunteers to present their thoughts to the class. This will lead the class to Activity 2, which can be done within the same class or during another class time.

Activity 2

1. This is a pair or group work activity, depending on the class size. Ask the students to decide on a country where they would like to create a public square. Tell the students that each pair/group will do some research about the country in terms of its identity and culture. Encourage the students to think about a creative, open, and inviting space that would appeal to a younger generation but keep in mind the importance of preserving the country's culture and identity.

2. Tell the students that each pair/group should work together to design one collage and create it on paper (drawing) or with computer software, including symbols such as colors, statues, and type of plants and flowers. They can design their collage on paper, a PowerPoint slide, a display board, or any other ways that work for them. Give the students time to complete this assignment at home. Tell the students to use photographs from the internet, capture the photographs on their own, or choose to draw the symbols that they want to include in their collage. They should not think about the architecture of the public square for this assignment—only the symbols that represent the culture and identity of the place to be included in their square.

   Let the students know when they need to bring their collage to class to present in pairs or as a group. Also, let the students know that each person in the pair or group must speak when presenting.

CAVEATS AND OPTIONS

1. At each stage of the activity, remember to check with the students that the instructions are clear. Answer questions as needed. Inform students about how much time is allocated for that stage of the activity and then proceed.

2. Remind students to speak clearly and loudly when presenting. If they have been focusing on additional skills, remind them to concentrate on those, too.

3. In Activity 1, have students continue to focus on their original public square. Give them a photograph (or give them the URL for a photograph) that has a broader/larger picture of the square and the area around it. This may help them to find more symbols near their public square.

4. To find the names of additional public squares, go online and search with this phrase: "list of public squares worldwide."

APPENDIX: *List of Public Squares (representative sample)*

Note: Photographs can be obtained from the internet and must be credited.

- Ba Dinh Square (Vietnam)
- Black Star Square (Ghana)
- Confederation Square (Canada)
- Congress Square (Slovenia)
- Federation Square (Australia)
- Grand Parade (South Africa)
- Gwanghwamun Square (Korea)
- Merdeka Square (Malaysia)
- Millennium Park (Chicago, USA)
- Naqsh-e Jahan Square (Iran)
- Plaza de la Independencia (Ecuador)
- Plaza Hidalgo (Mexico)
- Plaza Mayor (Spain)
- Sanam Luang (Thailand)
- Shibuya District (Japan)
- Taksim Square (Turkey)
- Tiananmen Square (China)
- Times Square (New York, USA)
- Trafalgar Square (England)

IV

Simultaneous Presentations in Pairs

Wendy Sagers

Levels	*All*
Aims	*Speak in the specific context of oral presentations*
	Build confidence
	Increase fluency and eye contact
Class Time	*≈ 50 minutes*
Preparation Time	*20 minutes*
Resources	*Index cards or laptops/tablets*
	Rubrics or evaluation forms

Students often make presentations in classes that emphasize listening and speaking skills. Some students are so nervous when presenting in front of a class that their speaking ability is compromised. An alternative type of presentation can be very effective for developing skills for both the presenters and the audience members—simultaneous presentations in pairs.

PROCEDURE

1. Introduce a topic that you wish the students to prepare and present. Tell students that they can use notes for their presentation, either written on index cards or on laptops/tablets.

2. On presentation day, divide the students in your class into pairs. Give the students simple rubrics or evaluation forms to complete when they are listening. Include a space for "What I liked best about this" and "Areas to improve." Each student earns participation points for completing these evaluation forms.

3. Assign one partner from each pair to present first. All pairs present simultaneously with one partner as the presenter and the other as the audience. Circulate among the pairs, making notes regarding pronunciation, fluency, and eye contact. The students switch roles and complete the second presentation. Then students ask each other questions and give verbal feedback. Students take time to revise their own presentations.

4. Reassign pairs so that every student has a new partner. Follow the same procedure so that everyone has a second chance to present, evaluate, and revise. Finally, students submit their notecards or electronic notes and give completed evaluation forms to the instructor.

CAVEATS AND OPTIONS

1. This format allows students to communicate in pairs, removing the pressure of talking in front of a large group. Students are more willing to ask questions and give both positive and negative feedback when only one or two others will hear it. Nearly every presenter has more confidence, greater fluency, and eye contact when giving the presentation the second time.

2. Simultaneous Presentations in Pairs works best when used two or more times during the term, because this allows students to become familiar with the format while boosting confidence. When all students have nearly the same topic, this format works well because students and instructors are not bored by listening to multiple, nearly identical presentations. For large classes, it can also reduce the number of class sessions dedicated to presentations.

REFERENCES AND FURTHER READING

Instructors at Tokyo International University of America at Willamette University in Salem, Oregon, USA use this technique when preparing students to go present or interview outside their classroom (www.tiua.edu). This activity is adapted from a session titled "Collaboration With a High School Global Issues Class: Real Life Pronunciation Practice Outside the IEP Classroom" presented by Christine Nile of TIUA at an ORTESOL Fall Conference in November 2010.

Sagers, W. (2017). Simultaneous presentations to small groups. *ORTESOL Quarterly, 40*(1), 6.

IV

A Poster Session

Jean Kirschenmann and Sally La Luzerne-Oi

Levels	*Low intermediate to advanced*
Aims	*Practice speaking in a low-stress setting that simulates an academic or professional event*
Class Time	*≈ 1 hour (variable)*
Preparation Time	*30 minutes +*
Resources	*Sample posters*

Poster sessions are authentic, interactive, multimodal alternatives to traditional student presentations. They offer a change of pace and are less intimidating and time-consuming than speeches. Additional benefits are that poster sessions involve listeners as much as speakers; require critical, spontaneous thinking; and provide an authentic context for repeated English practice. They can be used as a stand-alone speaking and listening activity or as a culminating experience for a unit of study.

PROCEDURE

1. Explain that a poster session is
   - a gathering with short, illustrated, simultaneous presentations given by many speakers as listeners move from poster to poster.
   - a common presentation format in academic and professional settings.
2. Give an example poster presentation suitable for your students.
3. Lead a class discussion about your example poster presentation. Discuss with students how long you spoke, how you positioned yourself in relation to the poster, what was on the poster, and how you made it.
4. Show students what kind of poster materials to use and discuss where to obtain them. If desired, give written directions and deadlines. Consider including some of the following guidelines:
   - Center your title on the top of the poster.
   - Place information on your poster so it reads from left to right.
   - Use lettering (text) that can be seen from 6 feet (about 2 meters) away.
   - Use a minimal amount of text. Use short sentences, simple words, and bullets to illustrate discrete points.
   - Use color. However, more than three colors can detract from your poster.
   - Use pictures/graphics to illustrate or further explain your words.

- Strive for balance between text and graphics and between too much and too little information. Your poster should have enough information to communicate without your spoken words.

5. Explain the format your class will follow on the day of the poster session.

- Option A is to divide your class into two groups. One group presents while students in the other move from poster to poster to hear (and speak with) the presenter. Then they switch roles.

- Option B is to invite another class to visit while your students present.

6. Help students understand that

- presentations are simultaneous, not one-by-one.

- they will need to repeat their presentation several times whenever new visitors come to their poster.

- listeners should not be passive. The experience is a conversation with a friend rather than a presentation to a class.

- the conversation is more important than the poster.

7. Have a practice activity during which students bring their posters and practice with a partner in class. Emphasize that listeners should ask for clarification or other information. This practice session also allows you to help students make adjustments to their presentations.

8. On the day of the poster session, make sure the listeners understand that they should move from one poster to another, listening to each presentation, asking questions, and interacting with the presenter.

9. Save a few minutes at the end for debriefing. Ask volunteers to explain how this experience differed from their previous experiences giving presentations in English.

CAVEATS AND OPTIONS

1. Depending on the group of students you are working with, you might liken this activity to a show-and-tell talk, cocktail party, or speed dating.

2. There are numerous ways to make a poster: Post-it notes on paper, mini–hand-held posters, and digital posters on electronic notepads.

3. Presenters can stand in one place with their posters affixed to a wall or on a table, mingle with classmates, or sit/stand in two lines with one line moving to the next person after each presentation.

4. Consider giving the listeners a task, such as asking at least one question, noting new ideas, or writing about their favorite presentation.

5. Students sometimes spend too much time with one or two presenters, leaving others without visitors. If necessary, have visitors move in an established direction and ring a bell or flash the overhead lights to alert them when it is time to move.

6. If some students do not want their posters, keep them to use as samples in the future.

IV

REFERENCES AND FURTHER READING

Kirschenmann, J. (2007). Poster sessions as an alternative to speeches. *Language Teaching, 31*(6), 17–18.

La Luzerne-Oi, S., & Kirschenmann, J. (2009, March). *Enhancing oral fluency classes with poster sessions*. Paper presented at the meeting of TESOL International Association, Denver, CO.

Discussion and Facilitation: Leading a Presentation

Kia Dennis

Levels	Advanced
Aims	Practice fluency
	Share and disagree/support an opinion
	Practice making a presentation
Class Time	30–40 minutes (per presentation)
Preparation Time	0–10 minutes
Resources	Television or projector screen (optional)

Presentation and discussion facilitation exercises are popular in advanced and academic English courses because they allow students to practice skills that are necessary to succeed in academia. This exercise requires students to practice skills that are necessary when making a presentation or communicating in an academic setting, such as speaking clearly, stating and supporting an opinion, respectfully disagreeing, and engaging an audience.

PROCEDURE

1. Give the students this assignment several days prior to making their presentation. Advise them to allot 30 minutes–1 hour to complete the assignment. Explain that this exercise requires each student to select a news video, TED Talk, YouTube video, audio program, or other lecture to introduce, show to the class, and lead a discussion on regarding content and vocabulary. Their selected media should be 5 minutes long, and the discussion portion of the presentation should last the remaining 20–30 minutes. Students may use visual aids such as the board, their computer, or a worksheet during their presentation, but they are not required to do so.

2. Each student prepares prelistening questions, comprehension questions, and discussion questions.

3. On presentation day, the student presents their prelistening questions to the class to familiarize them with the topic. Then the student shows/plays the media.

4. Immediately after the viewing/listening, the student presents the comprehension questions for the class to ensure that the class comprehended the main points and the important vocabulary.

IV

5. For the remainder of the time, the student presents the discussion questions, which allows the class to discuss their opinions and thoughts about the media. Here is the criteria for questions:

Prelistening Questions

a. At least two initial discussion questions about the topic in general.

b. At least five vocabulary items with explanations or definitions.

Comprehension Questions

c. At least two questions to check student comprehension.

d. Questions *should not* all be simple multiple-choice or yes/no.

Class Discussion Questions

e. At least three questions intended to encourage class discussion.

f. Questions must be open-ended; they will deal with belief and opinion rather than simple fact.

CAVEATS AND OPTIONS

1. There are other ways to use this activity. It can be done as a group project by assigning two or three students to pick a video and facilitate a lesson. It can also be done with a chapter book by assigning students chapters in a book to facilitate discussion. In very large classes, multiple groups can have one person present in each group on assigned days.

2. Consider spacing out this activity over the entire course. For example, in a course that meets 4 days a week, each week 2 students can present.

Discussion and Facilitation: Strengthening Skills in Class Activities

Lisa Leopold

Levels	*Advanced*
Aims	*Hone facilitation and academic discussion skills*
Class Time	*50 minutes*
Preparation Time	*20 minutes*
Resources	*Controversial discussion prompts*
	Discussion role-play prompt (Appendix)
	List of students' names

F acilitating and participating in class discussions are the oral skills East Asian international graduate students in nonscience and nonengineering fields reported as most difficult (Kim, 2006). This activity helps English for academic purposes students hone their facilitation and discussion skills and can be taught independently or after students have learned how to express agreement, disagreement, and clarification in pragmatically appropriate ways from authentic materials (see Bardovi-Harlig, Mossman, & Vellenga, 2015).

PROCEDURE

1. Before the activity, prepare discussion prompts about controversial topics. The number of prompts equals the number of students divided by three. (If there are 12 students in the class, prepare four different prompts.) An example of a prompt is, "Do you think the world should consider nuclear energy as a replacement for fossil fuels? Why or why not?"

2. Put students' names in an envelope. Explain the discussion format. When a student's name is drawn, the student comes to the front of the classroom and speaks. The first speaker has 2 minutes to respond to the prompt. Meanwhile, all other students take notes in case their name is drawn as the next speaker. The second speaker whose name is drawn has 1½ minutes to paraphrase the first speaker's response and state agreement or disagreement with the first speaker's perspective. The third speaker has 1 minute to summarize the main points from both speakers and pose a thought-provoking follow-up question to both speakers, who have 2 minutes (collectively) to respond. This is the procedure for one round of discussion.

3. Then, you and students who have already spoken record expressions the speakers used to state their opinion, agreement, disagreement, or pose clarification questions. After class, either you or students check the frequency of those expressions in the MICASE Corpus (http://quod.lib.umich.edu/m/micase/) and report on the findings in the next class.

4. The cycle outlined in Steps 2 and 3 repeats until all students have participated as speakers and all of the different prompts have been answered.

5. Begin the second activity. Students, in teams of four (playing the roles of facilitator, Discussant 1 or 2, or audience member/observer) discuss an issue for 15 minutes according to the directions in the Appendix (or discuss an alternate topic you've prepared). Circulate among discussion groups and record students' expressions of agreement, disagreement, or clarification so you or students can later check their appropriateness and frequency in the MICASE Corpus and report on the findings in the next class.

CAVEATS AND OPTIONS

1. These activities may be adapted to train students to prepare for a panel presentation: the facilitator role is similar to that of moderator; discussant roles are similar to panelist roles.

2. For larger classes, it would be much more time efficient for students to complete Steps 2 and 3 in small groups. The names can still be put into an envelope, and the previous speaker can draw the next speaker's name. This is a good technique to "keep students on their toes."

3. After the students work with the MICASE Corpus, it is helpful to discuss it in the next class. If they looked up the expressions, ask, "What expressions did you hear your peers use to state their opinion, agreement, disagreement, or pose clarification questions?" Divide the students into four groups—each in charge of answering one of those areas. Then ask them to rank, by frequency, the expressions that were found in the MICASE Corpus (noting any expressions that were not found—which may be ungrammatical). If you have searched the corpus (which is only ideal if the activity is done as a whole class—because otherwise you will have missed expressions from some of the groups), then the results can be presented to students on a handout. The handout would explain the frequency of expressions students used that were found in MICASE. In both cases, it's preferable to limit the search to native speakers (if the goal is to learn expressions native English speakers use).

REFERENCES AND FURTHER READING

Bardovi-Harlig, K., Mossman, S., & Vellenga, H. (2015). Developing corpus-based materials to teach pragmatic routines. *TESOL Journal, 6*, 499–526.

Kim, S. (2006). Academic oral communication needs of East Asian international graduate students in non-science and non-engineering fields. *English for Specific Purposes, 25*(4), 479–489.

Elevator Pitch Competition for Environmental NGOs

Julie Vorholt

Levels	High intermediate to advanced
Aims	Hone speaking skills, focusing on concise, clear expression in a persuasive style
Class Time	3 class periods (variable)
Preparation Time	15 minutes
Resources	YouTube clips of elevator pitches

An elevator pitch is a short speech that successfully delivers a sales pitch in the time it takes for an elevator to travel from the first floor to the top floor of a building. This is based on the premise that a business person must always be prepared to sell their venture to a prospective client, no matter the location or the brevity of the interaction. Elevator pitches spread from the corporate world into academia, where many business programs now have their students compete to give the best pitch. The following activity was created for a content-based English as a second language class focusing on environmental issues. Students from many disciplines appreciate practicing their ability to speak concisely and eagerly vote on their classmates' pitches to select the top speaker.

PROCEDURE

1. Introduce the term "nongovernmental organization" and its abbreviation, NGO. Describe the functions of an NGO and give examples. Connect the term to the field of environmental issues. Ask the class to provide examples of NGOs, such as World Wildlife Fund and Greenpeace.

2. Discuss the reliance of NGOs on financial donations and the need for the directors of NGOs to garner support for their organization. Directors must be prepared to describe the organization's focus and needs to others.

3. Introduce the concept of an elevator pitch. Provide a definition and give examples of its ubiquity in the corporate world, business programs, and a variety of academic fields.

4. Describe the assignment to the class. Tell students:

   Imagine that you are the director of an NGO that supports the environment. You have been invited to participate in this year's Environmental NGO Elevator Pitch Competition! You will give an elevator pitch of 2½–3 minutes to convince us to donate money to your NGO. This year's prize is one million dollars, which will be donated to your NGO.

IV

Other directors will compete against you. The audience's vote will decide which NGO receives the prize.

5. Lead the class in evaluating the strengths and weaknesses of some elevator pitches. Go to YouTube and search for "elevator pitch winners." Watch and comment on each video.

6. Students may note that some speakers talk so quickly that it's not possible to catch every word or even every main idea. Extend this analysis into a consideration of audience and the importance of clearly communicating your pitch at an appropriate pace, one that is fast enough to include key information within the time constraints but not so fast as to cause important details to be missed.

7. Demonstrate for the class the process of completing online research on one environmental NGO. Identify the problems that the NGO is trying to solve. Look for examples of how people can support the organization through volunteerism and other actions. Evaluate the NGO's financial health by looking for reports on its website. Visit the website for Charity Navigator (www.charitynavigator.org), an independent group that assesses how responsibly charities in the United States spend their donations.

8. For homework, students do research and select the environmental NGO that they want to represent in the competition. It's best to have each student select a different NGO. A listing on Charity Navigator is not required.

9. In the next class, students announce the name of their environmental NGO. Address any questions or conflicts, such as multiple students selecting the same organization.

10. Provide students with additional guidelines for their elevator pitch. For homework, students prepare and practice their elevator pitches.

Notes on Content

- Include interesting, clear explanations with strong supporting facts that persuade the audience to award the prize to your NGO.

- Cover the following points, in this order:

Hook	Generate curiosity.
What	Describe the problem you're solving.
How	Describe how your NGO is working to solve the problem.
Why	Explain why your NGO and you are passionate about this issue.
Call to Action	Inspire people to act by voting for your NGO.

Notes on Delivery

- Do not use props or visual aids.

- Do not read from a piece of paper. One or two notecards may be used if desired. Notecards will be collected after the elevator pitch and checked for usage of keywords and target phrases. (Every word should not be written down.)

11. In the next class, students present their elevator pitches. The audience listens and takes notes. After the presentations conclude, the audience votes and a winner is announced.

CAVEATS AND OPTIONS

This activity may be adapted to give students more time and support. As a class, students could work together to research an NGO and prepare and give the elevator pitch for practice. Another option is to include an in-class workshop focusing on locating content for the elevator pitch. Students may be given a list of facts to research and include in their elevator pitch, such as the year that the NGO was founded, its motto, its main goals, a description of its social media presence, and more.

Group Presentation of a Community-Based Business Plan

Stephanie N. Marcotte

Levels	*High intermediate to advanced*
Aims	*Practice fluency in both informal and formal speaking and listening*
	Develop a business plan that supports local economy
	Collaborate to develop a group presentation
	Practice taking notes during a presentation
Class Time	*2 hours*
Preparation Time	*1 hour*
Resources	*Projector and computer*
	Multiple colors of marker/chalk for board
	Computer lab (or 1 computer per group of 3–4 students)
	Stack of Post-it notes
	Fake $10,000 dollar bills, 5 bills per group, plus an additional 5 bills
	Handouts (Appendixes A–D)

PROCEDURE

1. Welcome students to class. Ask them to brainstorm a list of businesses that they like, use, and/or would recommend. After everyone has contributed and the board is full, ask students which of the businesses are local businesses. Circle these in blue. Then, ask students which of these businesses give back to the local community. Circle these in red. Ask students what they notice.

2. Put students into small groups of three or four (depending on the size of the class). Make sure that the groups are varied in terms of first language. Provide groups with five cut-out question strips discussing business, local business, and nonprofit businesses (Appendix A). Give each group about 10 minutes to discuss these questions and prepare to share their thoughts with the larger class.

3. Review the questions and responses as a group. During the discussion, take notes of the student responses in a Google Doc to share with the students or post to an online classroom platform (if available).

4. Project or write the following questions on the board:

    a. What businesses are needed in this area or in the area in which you live?

    b. What businesses would thrive in and be beneficial to this area?

Have students write individually in response to these questions for about 5 minutes.

5. After 5 minutes, have students share with their small group and create a list of five possible ideas. Give each group five Post-it notes to write down their five possible business ideas. Have each small group share with the larger class. Write or type notes to record student thoughts and examples.

6. Take out a stack of fake $10,000 bills. Tell students the following:

> I have recently won the lottery and I am willing to help fund local entrepreneurs that hope to create local businesses in the area. However, the businesses that I help fund must adhere to the following: They must (1) create local jobs for people of all educational backgrounds, (2) use a building or factory that already exists in the community, and (3) have a plan to donate at least 15% of the total yearly earnings to local programs.

Project/write Points 1–3 on the board.

7. Explain that each group is eligible to receive $50,000 dollars (in fake money). To receive the first installment of money, each group must select a business idea, location, and business name. Distribute one handout to each group to document their answers (Appendix B). Walk around to groups and monitor progress. When a group finishes their handout, review it. If their idea is approved, give them $20,000. If their idea is not approved, tell the group to revise their idea and submit it again.

8. After each group receives approval for their idea, they create their detailed business plan. Give each group one handout with guiding questions for their business plan (Appendix C). Groups work independently on this.

9. When a group finishes their detailed business plan, review and evaluate it. If it is approved, give the group an additional installment of $10,000.

10. Introduce the next phase in this activity. Tell each group to take their business plan and turn it into a formal presentation using PowerPoint, GoogleSlides, or Prezi. Each group must work together using only one computer to prepare an 8–10 minute presentation to be given to the class. Everyone in the group must speak. (Write or type these directions for students to review.)

11. Before students start working on the computer, draw a web on the board. On the inside of the web, write "Formal Business Presentation." Have students think about what is required during a formal presentation, come to the board, and document their answers. Draw attention to formal language, posture, and voice projection.

12. Each group then starts to create their presentation to formally present their business plan to the class. Groups work independently. Monitor student and small group progress and remind students to practice what they will say for each slide.

13. On presentation day, small groups take turns presenting their business plans to the larger class. While a group presents, the class completes a handout with a graphic organizer to see if each group meets the requirements (Appendix D).

IV

14. After all of the presentations, walk around and give each group their remaining $20,000. Then, tell the class, "I have taken too much money out of the bank and I have an additional $50,000 dollars. I would like to donate this money as well."

15. Tell the students to review their notes from the presentations. Initiate a class vote on which team should receive the additional funds. Make sure that votes are anonymous. Then, present the winning group with their additional funding.

CAVEATS AND OPTIONS

1. Remind students to incorporate formal academic language. Brainstorm some examples of words and phrases that might be used during a formal business plan presentation.

2. Have students create notecards for their presentation. Together, talk about what should go on the notecards and why they are important.

3. Use authentic materials from businesses in the area to help stimulate ideas and discussions.

Mock Parliament: Discussing Changes in the Law

Elena Amochkina

Levels	Intermediate to advanced
Aims	Practice public speaking and active listening
Class Time	40 minutes–1 hour
Preparation Time	None
Resources	Timer

Mock Parliament is an activity in which students devise, present, and discuss proposals of changes in the law. Though the activity is aimed at a wide range of language learners (adults and young adults), it can be of special interest for students and professionals of law, politics, international relations, and social sciences. Depending on the level and focus of the group, the activity can easily be adapted to the particular needs of the students. Variation is possible in the choice of topics (e.g., laws of a given country, school or university rules, animal protection, intellectual property law), the length and the style of oral presentation, and the time given for preparation.

This activity allows students to combine and practice different kinds of speaking—prepared and spontaneous, monological and dialogical—as well as active listening and note-taking. At the same time, a special focus can be put on the acquisition of new vocabulary, the effective use of stylistic and rhetorical devices that make the speech more convincing, or the peculiarities of speaking to an audience. Peer assessment, which is intrinsically involved in the activity, adds to the motivation of the students, and the game-like format makes the learning environment more relaxed.

PROCEDURE

1. Lead the class in brainstorming the rules and laws they dislike in their country/city/school, including the laws they would like to change, introduce, or repeal.

2. Divide the students into pairs or groups.

3. Explain that they are going to turn into members of government and act as members of parliament (MPs) discussing draft laws of their own making. Each student/group should come up with an idea of a new law or a change in the law and convince the "parliament" that this change is needed.

4. Explain that after each presentation of a draft law, there is a discussion (questions and comments from the audience), or the draft law fails automatically. The "sponsors" of the bill should answer the questions and react to the comments.

IV

5. Set the time limit for each speaker (from 1–5 minutes, depending on the number of students and their level of proficiency).

6. Give the students about 10 minutes to prepare. Provide paper for brainstorming. Encourage the students to put down their ideas, the key vocabulary, and a brief plan of their introductory speech (but not the full text of that speech).

7. When everyone is ready, the session of parliament can begin. Each student or group introduces their draft law and discusses it "on the floor of the parliament," followed by secret voting by the class. A simple majority vote decides whether the law is passed. Announce whether the law passed or failed.

CAVEATS AND OPTIONS

1. Make sure that the topic (or range of topics) is familiar to all the students, inspiring, and easy to discuss. The students are more likely to engage in the discussion of something that directly affects them.

2. The activity can be done in one class or can be split in two parts to allow more in-depth preparation at home.

3. During the discussion period, one option is to set a minimum of three questions or comments for each presentation. This can be helpful with less active groups.

4. In lower level groups, active vocabulary can be introduced before or during the brainstorm. Also, help out the students with new words while they are preparing their introductory speeches.

5. In more advanced groups, a special emphasis can be placed on learning and practicing stylistic and rhetorical devices that make public speech more convincing. These can be discussed separately before the students start to prepare their speeches.

The Five-Paragraph Debate

Gunther Wiest

Levels	*Intermediate to advanced*
Aims	*Apply functions and vocabulary to real life*
	Grapple with intense dialogue
	Improve accuracy
	Acquire a greater knack for the five-paragraph essay
Class Time	*75–90 minutes*
Preparation Time	*None*
Resources	*Student notebooks*
	Student lists of functions and vocabulary
	Whiteboard/Smartboard/PC with projector

This innovative style of debate promises abundant practice of previously encountered functions and vocabulary, all depending on the level of students and the course curriculum. Time constraints imposed during most of the activity create the impression of a simmering stew whose lid will suddenly burst off. Students gain patience in addition to greater confidence in defending opinions and facts. They walk away with a heightened sense of the power of structured speech and, subsequently, more enthusiasm for speaking's partner in productive skills, writing.

PROCEDURE

Preparation

1. Lead a class discussion and elicit examples of good topics for debate, over which the class is almost evenly divided. One or more nonpolarizing, noncontroversial topics will probably be offered. Delicately portray them as bad examples.

2. Tell students to think of units previously covered and topics which would afford lots of target vocabulary practice. Designate groups of three or four and have them discuss their ideas, choose the "best" one, and present it with the entire class listening. Write this one best idea from each group on the board or type them on a computer connected to a projector/interactive whiteboard. Students vote on their two favorite topics. Tally the votes (the total should equal double the number of students). Quickly judge whether the winning topic is controversial enough for a heated debate and suggest some restructuring if it isn't.

3. Ask who strongly agrees with the topic. Hands will rise; make five of them the Pro team. In turn, five of those who strongly disagree become the Con team. (Note: If the class has more than 20 students, place six on each team.) The

IV

remaining students become the Commentators. Next, discuss the importance of strong organization in both speaking and writing. Bring up the five-paragraph essay as an example. Briefly elicit from the class what makes a good five-paragraph essay in terms of the major sections: introduction, body, and conclusion. Explain that they will participate in an oral debate that follows the structure of a five-paragraph essay.

4. Pro and Con students sit in teams and decide who will present each section orally. The sections are 1) introduction; 2) Body 1; 3) Body 2; 4) Body 3; and 5) conclusion. (Write the sections on the board or tell students to write the sections in their notebooks.) Tell students that outlines or phrases may be jotted down, but not long sentences, which might negatively affect delivery. Commentators do likewise with what they would have said if on a Pro/Con group, plus plans for individual tackling of opposing viewpoints. All students should target both functions and vocabulary for personal use. (Note: The 10–20 minutes needed for finishing one's outline could be allotted now or it could constitute homework.)

Activity

5. Before opening the debate, verify that at least 1 hour of class time remains and that all students have outlines and other necessary materials in hand. Remind the class that everyone must speak for at least 2½ minutes (in total, not at length). (Note: This number is adjustable, depending on the head count. It's not possible to track the time used once someone has the floor, so estimates will do.) Further, remind students to look at other classmates while speaking, and not at you because you'll be busy taking notes and moderating.

6. Starting with the introduction of the Pro team, each student gives their mini-speech. The order follows a five-paragraph essay, but bounces from one team to another (i.e., Pro-Intro, Con-Intro, Pro-Body 1, Con-Body 1, etc.). Review these guidelines with the class:

   a. Commentators may interrupt anyone speaking at any time provided that they don't do this excessively or without any coherence.

   b. Only the Pro/Con team member who was interrupted while speaking can respond.

   c. Other commentators may join this extended discourse, but Pro/Con representatives other than the one speaking may not.

   d. If there are six students in Pro/Con groups, the sixth should give a second conclusion attuned to the input of the commentators.

7. Begin and continue the mini-speeches until every Pro/Con student speaks. Then announce that all commentators are blocked from speaking for 5–10 minutes (depending on the amount of time left and on how dominant they have been). At this point, any Pro/Con member can speak to any other Pro/Con member, as well as gain more practice in both interrupting and holding the floor (previously monopolized by commentators).

8. When the allotted time concludes, prepare to introduce the final stage. Carefully gauge the time left so that this stage won't last more than 10 minutes. Let the students know that the debate is about to change dramatically. Remind them

that they must use functions when chiming in, as well as techniques such as raising one's voice, using body language, and even standing. Unblock the commentators and continue with an open debate.

CAVEATS AND OPTIONS

1. The acoustics and sound leakage of the classroom must be considered beforehand.

2. A class with as few as 10 students could try this, provided that you make adjustments.

3. While the students go back and forth with their mini-speeches in Step 6, headway may be gradual. Know that the slow progression replete with interruptions demands a good deal of patience. During this "simmer stage," the commentators have the upper hand.

4. During the open debate in Step 8, rather than overtly helping shyer students to join the ruckus, you could alter the dynamics by individually blocking any extreme talkers for whom you've already filled out notes.

5. Require students to turn in both the outlines they had prepared and a list of functions and vocabulary used and recorded during the debate (when useful to your grading scheme).

6. Brief closure is highly recommended if the debate really hits home with the students. They should see that increased ease with lively speech outweighs the risk of bruised feelings.

IV

Understanding the Oral Defense Process: Students as Ethnographers

Joseph J. Lee

Levels	*Advanced*
Aims	*Raise awareness of the organization, management, and expectations of the oral defense of thesis/dissertation*
	Practice speaking and active listening
Class Time	*50–75 minutes (in 2 class periods)*
Preparation Time	*5–10 minutes*
Resources	*Handout (Appendix)*

The context for this task is an oral communication course that focuses on developing students' academic and professional communication and presentation abilities. In university settings, many students, particularly graduate students, are expected to write and orally defend their thesis/dissertation. Yet students are often unaware of the processes involved in the oral defense portion of their thesis/dissertation. The focus of this task is to raise students' awareness of the organization, management, and expectations of the oral defense by acting as a sort of ethnographer of communication. Students interview their thesis/dissertation supervisors to gain a deeper understanding and appreciation of the oral defense process.

PROCEDURE

Part 1

1. Ask students to review the set of interview questions in the Appendix.
2. Put students into groups of three or four and ask them to come up with other questions of potential interest.
3. Ask each group to share the questions that they have come up with.
4. Instruct students to contact their thesis/dissertation supervisors to set up a time to interview them.
5. Instruct students to interview their supervisors outside of class with the set of interview questions in the Appendix and other student-generated questions, and type up a short report in a question-answer format.

Part 2

1. Put students into groups of three or four and ask them to share the insights gained from the interviews and come up with a list of similarities and differences.
2. Ask each group to share their findings with the class.

3. Ask students what they have learned from their classmates and what changes they might negotiate with their supervisors.

CAVEATS AND OPTIONS

1. Parts 1 and 2 will need to be done weeks apart for students to have enough time to interview their supervisors.

2. Some students may be preparing for their thesis/dissertation proposal (or prospectus) rather than the thesis/dissertation proper. For these students, minor modifications to the set of interview questions will be needed.

3. A few students may experience challenges in interviewing their supervisors. In such a case, the student may interview another student who has successfully defended his or her thesis/dissertation with the same supervisor.

REFERENCES AND FURTHER READING

Foss, S. K., & Waters, W. (2007). *Destination dissertation: A traveler's guide to a done dissertation.* Lanham, MD: Rowman & Littlefield.

Swales, J. M. (2004). *Research genres: Explorations and applications.* Cambridge, England: Cambridge University Press.

APPENDIX: *Set of Interview Questions*

1. How long should the defense be?
2. Will the defense be a formal presentation, followed by questions from the committee, or will it be an informal conversation?
3. Who will introduce the candidate? The supervisor (chair) or the candidate?
4. Will the chair outline the procedures of the defense?
5. What types of opening statement should be made?
6. How much introduction, literature review, methods, results, discussion, etc. should be covered?
7. Should PowerPoint slides and/or handouts be prepared?
8. Will the defense be open to the public or closed to only the committee? Who can and will attend the defense?
9. Who should schedule the defense?
10. Who will contact the committee to arrange the defense date?
11. When should the committee members receive the thesis/dissertation?
12. What role will the supervisor (chair) play?
13. Will the supervisor (chair) write down questions asked and by whom? Should an audio-recorder be brought?
14. Will the supervisor (chair) prepare a list of potential questions that might be asked in advance?
15. Are there other questions?

IV

What's My Word?

Chris Banister

Levels	*Intermediate to advanced*
Aims	*Develop spoken fluency and active listening*
Class Time	*Variable*
Preparation Time	*10 minutes*
Resources	*Small pieces of paper*
	Definitions, ideas, and examples of strategy for discussion

Guessing games have formed the basis of many successful language classroom activities that look to promote spoken fluency. This activity uses group discussion to prompt business English students to develop their oral fluency skills with the twist that students will also find themselves listening very actively to their peers because of the inherent gamification and dual nature of the task. The activity also ties in nicely with any focus on strategies in business English lessons.

PROCEDURE

Phase 1: Preparation

1. Before class, select some business-related words that you would like students to use during oral practice. Choose single items, not phrases or collocations, such as *invest* or *profit*. Write the words on a list and assign each word to one student, writing the name of the student next to the relevant word.

2. Write the words on small slips of paper along with the assigned student names. Write a few additional, unassigned business words on extra slips of paper.

3. In addition, gather definitions, ideas, and examples of strategy from the world of business and beyond to share with students.

Phase 2: Activity

1. In class, ask students what a strategy is and briefly discuss definitions, ideas, and examples from business and beyond. Tell them that they are going to participate in an activity in which strategy will be extremely important and that they will work on improving their oral fluency at the same time by discussing some business topics.

2. Write some business topics on the board (e.g., sustainability, luxury brands, important entrepreneurial skills). These are best selected from areas previously studied so that students are more likely to have something to say about them. Ask students for additional ideas they would like to discuss and add these to the

list until you have at least six or seven ideas. These form the frame for students' discussion. Write the name of the activity (What's My Word?) as a title for the list you have constructed.

3. Put students into groups of three to six, preferably sitting in a circle. Refer to the activity title explicitly now (What's My Word?) and tell students that they will each be given a business-related item of vocabulary on a piece of paper, that it is secret, and that when they receive it they can secretly write it down to remember it, but should not show it or say it to anyone at this stage.

4. Show each student *their word only* and double check that you have recorded the student's name on your list next to the word you have assigned to them.

5. Explain to students that the aim of the game is to use the word in the conversation so naturally that other students hardly notice it. Explain that you, the teacher, or a nominated student will act as a "listener," sitting discreetly outside the circle and noting the number of times that each student uses their word. (Only one listener can monitor one group, so if you have more than six students, you will need multiple groups and need to appoint listeners.)

6. Tell students that the aim of the game is to be the person in the group who uses their word most in the conversation—but there is a catch. At the conclusion of the activity, the other students have one chance (as a group) to guess what each student's word was. If they guess correctly, then the user of the word is "out" and cannot win no matter how many times they used the word. If no one guesses the word, it is the person who used their word most who wins. At the end of the discussion, the group is given the chance to guess each person's word.

7. Tell students that any acceptable form of the assigned word used counts (e.g., if the word assigned is *profit*, then *profitable* is acceptable). Encourage students to speak audibly and clearly to aid the listener. The listener's decision is final! Check understanding carefully at this point and clarify any questions.

8. Remind students that it is up to them to ensure that the conversation stays as one conversation and to use polite interruptions to allow turn-taking.

9. Tell students to start the activity and, as they discuss the topics, you should discreetly note each time you hear their word used.

10. At the end, give the group a chance to guess each student's word. This can become a short discussion activity in itself.

CAVEATS AND OPTIONS

1. This activity is relatively complex to explain and an example run is often necessary. However, once students understand the aim, they can get quite involved in devising strategies to win, such as using distractor words repeatedly to mislead the group.

2. Have additional words ready in case students are unfamiliar with their assigned word.

3. For large classes, do a demo with a small group first and have multiple sets of word cards ready.

4. Though this activity fits seamlessly into a business English course focus on strategy, there is no reason this activity could not be used with general English/nonbusiness English classes, too. The list of topics at the beginning could be more general (e.g., hobbies, work, food and drink from your country), and the words assigned could be more general vocabulary items.

5. Although the focus is fluency, the listener (whether teacher or student) can note language use for later/delayed language feedback in line with best practice when developing oral fluency.

6. After an initial round with teacher-selected words, learners could choose their own words from their coursebook (although you might need to judge the relative difficulty of items chosen before they begin).

Cartoon Speaking Presentations

Janet Pierce

Levels	*All*
Aims	*Develop fluency*
	Speak in specific contexts for oral presentations
Class Time	*2 (43-minute) class periods*
Preparation Time	*Variable*
Resources	*Colored pencils*

At the beginning of the year or after various vacations/breaks or content covered within the school year, students can get to know more about each other and what they are learning, practicing their fluency and conversation skills on topics with which they are familiar or have learned as they present their vacation/content-specific cartoons. Students spend one class creating a one- to four-box panel of pictures showing themselves doing different activities. Students spend another class presenting their cartoons (1–3 minutes per student) and answering any questions that their classmates have about their cartoon.

This activity can be adapted to all grade levels and all English proficiency levels, depending on the number of boxes used, the number of activities depicted, and the addition of summary sentences and conversation balloons included in each box panel. Students become more comfortable with each other, practicing their speaking skills in a nonthreatening environment.

PROCEDURE

1. To prepare for this activity, decide if the focus will be vacation/breaks or content covered in class. Prepare white paper by folding it into two to four sections. Kindergartners may draw one large picture, first and second graders may draw two to three pictures, and students in more advanced grades or levels may draw three to four pictures.

2. Tell students to draw pictures of different activities that meet the selected focus of this activity. Draw one picture in each box. Hand out the sheets of folded paper and colored pencils. If students prefer, they can use a regular pencil to start and color it afterward.

3. Explain this is not graded on artistic ability. They may draw stick figures (demonstrate what that means) and then put clothes on the people. Students at the beginning levels draw pictures to talk about. Students at the developing to expanding levels may add conversation balloons of themselves saying something and a summary sentence at the bottom of each picture.

IV

4. Show students examples of what you want them to do. Stress that students should have a different activity for each picture they are drawing.

5. Ask students to think of a title for their cartoon, offering suggestions they can copy from the board, and show them where to put their byline or their name.

6. When all students are done with their pictures, explain each student will present in the next class period, and they may ask each other questions after the presentations.

7. Students take turns presenting their cartoons, pointing to the pictures as they talk to their classmates.

8. After the presentations, students ask each other questions about their activities.

9. Students turn in their cartoons for you to put into a vacation-specific or content-specific titled booklet for all to look at and read.

CAVEATS AND OPTIONS

1. Remind students to speak loudly and show the pictures as they talk. This may be graded on a 1–5 point basis on a rubric for speaking (1 = student tried, 3 = student spoke loudly *or* clearly, 5 = student spoke loudly *and* clearly). If this is graded for speaking, let students know beforehand how they will be graded. The first time students present, you may choose not to grade them.

2. Students may be graded on their cartoon work if desired, giving points for the student following directions to include whatever number of box panels are required, if it is colorful, and if it has any required/understandable/accurate information, such as summary sentences or conversation balloons.

3. Use the cartoon booklets after holidays so that students may share their own impressions and actions over the different holidays, helping others to become familiar with how various cultures view the holidays.

4. Adapt the cartoon idea to various subject content being studied to show how well students understand the information, such as a discussion about a historical event, with students choosing to depict the people of that time period in conversation and activities they have done.

5. In the booklet, include your class and also other English as a second language classes. The pictures can be assembled in one volume and shared within your school community.

Family Survey

Robert J. Meszaros

Levels	*All*
Aims	*Generate ideas*
	Bring ideas of family members into the class discussion
	Develop fluency
Class Time	*25–35 minutes + (over 2 class periods)*
Preparation Time	*10 minutes*
Resources	*Handouts (Appendixes A and B)*

This activity uses input from family members to form part of the content for a class survey and discussion. This is useful when teaching young students or teenagers as it will help promote important dialogue between students and their families about what is happening in the classroom. When teaching character traits or topics with a moral dimension, this can help bring a family member's opinions and values into the class discussion, which is especially important in English as a second language settings where there are a variety of cultures present in the classroom community and in any classroom settings where the teacher may not share the culture of the students.

PROCEDURE

Day 1

1. Give students the "Responsibility" handout (Appendix A). Explain and model the task. Tell students to complete it for homework.

2. Outside of class, students should survey their family member orally. They may do this in their first language and then translate the answers into English on their handout. If the family member can answer in English, answers may be given in English.

Day 2

3. Give students the "Class Survey" handout (Appendix B). Tell students to fill out the first row with their answer and their family member's answer in point form.

4. If necessary, demonstrate how to conduct the class survey, making sure that students know how to ask the question, how to ask for spelling, and how to ask for something to be repeated using English.

5. Give students 10–15 minutes to walk around the classroom, survey their classmates, and write down their answers. Walk around and help students as needed and make notes of any common errors to be addressed with the class later.

6. Put students into groups of four to review their answers and select their three most interesting answers. Then ask each group to share that with the rest of the class. Record the answers on the board or ask a student to do that.

7. Discuss the answers on the board with the students and give any feedback on what you heard (common errors).

CAVEATS AND OPTIONS

1. Students can do several different types of oral tasks with the answers on the board (Step 7). They can work in groups and rank them from best to worst, separate ideas from students and those from family members, or compare and contrast answers from students and family members.

2. Students can use the ideas from Step 7 in a subsequent group discussion on the same topic.

3. Students could follow up with an individual or group writing task. This can be a poster, a survey report, or a letter to their parents or other family members sharing what they learned. They could also create a document or project online using a tool like Padlet (https://padlet.com).

4. This type of survey can be done for teaching any character trait that is encouraged by your school or district. It can also be done using the topic of "How to be a good student," "How to learn English," or "Yearly goals" at the beginning of a school year. This technique can be assigned after holidays to investigate how different students celebrated. It can likewise be used for discussing any current event, such as important events in the news. For adult classes, this can be used to survey others about current events, holidays, or any important or controversial issue.

5. Students can also complete Step 6 by recording their group's answers with an online tool, like Padlet or Seesaw.

Ordering Food in a High School

Melissa Quasunella and Hannah Massengill

Levels	Low beginner; Grades 9–12
Aims	Link classroom tasks to authentic high school experiences
Class Time	35–40 minutes
Preparation Time	10–15 minutes
Resources	A computer with internet connection, speakers, and projector
	Handouts (Appendixes A–D)
	Access to a cafeteria

This activity is for U.S. high school English language learners who are Entering or Emerging, according to the WIDA framework. The WIDA standards were considered when developing these activities. The activities incorporate language comprehension and development through meaningful tasks while contextualizing language skills to facilitate acquisition. The teacher's role is to motivate students and facilitate their language and cultural input. The teacher should also strive to relieve students' anxieties about entering a new school in the United States. The students' role is to take initiative in their learning so they can successfully manage everyday tasks in a U.S. high school.

PROCEDURE

1. Show students the "Ordering Food in the Cafeteria" video twice (www.youtube .com/watch?v=6iJdy_BJhJk). Point out the use of the question, "What would you like to eat/drink?" Introduce other useful phrases, such as, "I'd like . . ." and "How would you like to pay?"

2. Play the "Melissa Quasunella" video (www.youtube.com/watch?v=0Uwhh S0YMjM) to model a student ordering food from Scenario 1 from Appendix A. Distribute the "Cafeteria Vocabulary" handout (Appendix B). Review the words with the class. Emphasize the meaning of *lunch worker* and *student*.

3. Distribute the "Jazz Chant" handout with lyrics (Appendix C). Put the students into Groups A and B. Have them sit across from each other at a long lunch table in the cafeteria. Ask Group A to chant the role of the lunch worker and ask Group B to chant the role of the student. Then ask the groups to change their roles and chant for the other role.

4. Distribute the handout, "Cafeteria Role-Play (Visual Scripts)" (Appendix A). Direct the students to form two small circles. Students in the inner circle act as the lunch workers and those in the outer circle act as students ordering food.

IV

Students practice saying the different scenarios from Appendix A. The students in the outer circle rotate between scenarios. Once they have made their way around the circle one time, the students change roles.

5. Explain that during lunch today, students have the opportunity to practice ordering their lunch in the cafeteria. Pass out "Conversation Fill-In" handouts (Appendix D) to students. Read the lines to the class and ask them to complete it. Refer students to their "Cafeteria Vocabulary" handout (Appendix B) to copy the words and to check spelling.

CAVEATS AND OPTIONS

1. Bring the groups together and ask for volunteer groups to present Scenarios 2–4 from Appendix A in the actual lunch line. Informally assess students' intelligibility, vocabulary usage, and use of appropriate expressions (those that were explicitly taught in the warm-up activity) while they perform the role-plays.

2. Monitor students when they actually order food from the cafeteria workers at lunch and provide students with feedback on how to improve their intelligibility if necessary.

3. After showing the video in Step 3, the class can continue the activity in the cafeteria. If one is not available, set up a classroom cafeteria for this activity.

4. To extend this activity, assign students to create a picture dictionary of their own; a published example (e.g., Gramer, 2003) could be shown as a model. You can also create more guided practice activities. The activities here were adapted from the fluency circles in *Jazz Chants* (Graham, 1978, p. 336).

REFERENCES AND FURTHER READING

Celce-Murcia, M., Brinton, D. M., & Goodwin, J. M. with Griner, B. (2010). *Teaching pronunciation: A course book and reference guide* (2nd ed.). New York, NY: Cambridge University Press.

Graham, C. (1978). *Jazz chants.* New York, NY: Oxford University Press.

Gramer, M. F. (2003).*The basic Oxford picture dictionary* (2nd ed.). New York, NY: Oxford University Press.

Pescadora99. (2017, August 1). *Melissa Quasunella* [Video file]. Retrieved from https://www.youtube.com/watch?v=0UwhhS0YMjM

Retzkin, D. (2015, September 20). *Nehs: Ordering food in the cafeteria* [Video file]. Retrieved from https://www.youtube.com/watch?v=6iJdy_BJhJk

Structured Sing-Along

Jeff Popko

Levels	*All; Grades K–3*
Aims	*Develop oral fluency*
Class Time	*20 minutes*
Preparation Time	*20 minutes*
Resources	*Video of children's songs with subtitles (see References and Further Reading)*

Songs that allow children to sing and act out the lyrics help them to acquire English pronunciation, rhythm, intonation, grammar patterns, and vocabulary while having fun using authentic language. In this activity, first, students listen to a fun, simple song with a repetitive refrain that uses basic grammar and vocabulary while watching a video cartoon of characters acting out the lyrics. Second, the students listen to the song while acting out the lyrics. Finally, students sing along with the song while acting it out. Using a number of songs as warm-up activities through the semester can give children a foundation for language acquisition and can act as a gateway to English literacy.

PROCEDURE

1. Pick a song that contains some key aspect of language from your curriculum. A good source for songs is Super Simple Songs (http://supersimplelearning.com/). Animal songs are popular, such as "Good Morning, Mr. Rooster" for greetings or "My Teddy Bear" for possessives and/or parts of the body.

2. Play the video for the class. Meanwhile, talk through, sing, and demonstrate the movements.

3. Play the video for a second time. Act out the movements and sing along. The students act out the movements.

4. Play the video for a third time. Act out the motions and speak one line at a time. The students repeat after each line and act out the motions.

5. Play the video for a fourth time. Walk around the room, prompting the class. Students sing along and act out the motions.

6. Build on the language of the song for your activity. For example, "Good Morning, Mr. Rooster" can be changed to *Good Afternoon, Mr. Ramirez*. After "My Teddy Bear" has two eyes, use realia to teach new vocabulary (e.g., "My rooster has two wings,") or teach questions and answers (e.g., "Does your teddy bear have two noses? No, my teddy bear has one nose.")

IV

CAVEATS AND OPTIONS

1. The younger the students, the more often they will enjoy repeating the same song. As students mature, they will find multiple repetitions boring. Kindergartners tend not to tire of songs they like, but by second grade children grow restless by the third repetition.

2. Find materials that are appropriate for the language level of the students, not just for the age level. Mother Goose rhymes are great for native speakers, but they are often well beyond the comprehension level of English learners. Look for materials (like Super Simple Songs or www.Littlefox.com) created with English learners in mind rather than just searching for "children's songs."

3. Play the video without sound to pique interest.

4. With older students, after playing the video for the third time, work in groups to add stanzas with other vocabulary they know.

5. To transition to literacy, play the song first without the subtitles. Second, play the song with the music and subtitles on. Finally, play the song with the audio turned off, focusing students' attention on the subtitles. As a follow up, have students write down the lyrics as they listen to the song.

6. With a more complex song (e.g., "Let's Go To the Zoo"), have students brainstorm content that was not in the song and create new stanzas.

The Country That I Want to Go To

Gerry McLellan

Levels	*Low intermediate to advanced*
Aims	*Practice presentation skills*
	Learn how to structure a speech and think about content
Class Time	*Up to 6 (50-minute) class periods*
Preparation Time	*1 hour–90 minutes*
Resources	*Handouts (Appendixes A and B)*
	Teacher's notes (Appendix C)

ome students in university could benefit from additional review of basic writing and presentation skills, such as how to structure an essay or short speech. At the junior high level, teaching these basic concepts is an attempt to provide students with solid building blocks for these future endeavours. The following activity is a simple way to provide cultural awareness, help students structure a speech, learn how to do research, and encourage them to make presentations in English.

PROCEDURE

1. Before class, make a set of flashcards showing famous landmarks from 16 countries. A list of countries is provided in Worksheet A, Activity 3 (Appendix A). Any 16 countries are fine. Each flashcard should show a picture of the country and possibly its capital. Also, plan a short speech (if teaching alone) to inform students of "the country that you want to go to." Use the template provided in Worksheet A, Activity 5 (Appendix A) or follow the Sample Speech (for one teacher) or Sample Conversation (for two teachers) in the Teacher's Notes, Activity 1 (Appendix C).

2. Write the title of the topic on the board and elicit from students the meaning in their own language.

3. Present the short speech. Ask students questions to check comprehension using Worksheet A, Activity 1 (Appendix A). Check vocabulary after this using Worksheet A, Activity 2 (Appendix A). (Information for teachers can be found in the Teacher's Notes, Appendix C, Activities 1 and 2.)

4. Show the grammar point on board: "I want to go to_____, because_____. I have three reasons."

5. Show the flashcards of famous places and have students provide information, such as the following: name of landmark, name of country, capital city, famous place, famous food, drink, sport, mountain, sea, person, and so on. Students

should complete the chart about the famous places found on Worksheet A, Activity 3 (Appendix A). Then, the class can share their answers.

6. Have students work as a class to practice asking and answering questions based on the country they want to go to. This makes a good Bingo game, as shown on Worksheet A, Activity 4 (Appendix A).

7. Tell students that they are going to prepare a short speech about a country that they want to go to. (The speech should be around 90 seconds for students in Grades 6–9 and longer and more difficult for more advanced students.)

8. In the next class, students do research on the country they want to go to. Then, they prepare to give their speeches. They can use the outline on Worksheet A, Activity 5 (Appendix A).

9. In the next class, students make group speeches. Before the speeches begin, distribute Worksheet B (Appendix B) to the class. Review Activity 6. Put students into groups of four. Students make their speeches in these groups and their peers evaluate their speaking using the form in Activity 6.

10. Each group selects the best speaker in their groups. The students create and write true or false questions based on the best speech on Worksheet B, Activity 7 (Appendix B).

11. In the next class, the 10 best speakers make speeches and the other group members ask true/false questions. Other class members judge the best speeches using Worksheet B, Activity 8 (Appendix B). Collect all of the Worksheet B handouts from the students. Write comments on the speeches given in small groups and in front of the whole class in Activities 6 and 8.

12. In the final class, the remaining class members make speeches. There is no need to have a true/false section.

CAVEATS AND OPTIONS

1. Try to elicit as much information as possible from students at the beginning to ensure that all class members have an idea about different countries.

2. Explain that they have to speak loudly, clearly, and slowly, and that they must make use of eye contact.

3. Show them in advance the basic essay structure of introduction, main body, and conclusion, and elicit what information goes into each section.

4. Give an example of how to make use of a mind map. Use the students' country for this as they will be familiar with it and can't talk about it in their presentation. If students come from different countries, use the country where they currently live.

5. Remind them that they have to teach other students something during the speech. Give two speeches to the class. Without telling them, make one speech boring and one ideal. After giving both speeches, discuss the strengths and weaknesses of each.

Vocabulary and Pronunciation Slap

Steven G. B. MacWhinnie

Levels	*All*
Aims	*Develop word recognition ability*
	Practice pronunciation
Class Time	*5–15 minutes*
Preparation Time	*5–10 minutes*
Resources	*Flash cards (teacher created)*

This is a common activity used to teach vocabulary listening skills to younger learners. Any type of vocabulary can be used, from simple words to full sentences for older learners. In this variation, pronunciation is also focused on as students must correctly identify the card and then read it back to the teacher before being awarded a point.

This activity is suitable for busy teachers who need a warm-up or ending activity to review vocabulary without much preparation. Once students know how to play this game, it can be set up quickly, allowing for maximum game time. As students must listen carefully to identify the correct card, their attention remains focused.

PROCEDURE

1. Before class, prepare a set of flash cards. Depending on how large you would like the word to be written, use an index card or a sheet of paper for each word.

2. Begin by teaching the target vocabulary using the flash cards.

3. Place the flash cards face up on a large table or the floor and have the students gather around. (You may wish to divide the class into groups if there are too many students to easily make a circle. Have several identical sets of flash cards for each group.)

4. Call out a word from the cards, and the student who can slap the card quickest gets a point.

5. The student should pick up the card and say the target vocabulary word. If the word is correctly selected and correctly pronounced, the student earns a point and keeps the card to indicate they received that point.

6. Continue to call out words until all of the flash cards are gone.

7. Total the number of cards collected to determine a winner.

IV

CAVEATS AND OPTIONS

1. For young learners who have energy to spare, the cards may be placed across the room, and the students must run to get the target card. This is good for high-energy classes when you want to let the students release some energy.

2. This activity can be made easier or harder depending on the vocabulary words. If you wish to teach listening skills, the word might be used in a sentence, and students have to react when they hear that word in context. Additionally, you can require that after identifying the card, students use that word to create their own original sentence.

3. Call the first word, then have the student who identified that card call the next, and so on. This allows the students a chance to better engage with the activity. More advanced students may enjoy the chance to make rather unusual and strange sentences that incorporate the chosen word.

4. Include a fluency component by asking a follow-up question. For example, the student may correctly guess and pronounce the target word "rain" to earn 1 point. Next, ask a question, such as, "How would you describe the rain that we had yesterday?" If the student correctly answers, they may earn another point.

Walkie-Talkie Role-Play

Jennifer Russell

Levels	*Intermediate to advanced*
Aims	*Develop fluency*
Class Time	*≈ 1 hour*
Preparation Time	*1 hour*
Resources	*Index cards*
	Pictures of different careers that use walkie-talkies
	List of walkie-talkie codes and lingo
	Example of a dialogue (Appendix)

Ⓡ

As a child, did you and your friends ever grab some walkie-talkie radios and pretend to be secret agents or military personnel on an undisclosed mission? Children love to role-play and embark on secret investigations or undercover operations. In this activity, students pair up and assume the roles of police officers, ambulance drivers, firefighters, and other heroic figures. Students randomly pick two objects and a location where their scenario will take place and write a dialogue using these prompts.

PROCEDURE

Before Class

1. Before class, organize materials. First, prepare two sets of index cards. For the first set, write the name of one person or the name of one object per card (a banana, Taylor Swift, a donut, etc.) that will be involved in the dialogue. Make one card per student. For the second set, write a location (e.g., lake, grocery store, mall) where their scenario will take place. Make one card per pair of students. Be creative with objects and locations, making sure they are culturally and linguistically accessible. Make extra cards so that there are some options if necessary.

2. Locate pictures of radios and different careers that use them, such as security guards, police officers, and school employees.

3. Go online to prepare a list of "codes" that are commonly used with radio communication, such as *10-4*, *copy*, *affirmative*, and *stand-by* (see References and Further Reading). Search "walkie-talkie code list," "universal rules of radio communication," or "two way radio etiquette."

IV

In Class

4. Begin the activity with an explanation of the use of a walkie-talkie. Show the pictures of radios and different careers that use them.

5. Write up to five codes that are commonly used with radio communication on the board. Ask students if they recognize any of these words. Explain to students that they will work in pairs to write walkie-talkie dialogue scripts using prompts and radio codes.

6. In pairs, have each student draw a card from the first set of cards (people or objects) to use in the dialogue. Then have each pair draw one card with the name of a location where their scenario will take place.

7. In pairs, students choose the career they want to act out from a list.

8. Next, show students an example dialogue (Appendix). Invite a student to act out a part to model the activity with you.

9. Continuing to work in pairs, students write their scripts and practice their dialogues, adding gestures and emotions.

10. Pairs combine to form groups of four and perform their dialogues within their small group. After one pair performs, the other pair gives them feedback and then the next pair performs and receives feedback.

11. Volunteers perform in front of the class.

CAVEATS AND OPTIONS

1. Specify the length for the dialogues, such as the number of lines per student.

2. In the sample dialogue provided, the different expressions and idioms may need to be reviewed.

3. Dress up in a costume and explain the directions of the assignment in character. Treat students as if they are really going on a mission with walkie-talkies and you are their leader. For example, perhaps some animals escaped from the zoo and everyone must work together to find them. Dress in a beige jacket and hat with the picture of an animal on it (to illustrate your connection with the zoo) or in another appropriate costume.

4. Decorate your classroom to create a scene for performing the radio scripts. For example, to create a jungle scene, play sounds from the jungle. Allow students to sit on the floor and/or under their desks to act out their scenes.

5. Students can make their own walkie-talkies out of air dry clay prior to the activity.

REFERENCES AND FURTHER READING

Sources on radio codes and etiquette

- CommUSA, "Walkie-Talkie '10 Codes'": www.commusa.com/walkie-talkie-10-codes

- Military English Stanag 6001, "Radio Communication Rules": www.stanag6001.com/radio-communication-rules

- Quality 2-Way Radios, "Two-Way Radio Etiquette": https://quality2way radios.com/store/two-way-radio-etiquette

Part V

Speaking and Technology

- **Developing Fluency and Accuracy Using Technology**

- **Developing Pronunciation Using Technology**

- **Spoken English for Academic and Professional Purposes Using Technology**

Angry Birds and Directions

Tingting Kang

Levels	Low intermediate
Aims	Practice giving and following directions
	Develop teamwork ability
Class Time	20 minutes
Preparation Time	5 minutes
Resources	Tablet with the game "Angry Birds" installed
	Wireless internet connection
	Projector
	Eye cover/sleep mask

Various activities have been developed and used to teach directions. One of the classic activities is to ask Student A to give directions to Student B. Student B follows the directions that Student A gave and finds the destination on a map. In this activity, the physical map is replaced by a popular virtual game, Angry Birds. Student A gives directions to Student B, whose eyes are covered, to play the Angry Birds game. Because Student B's eyes are covered, if they want to win, Student A has to give very clear directions, and Student B has to listen to the directions very carefully. Because they are playing a game, the process is more intense and the outcome is more intuitive than finding a destination on a map.

PROCEDURE

1. Connect an iPad to the projector and show students how to play Angry Birds. Tell the class, "The goal in each level is to get rid of the pigs. Start the game by pulling back the slingshot with your finger on the screen. Lift your finger off of the screen when you are ready."

2. Write down the following instructions on the board. Then, demonstrate them using Angry Birds. Write: go up/down/left/right/forward/back, stop, pull back, touch the screen, lift your finger.

3. Ask two students to come to the front of the class and play Angry Birds. Cover Student B's eyes with an eye cover or a sleep mask. Begin the game. While the class watches, Student A gives directions by using the instructions that they just learned and Student B listens to the directions and plays the game using an iPad.

CAVEATS AND OPTIONS

1. If time allows, ask more students to do this activity in front of the class. Record their scores on the board and find a winner in the end.

2. If there are enough iPads, an option is to divide the students into pairs and give each pair an iPad to do this activity. This will give individual students more time to practice.

Creating Mini–TED Talks to Increase Speaking Fluency

Zuzana Tomaš

Levels	*Intermediate to advanced*
Aims	*Improve oral summarizing skills*
	Practice speaking fluency
	Learn new vocabulary
Class Time	*45 minutes–1 hour*
Preparation Time	*0–90 minutes*
Resources	*Access to TED talks*

This activity revolves around TED Talks (www.ted.com). These online talks range from relatively informal, high-interest stories to highly academic, lecture-like presentations and are easily accessible online. Because of the large variety of topics and high-interest content, TED Talks have been shown to motivate second language learners (DaVia Rubenstein, 2012). Though TED Talks lend themselves to a large range of activities, this activity has been designed to help students with increasing fluency in oral summaries—a valuable skill in various social (e.g., personal introductions, small talk) and academic (e.g., article or lecture summaries) tasks.

PROCEDURE

1. Guide students to select a TED Talk that they find engaging and accessible.

2. Ask them to watch the selected TED Talk three times. The first time, they should watch it for main ideas and general understanding. The second time, they should take notes to guide their subsequent summarizing. The third time, they should pause and take notes on useful language that they plan to use in their summarized versions of the talks. (*Note*: Direct copying is acceptable in this task; students can learn and use the exact vocabulary and/or phrases used in the original talks. You may require that students give credit to the original source and acknowledge that they have copied language chunks in their mini-talks.)

3. At home, students practice preparing mini–TED Talks of 2–4 minutes in length; they are based on the original talks. In class, they present to each other in small groups of three or four. To provide further fluency practice, students can then be encouraged to present their talks to the whole class, thus totaling three to four total repetitions, which is a prerequisite for fluency practice.

4. The activity may end there or be extended by focusing on more general speaking skills. Encourage students to relate different ideas from TED Talks to their own lives in group or class discussions.

CAVEATS AND OPTIONS

1. To save on preparation time, students can select the TED Talks.

2. To support students who may be anxious about continuous speech in front of peers, model the task, have students first present to you, or shorten the expected mini-talks.

3. Students can be challenged to teach a limited number of useful expressions from their TED Talks to their peers, following their presentations.

REFERENCES AND FURTHER READING

DaVia Rubenstein, L. (2012). Using TED Talks to inspire thoughtful practice. *The Teacher Educator, 47*(4), 261–267.

Google Earth Field Trip

Emma Tudor

Levels	*All*
Aims	*Practice using adjectives and comparatives*
Class Time	*15–20 minutes*
Preparation Time	*5 minutes*
Resources	*Internet and projector with screen*
	Laptop, tablet, or phone with internet (1 per pair of students)

Bringing the outside world into the classroom with the use of Google Earth maps adds relevance to the class. Students can explore their home city as well as their classmates' or take a virtual tour around national parks, the International Space Station, volcanoes, oceans, and more. Students describe and compare different locations as they explore the area, practicing their speaking fluency skills and grammatical accuracy of adjectives and comparisons.

PROCEDURE

1. Choose a location on Google Earth that will engage and interest your students (e.g., the city you are in or a World Heritage Site). Display the image on the board/screen and explore the area on Google Earth. An option is to ask students which direction they want to go in by calling out directions to lead you to where they want to explore. As you explore the area, elicit some adjectives from students to describe the location and note these on the board.

2. Choose a second location on Google Earth that contrasts to the first location and explore the area. Elicit more adjectives from students to describe the new location and note these on the board.

3. Ask students to make comparisons of the two places, using comparatives. Note these sentences on the board or invite students to do so.

4. Put students into pairs or groups of three. Give them a device (laptop/tablet/phone, etc.) linked to the internet to share. Ask each pair or group to choose two or three locations in the world they would like to explore.

5. Tell the students to go to Google Earth and explore their first chosen location, describing the area using adjectives, and then go their second location, describing the area using adjectives as well as comparatives to the first location. While students are speaking, monitor and make notes of any errors they are making; do not address them at this time.

V

6. Once students have described and compared their locations, address any accuracy errors you heard while monitoring. Write the incorrect utterances on the board and invite students to come to the board to correct them.

7. Repeat the activity by mixing up the pairs/groups and choosing different locations. As students speak, their accuracy using adjectives and comparatives should improve as they address their previous errors.

CAVEATS AND OPTIONS

1. To ensure a wide range of adjectives are used and comparisons are possible, encourage students to choose locations that are very different.

2. If students find it challenging to choose which locations to explore, offer suggestions, such as students' home cities or options from the Google Earth gallery (e.g., a World Heritage Site, an ocean, or the International Space Station).

3. The locations chosen need to be viewable from the Google Earth street view to allow for a realistic and in-depth exploration, as some Google Earth images are only photographed from above. If a student chooses a location without street view, encourage them to pick a different location.

4. An alternative option to Google Earth is to use live webcams or virtual field trips that are offered online.

5. To expand the activity, students could plan a scavenger hunt around the location using directions to navigate through the area.

International Video Chats

André Hedlund

Levels	**Beginner**
Aims	**Practice fluency through impromptu speaking and interviewing**
Class Time	**90 minutes**
Preparation Time	**None**
Resources	**Internet connection**
	International friends, colleagues, or acquaintances to contact online
	Handout with practice telling time (optional; see Caveats and Options)
	World Time Zones Map: card stock, cardboard, colored pens, toothpicks, hot glue, old erasers, paper plates, and either a world atlas or a projector connected to the internet

Curiosity and critical thinking are aspects that need to be promoted in the classroom. Most of the time, however, the students are only in touch with the teacher as a source of more authentic language in English as a foreign language learning settings and are exposed to a limited range of information concerning different parts of the world where people speak English both as a second and as a foreign language. This activity is meant to show the students that they can communicate, even as beginning English language learners, with people around the world.

The idea is to have students use FaceTime or Skype with people in different countries (and time zones) to learn about the time and, consequently, see how time zones work. They will each ask simple questions to learn the time where the guest is speaking from. Arrange with international friends, colleagues, or acquaintances to be available during class to pick up their cell phones and talk to your students.

PROCEDURE

1. Remind the students of the question, "What time is it?" by elicitation. If they do not know this structure, teach them, and write it on the board. Drill it a few times to get the pronunciation and intonation right.

2. Write on the board: "It's . . . ." Make sure they know when to use "o'clock." Direct students to work in pairs. One student asks, "What time is it?" and the classmate answers, "It's . . . o'clock." Invert roles. (*Note*: See Caveats and Options for alternatives about how to present this step in the activity.)

3. Tell the students that they will interview someone in a different country. They need to learn their names, where they are speaking from, and what time it is

V

there. They need to work together so that someone asks the questions and someone writes the answers. This will allow the students to use *where* and *what* with the verb *to be*. Rotate students' position so that everyone gets the chance to ask and write. At this point, have the class talk to at least one person online.

4. Build a World Time Zones Map with the students. (See Resources for a list of materials to gather.) Have a world atlas (or a projector and internet connection) so that the students can find different locations. Decide if the class will make one clock or more, depending on the size of the group. Guide students in creating one or more clocks, following these steps:

   a. Copy a map on the card stock,

   b. Use the paper plates to make the clocks,

   c. Use the cardboard to make the hands of the clocks,

   d. Use hot glue, toothpicks, and the eraser to hold the hands together and still allow them to rotate.

5. When the World Time Zones Map is ready, help the students locate and mark on the map all the places they learned about when interviewing the guests. Then, get the students to set the hands of one clock to the correct time in one of the places and set the hands on another clock to the time in the location of the classroom. Ask them the time difference to practice the term *hours*. Tell students to ask, "What is the time difference?" and answer, "It's . . . hours."

6. Hang the World Time Zones Map on the wall and get students to work in groups of four to ask each other the time and practice the answers. They must rotate the hands of the clock every time someone asks about a different country.

CAVEATS AND OPTIONS

1. In Step 2, when students practice telling times, they may complete an activity in their books, on a handout, or on the board. To locate a handout or ideas about what to include on one, search online using the phrase "ESL practice telling time on the clock." You may prefer to have students work in pairs to complete the activity together or to have each student first work individually and write down answers and then discuss the answers with their partner.

2. Make sure you help the students with the pronunciation of peoples' names and the countries. You can also have students ask all of the guests about the pronunciation as they may have slightly different answers.

3. For a large class, you can divide students into many different groups, and they can work on different World Time Zones Maps at the same time. Ask them to use different colors and compare them at the end.

4. Remind the students to tell the guests their names, where they are from, and the time in their classroom so that they can practice their fluency and pronunciation.

5. This could be included as a weekly warm-up activity or a routine in which one new person in a new location is contacted every week. Another option is to have a different theme each week. For example, "food" could be a theme and students could ask questions such as, "What is the last meal you ate? What is the next meal you will eat?"

Lights, Camera, Action in Autos

John Schmidt

Levels	High beginner to advanced
Aims	*Expand fluency and creativity in spoken English*
	Practice spoken English interactively in a fun context outside of class
	Use English in a recorded, improvised role-play
Class Time	*35–45 minutes*
Preparation Time	*None*
Resources	*A parked student or instructor car*
	Cell phone video camera(s)
	Auto-Related Role-Play Situations (Appendix)

Lights, Camera, Action in Autos gives students an opportunity to produce and perform a skit, creatively employing their oral English skills in an imagined context revolving around a car and those involved with it. In addition to giving students a visual and audio impression of their English performance in a fictional context, the video recording offers an engaging and entertaining perspective into using English interactively while enhancing oral fluency.

PROCEDURE

1. Organize groups of four to five students. Ask students to decide upon an auto-related situation. (See Appendix for examples.) Students discuss, decide upon, and develop a storyline in 5 minutes, including a problem to resolve.

2. Students assign each other roles or characters. Alternately, a group member might play the role of director, camera operator, or sound engineer (using cell phone apps for sirens or other sounds). Classmates from other teams could be recruited as extras or as the production crew.

3. With broad plans for the improvised role-play in mind, you and the students move outside from the classroom to a parked student or instructor car(s). Although the windows are opened for the camera(s) and for interaction with characters outside of the car, the car remains parked and turned off at all times.

4. Student actors and crew take their places inside and outside the car as the camera operator(s) prepares to film through the car windows and/or from the back seat.

5. The director declares, "All quiet on the set. Lights, camera, action!" Filming begins, as classmates from other groups observe from outside the view of the camera lens.

V

6. There are no "retakes" at this time unless absolutely necessary to complete a recording, and subsequent student groups proceed to shoot their films.

7. Outside, in class, or on student social media sites, with hilarity and pride for having produced a (mini) movie in English, view the videos.

8. Consider options for optional, follow-up activities.

CAVEATS AND OPTIONS

1. This is a fluency fueled activity, but in the excitement of improvising and character acting in a car, language accuracy tends to "fly out the window" (pun intended). Students might welcome the opportunity to improve on their first take by completing an assignment outside of class to write lines and scripts.

2. Check student work and have groups reshoot more polished productions during or after subsequent classes. Students preparing to script and reshoot their videos could surf the internet for videos and other sources that would provide examples of their auto situations, expressions, and relevant vocabulary.

3. After students determine categories for film award nominations and after viewing the videos, students vote for award winners. A filmed classroom awards ceremony includes a master of ceremonies; celebrities announcing nominees; and opening envelopes and announcing the winners, who give acceptance speeches.

4. Introduce a grammatical focus into the activity, such modals, which are frequent in the following contexts: operating a car, rules of the road, driving etiquette, and planning trips. Characters could use modals in the skits to express ability, possibility, necessity and lack of necessity; give advice, forbid, and make deductions. Modals can be used to ask permission and make requests.

5. A variation on this activity is based on the television segment "Carpool Karaoke," from the American CBS "Late Late Night Show," in which famous entertainers sing hit songs while in cars. After students view "Carpool Karaoke" on YouTube, they select one of the songs, find the lyrics online, and learn them in order to imitate and film their performance. Students could learn the lyrics to a song of their choice and sing it while being filmed in a parked car, focusing on imitating the pronunciation and rhythm of the original singers.

APPENDIX: *Auto-Related Role-Play Situations*

Auto Situations/Contexts	Roles/Characters

Problems on the road
    Flat tire or mechanical problem
    Out of gas
    Stopped by the police
    Lost when on the way
	Driver
	Passenger(as)
	Mechanic
	Police officer(s)

Driving school	Student driver(s) Driving instructor or parent instructor
Buying a car, test driving a car	Driver (buyer) Family members or other passengers Car dealer or seller
Road trip	Family members or friends
Errands around town	Driver Family members or other passengers

Shadowing Fluency

Ranwa Khorsheed

Levels	**Intermediate**
Aims	**Practicing accuracy of pronunciation, intonation, focused listening, and reproduction of vocabulary**
Class Time	**20 minutes**
Preparation Time	**1 hour**
Resources	**Computer and speakers**
	Handout of a transcription (teacher created)

T he Shadowing Fluency technique has been used to train interpreters for on-spot interpretation into a target language. However, some English language teaching instructors have noted the efficiency of using this technique with language learners to learn accurate pronunciation and intonation produced by speakers of the target language. This technique also helps learners memorize, retain, use, and reproduce vocabulary within a suitable context.

PROCEDURE

1. Find a suitable recording with its transcription or prepare a suitable text recorded by a speaker. Make one copy of the transcription/text per student.

2. Give each student a written copy of the text.

3. Ask the students to read the text silently and practice the pronunciation of difficult words.

4. Prepare students for the first listening. Ask them to listen carefully, paying attention to the speaker's intonation and pronunciation. Play the recording for the first time.

5. This time, ask the students to read silently along with the speaker while looking at the text. Play the recording for the second time.

6. This time, ask each student to individually read aloud along with the speaker while looking at the text and also paying attention to produce the right intonation. Play the recording for the third time.

7. For the final playing, you could increase the speed of the speaker to about 1.5 times the original speed. Ask each student to individually read along with the speaker but without looking at the text. Play the recording for the last time.

CAVEATS AND OPTIONS

1. For large classes of more than 14 students, ask the students to read aloud as a group and not individually.

2. When playing the recording for the first time, pause at the end of every other sentence to make the students note different types of intonation by the speaker.

3. If it is a small group, monitor the students' speed and accuracy of pronunciation and intonation by making individual recordings for each student. Then, students could also benefit from these recordings by comparing their progress pre- and postpractice and noticing their points of weakness.

4. The difficulty of the recording can be adjusted according to the progress of the learners. A more difficult and faster recording could be used each time.

5. As an additional final step, ask for students to volunteer to read the text aloud, aiming to sound as much like the original recording as possible.

REFERENCES AND FURTHER READING

Baddeley, A. (2007). *Working memory, thought, and action*. Oxford, England: Oxford University Press.

Hamada, Y. (2015). Shadowing: Who benefits and how? Uncovering a booming EFL teaching technique for listening comprehension. *Language Teaching Research*, *20*(1), 35–52.

Smartphone Speaking

Marcella A. Farina

Levels	*All*
Aims	*Improve fluency and spoken accuracy via technology use*
Class Time	*Variable*
Preparation Time	*None*
Resources	*Smartphones and earbuds with microphones*
	Speaking prompt

Providing authentic, engaging speaking activities for language learners is a mainstay of increasing spoken competence in the target language. It is also essential to successful acquisition for students to notice and increase their awareness of their own production. Gathering student output for this purpose can prove particularly challenging for teachers not only because of the fleeting nature of speaking but also the time constraints of group settings.

Fortunately, the audio feature on smartphones today provides educators with an efficient and effective tool for capturing learner speech and a facilitated means of sharing those speech samples for self-, peer-, and instructor review. The following activity is applicable to any speaking lesson objective(s).

PROCEDURE

1. Seat students with as much space between them as possible. Have them face away from each other to minimize distraction.

2. Have students locate the audio recording device on their smartphones. For Apple devices, it's called Voice Memos and for Android, it's Sound Recorder. Tell students that carefully holding the microphone close to the mouth when recording can reduce ambient noise on the recording.

3. Use the same prompt(s) for the entire class. Typical response times are 30, 45, and 60 seconds, depending on the complexity of the prompt.

4. Prior to reading the prompt, remind students of the activity objective(s) and key elements characterizing an "excellent" response. Remind them to speak clearly and loudly. Encourage learners to stay focused regardless of the speaking around them. This may take practice but can be done.

5. Read the prompt aloud and signal the start of the response time by saying, "Begin speaking now."

6. While the students are audio recording their responses, monitor the time using your own smartphone. At the appropriate time, firmly say," Stop speaking now."

7. Have the students stop the audio recorder and save the audio file using an informative file label (e.g., Narrative_FernandezJuan). The file remains in the student's phone and can also be attached to an email, uploaded to a course website, or transferred via Bluetooth.

8. Have students listen to their audio-recorded response and self-evaluate their performance based on the activity objective(s) and guidelines you described earlier.

9. Elicit student feedback via a whole class discussion regarding areas they noticed as needing improvement and explore possible solutions.

10. Allow the class to re-record a response for the same prompt. Have them listen again, but this time compare the performances and share their thoughts with the class.

CAVEATS AND OPTIONS

1. The trick to efficiently managing this audio-recording activity is classroom management. Basically, all students should be talking at approximately the same time and then listening at the same time, rather than whenever they want. Start with only one or two tasks until the activity is well understood. It can also be helpful at first to write the steps on the board:

    #1 Start the audio recorder.

    #2 Listen to the prompt.

    #3 Speak/say your response.

    #4 Stop the audio recorder. Save your response.

    #5 Listen to your response. Check it.

2. Students should not write out and then read their responses. Minimal notes are acceptable, but ideally students should practice organizing their thoughts internally before/while they deliver their response. This is truly what is addressed by "speaking competence."

3. It is recommended to repurpose speaking prompts while students are adapting to the audio-recording activity in a whole-class setting. In addition, this repetition can improve speaking fluency (Nation & Newton, 2009), which can build learner confidence and, in turn, positively fuel further language gains.

4. It is not necessary for students to read the prompt, but if desired, it can be shown on an overhead projector (if not disruptive to the seating arrangement) or via handouts turned face down on the desks. If using a rubric, it can also be helpful to have a hard copy of that. Tell students not to write on these materials so that you can reuse them in the future.

5. With a group that is quite comfortable with the audio-recording task and each other, it is enriching to have students share their files with a classmate or two by simply exchanging phones for a few minutes or by transferring files via Bluetooth or email as mentioned before. Peer evaluations and feedback should mirror the activity objective(s) and teacher guidelines.

V

REFERENCES AND FURTHER READING

Nation, I. S. P., & Newton, J. (2009). *Teaching ESL/EFL reading and writing*. ESL & Applied Linguistics Professional Series. New York, NY: Routledge.

Star in a Viral Marketing Video

Sean H. Toland

Levels	*Pre-intermediate +*
Aims	*Improve communicative competencies*
	Develop cross-cultural awareness
	Enhance critical thinking abilities
	Practice presentation skills
Class Time	*1 hour–90 minutes*
Preparation Time	*5 minutes*
Resources	*Smartphones/tablets*
	Laptop with internet access
	Handouts (Appendixes A and B)

People all over the world are regularly viewing viral videos and sharing the links with friends on various social networking sites. Many companies are cognizant of this phenomenon and have found creative ways of integrating online videos into their marketing campaigns. Studying viral marketing videos is highly beneficial for English language learners (ELLs) in a number of ways. These entertaining online commercials can enhance students' speaking, pronunciation, and listening abilities. In addition, analyzing viral marketing videos can foster ELLs' critical thinking skills and cross-cultural awareness as well as stoke their motivational fires. The activity that follows draws on the popularity of viral marketing videos and uses them as a launching pad to get ELLs to create their own video plan and discuss it in an authentic language context.

PROCEDURE

1. Before class, select and preview the videos. For the first video, select one by Cup Noodles featuring the samurai. For the second video, use the video by Casey Neistat (see References and Further Reading).

2. Divide the class into small groups of three to four students.

3. Write the following terms on the board: *marketing, target market, setting, go viral, concept, character roles,* and *main message.* Give the groups 5 minutes to discuss the meaning of each one.

4. Bring the groups together. Elicit answers and provide corrective feedback.

5. Provide the class with an overview of the entire activity. Tell the learners they are going to watch a couple of popular viral marketing videos two times. During the

first viewing, they will sit back and enjoy the videos. During the second viewing, they will watch with a more discerning eye. Afterward, with their group members, they will complete a chart that scrutinizes each video.

6. Begin by playing the videos on a projector or getting students to access them on their smartphones.

7. When the first viewing is finished, distribute the "Viral Marketing Video Analysis Chart" (Appendix A) to students. Select volunteers to read each item on the chart. Check comprehension and review difficult vocabulary.

8. Give the groups 15 minutes to watch the videos again and complete the chart. When the time is up, get groups to read their answers to the class.

9. Distribute the "Star in a Viral Marketing Video! Plan" (Appendix B) handout. Get volunteers to read the information on the handout. Confirm comprehension and answer any questions.

10. Divide the class into pairs. Each duo has 15 minutes to brainstorm ideas for a viral marketing video that they will make and star in.

11. After 15 minutes, announce that time is up. Tell the students to come together as a full class. Model an example mini-presentation about a viral marketing video plan.

12. Provide the pairs with 10 minutes to prepare and practice their mini-presentations. Check each pair's progress and provide any necessary feedback.

13. When the practice session is finished, the duos rotate around the classroom, making a predetermined number of mini-presentations to other pairs. They will also listen to their classmates' presentations and ask and answer questions.

14. While the presentation session is taking place, write the following questions on the board:

    a. What was the most exciting or interesting idea for a viral marketing video you heard? Why did you like this concept?

    b. Do you think it would be difficult to make and star in a viral marketing video? Why or why not? What are some challenges that you would need to overcome?

    c. If you were a CEO of a company, would you use viral marketing videos? What are the advantages and disadvantages of using these videos in an advertising campaign?

15. When the mini-presentation session is finished, tell students to reconvene in their original groups of three or four students. Allot 10 minutes for the groups to discuss the three questions on the board.

16. Get volunteers from each group to share their answers. Provide feedback and answer any questions.

CAVEATS AND OPTIONS

1. This activity can be modified for ELLs of different proficiency levels. For example, lower level learners might need more time to complete the handouts and practice their mini-presentations. Thus, the presentation session can take place during the next lesson.

2. Students can find another viral marketing video and do an analysis of the video for homework. The new video can be shown and discussed in a small group during the next class.

3. As a follow-up to the activity, advanced learners can write an email/letter to a CEO of a company requesting sponsorship for their viral marketing video concept.

REFERENCES AND FURTHER READING

Neistat, C. (2012, April 9). *Make it count* [Video file]. Retrieved from https://www .youtube.com/watch?v=WxfZkMm3wcg

V

Storytelling With Cell Phones

Robert J. Meszaros

Levels	*All*
Aims	*Create and tell stories as a group*
	Develop fluency
Class Time	*20–40 minutes*
Preparation Time	*10 minutes*
Resources	*Student cell phones*
	PowerPoint
	Projector
	Handout (Appendix)

This activity is an expansion of "Storytelling With Pictures," which was published in the first edition of *New Ways in Teaching Speaking* (1994). Using the photos on students' cell phones makes this activity more student centered and meaningful, and the inclusion of technology is more engaging for students.

PROCEDURE

1. Before the activity, select four pictures from your cell phone and put them on PowerPoint slides.

2. Show students the slideshow with the four pictures. Have a student ask you these questions about each photo:

   a. When was the photo taken?

   b. What is happening in the photo?

   c. Why do you like it?

3. Then, ask students to take out their phones and find four of their favorite pictures that they would be willing to share with their classmates. Distribute and review handouts (Appendix). Tell students to prepare their answers to the three questions on the handout, which are the same as the questions you just modeled.

4. Put students in groups and ask them to take turns sharing their pictures in their groups. Students should listen to what members of their group say and take notes on the back of the handout or on other paper.

5. Ask each group to choose any eight pictures and create a story about them.

6. During Steps 4 and 5, circulate, help individual students, and take note of any common problems or errors to address later.

7. Ask each group to share their story with their classmates.

CAVEATS AND OPTIONS

1. Have a spare iPad or photos available for any students who don't have a cell phone.

2. If PowerPoint and a projector are not available, print out a copy of your four pictures for the class to see in Step 2.

3. In Step 2, ask the students to work in groups and guess the answers to the questions.

4. Students could move groups and do Step 4 several times to get additional speaking practice.

5. If writing a story is too advanced for your students, you can ask them to write a dialogue.

6. The number of pictures used in Step 5 can be adjusted according to each group's abilities.

7. Instead of presenting to the class, each member of a group could present their story to another group to increase the amount of student talk.

8. Students could be asked to take notes during Step 7.

9. Each group can post their pictures and story on Padlet (www.padlet.com), make a PowerPoint, or publish using another online tool.

10. Students can be assigned to take photos related to specific topics you wish to cover in class (e.g., food, family members, holidays, hobbies, tourist attractions, student's home/country) and then talk and write about that topic.

11. Students can be given time to take photos for this activity during class. This can be either in class or around the school. This works well during orientation, with students taking photos of their new school.

REFERENCES AND FURTHER READING

Mixon, M. (1994). Storytelling with pictures. In K. Bailey & L. Savage (Eds.), *New ways in teaching speaking* (p. 67). Alexandria, VA: Teachers of English to Speakers of Other Languages.

Student-Generated Podcasts as Speaking Portfolio

Bita Bookman

Levels	*Intermediate to advanced*
Aims	*Develop fluency*
	Practice impromptu speaking
	Increase confidence in speaking
Class Time	*30–45 minutes*
Preparation Time	*None*
Resources	*A computer with internet access and projector*
	Speakers and a microphone
	A free podcast account (see References and Further Reading)
	Podcast topics ideas (Appendix)

For many English learners, especially in English as a foreign language contexts, there are few opportunities to speak English outside the classroom. Student-generated podcasts enable students to use and practice English outside the classroom as frequently as they wish and at their own pace. Listening to other students' podcasts provides listening practice, and collaborative podcasts allow students to practice conversing and conversation strategies outside the classroom. Student-generated podcasts also allow teachers to monitor students' progress over time and provide individualized feedback.

PROCEDURE

1. Have each student create a free podcast account. (Two options are listed in References and Further Reading.) It is good practice to model in class how to set up an account and how to record a new episode.

2. Instruct students to email you a link to their podcast or post their links on the class website where other students can access them.

3. Once students have set up their free account and are familiar with how to record new episodes, instruct them to record new episodes every week. Assign a minimum number per week or allow the students to record as many episodes as they wish per week throughout the semester. Students may talk about topics that interest them or about topics that you assign. Encourage the students to speak on different topics and imagine different audiences. Consider leading a class brainstorming session and demonstrating how to record a short impromptu episode.

4. Depending on the learning objectives of the course, instruct students to focus on fluency (pace of speech, reducing pauses and repetition), accuracy (specific grammatical structures or new vocabulary), range (different vocabulary and grammar structures), and so on.

5. Have students listen and respond to each other's podcasts. This provides students with other audiences besides the teacher. Also, this provides students with listening practice outside the classroom. Most podcast servers have comment boxes below each episode where listeners can type comments.

6. Occasionally, listen to students' podcasts and provide feedback. The assessment criteria must align with the learning objectives of the course.

7. Include regular reflections, self-assessments, and peer assessments. Have students assess their progress by identifying their own strengths and weaknesses. To facilitate self- and peer assessment, provide students with a checklist or student-friendly rubric.

8. As portfolio assessment, evaluate the entire collection of episodes, or ask students to choose the episodes that they'd like you to evaluate.

CAVEATS AND OPTIONS

1. Based on your course learning objectives, develop a scoring rubric for assessment and evaluation. The rubric may include criteria such as number of posts; pace of speech; number of pauses, self-corrections, and false starts; sentence complexity; range of grammatical structures and vocabulary; and progress over time. Have students use the rubric for self-assessment and peer-assessment. Decide how to weigh the podcasts in terms of the overall point value assigned.

2. Students are able to make their podcasts public or private.

3. Give students a time limit for each episode (e.g., 1 or 2 minutes). Time limits will be helpful if you have large classes and limited time for listening.

4. Ask students to avoid reading from a script. Remind them that the purpose of this assignment is to practice impromptu speaking, and reading from a prepared script may not be helpful in building automatization. Do not give points for episodes that sound as if they are read from a script.

5. To increase motivation and promote autonomy, encourage students to choose topics they are interested in. See "Ideas for Topics" in the Appendix.

6. Students can work individually or collaboratively to record episodes. In collaborative episodes, students may interview each other, discuss different opinions on a controversial topic, or negotiate plans.

7. Students may choose to add music or sound effects to their podcasts, although this should not be required or considered in grading.

REFERENCES AND FURTHER READING

PodBean Support Center; How to create and record a podcast: http://help.podbean.com/support/solutions/articles/25000005043-podbean-how-do-i-record-and-publish-a-podcast-from-the-podbean-android-app-

Podcast software with free accounts: www.podomatic.com or www.podbean.com

APPENDIX: *Ideas for Topics*

short stories	book or movie reviews
weekend plans	favorite food/hobby/sport
celebrities	reflections on coursework
dreams and future goals	school life
poems	pros and cons discussions
new fads and trends	descriptions of objects/events/places
instructions, such as a recipe	explanation of graphs/charts
commentary on controversial issues	current news

Super Selfies

Martin Cooke

Levels	Intermediate to advanced
Aims	Increase teamwork
	Increase knowledge of the school or campus environment
	Develop fluency
	Practice using language based on gerunds and prepositions in a visual context
Class Time	20 minutes +
Preparation Time	10–20 minutes
Resources	Envelopes
	Computer with projector
	USB connector for cameras/camera phones (or high-speed wireless internet)
	Cameras/camera phones
	Task cards (e.g., Appendix)

This is a fun, teamwork-based activity that is great with larger classes. It works especially well if used with newly arrived learners who need to get to know their surroundings. Students participate in small groups of any size.

PROCEDURE

Before the Activity

1. Prepare Action Task Cards and Location Task Cards, similar to those shown in the Appendix.
2. Write each student's name on one envelope.
3. Place one Action Task Card and one Location Task Card in each envelope.

During the Activity

1. Divide students into groups of any size (six is ideal). Appoint a leader for each group. (This should be a responsible and trusted student.) Another member of the group will be their photographer.
2. Give each group leader their own envelope, which must stay sealed. Then, ask them to randomly select at least three more envelopes (on which student names

are not visible). When a student's envelope is selected, they must join their group.

3. When the activity begins, the student whose name is first in alphabetical order opens their envelope. Inside are two task cards with an action and a location. For example, if Alice opens her envelope to find cards that read *drinking water* and *under a tree,* the whole group must help Alice to get some water and find a tree, and the group's photographer must take a photograph of Alice performing her task there.

4. Once the first task has been completed, the leader hands the next person their envelope, and the whole group goes to wherever that person's location card tells them and take a photo of them completing the given task. This cycle continues until everyone takes their turn and completes their task.

5. During the activity, if anyone around the school or campus area asks what they are doing, the group must tell that person that they're playing "Super Selfies" and take a group selfie with that person—if the person agrees.

6. Once every member of the group completes their task, they must all return to the classroom immediately. The first group to return is the winner.

7. All groups must return to the classroom within the time limit imposed, even if they did not complete all of their tasks.

8. As each group returns to the classroom, give them a few moments to recover while the images are uploaded. When everyone is back in the classroom, show the images in succession. As each image appears, ask members of the group to explain what they or others are doing (e.g., I'm running away from a ghost on the running track. Kevin is playing air guitar outside the Student Affairs Office.) This stage can be hilarious! Also, it can be used to support or lead into a more focused language activity.

CAVEATS AND OPTIONS

1. This task requires a significant level of trust between teachers and students, and may only be feasible with younger learners if you can ensure that every group is supervised by a responsible adult or older student.

2. In all cases, everyone must be aware of their responsibilities before the activity begins, especially if a member of the staff does not supervise them.

3. If any task cannot be completed for some reason, such as safety concerns, lack of access, or weather conditions, the leader can suggest an alternative activity for the student(s) involved.

4. The group's leader is also responsible for timekeeping and must ensure that the group stays together until they return safely to the classroom.

5. The action and location tasks should be adapted to suit the environment of your school or campus. They must be realistic (especially if you have a huge campus area), safe, and culturally appropriate, and they should not disturb other classes or activities.

APPENDIX: *Task Card Samples*

Action Task Cards

Drinking water	Wearing a helmet	Giving someone a high five	Running in a race
Doing push-ups	Standing on one leg	Pointing to the sky	Reading an interesting book
Drawing a smiley face	Playing air guitar	Singing karaoke	Talking on the phone

Location Task Cards

On the running track	Outside the Student Affairs office	Next to a map of the world	In the cafeteria
In the convenience store	Next to a vending machine	Outside room E211	In an elevator
With a security guard	At the college entrance	Under a tree	Next to a park bench

Teaching Small Talk

Bryan Woerner

Levels	*Advanced*
Aims	*Developing fluency and speaking accuracy in specific contexts*
Class Time	*30 minutes–1 hour (daily over several class periods)*
Preparation Time	*2–4 hours*
Resources	*Recording device (microphone, digital recorder, phone)*
	Notebook
	Handouts (teacher created; e.g., Appendixes A–D)

Small talk is an important function in American society, culture, and work. The language is generally simple, but knowing what, when, and how to use it is complex. Research also shows that these conversations have a significant impact in how students learn English. This activity on teaching small talk to advanced English as a second language students includes dialogues, discourse analysis, and self-reflection. When choosing discussion prompts for this activity, it's usually best to avoid heavy topics (e.g., religion, politics, war, disease, or gossip) as they can make people angry or upset. Small talk is generally light and neutral. It is important to discuss this with students to avoid any cultural misunderstandings. The overall activity can be done in parts over the course of several days with students taking notes individually, listening as a class, and practicing in pairs.

PROCEDURE

Preparation

1. Instruct students to observe small talk conversations in their school, on mass transit, in the community, and so on, and to keep a written record of the situation (i.e., when, where, whom) and topics (e.g., the weather, television, sports, fashion, work, children, and news). This record will serve as a model for an activity.

2. Prepare three to five short sample small talk dialogues that use those topics. They are usually not more than a few turns per speaker—about three sentences or 20 words per speaker. An example is in the "Sample Dialogues" handout, Conversation 4 (Appendix A), where small talk focuses on the weather.

3. Prepare two or three short dialogues that are not small talk (e.g., giving directions, asking for and giving information). An example is Conversation 5 (Appendix A), where one person asks for and receives directions, but there is no small talk.

4. Record all sample dialogues for playback to students.

5. For several classes, before introducing the activity, greet students as they enter the classroom. Ask them about the weather, school, and/or their day.

The Activity

6. Begin with a discussion about students' experiences of social discomfort around native speakers of English. Ask them how they start conversations with people who are not their friends, family, or coworkers in their home country. What topics do they discuss in those situations?

7. Distribute the "Initiating Small Talk" chart (Appendix B) to students and review it. Tell students to record information about each dialogue in the chart. Play the dialogues for students. Play each one multiple times, focusing on

   • situation,

   • conversation topics,

   • identifying the small talk cue or "ice breaker" (e.g., "It's really hot out today!"),

   • identifying non–small talk situations (e.g., giving directions),

   • relationships of speakers,

   • pronunciation,

   • grammar (if appropriate), and

   • new or unfamiliar vocabulary.

   Using the chart, lead the class in analyzing the dialogues.

8. Provide students with the "Ice Breakers" handout (Appendix C), which includes sample small talk dialogues drawn from your observations with the ice breaker cue missing. Students select the appropriate ice breaker to complete each dialogue and then practice speaking the dialogues.

9. Provide students with the "Break the Ice Scenarios" handout (Appendix D), which includes sample small talk scenarios drawn from your observations. Have them create their own ice breakers to start small talk. Students practice these ice breakers with each other.

10. Refer back to the discussion on student experiences (in Step 6). Have students identify where they could have made small talk and prepare ice breakers for those situations as well as any new situations they can think of in their daily lives.

11. As an extension of this activity, have students keep a Small Talk Journal where they record their observations of small talk conversations they witness or take part in. Have them also record if the small talk became a big talk (i.e., longer conversations that go deep into a topic, express opinions, or cover multiple topics).

CAVEATS AND OPTIONS

1. For beginning students, follow the same general approach, but keep dialogues shorter, simpler, and focused on a grammar point. For example, students can practice expressing opinions using *like* and *don't like*.

   a. It's cold outside!

   b. I know! I *don't like* the snow.

2. For intermediate students, use the same approach, but include more complex grammar or functions. For example, students can ask for opinions using *do you think*.

   a. *Do you think* the American History Museum is interesting?

   b. Yes, but it is always crowded.

REFERENCES AND FURTHER READING

Biesenbach-Lucas, S., Couper, E., Leite, K., Woerner, B., & Yancey, J. (2005, April 16). *Using authentic dialogues for grammar teaching*. Presentation at Washington Area Teachers of English to Speakers of Other Language (WATESOL) SIGnificant Conference, Washington, DC.

Holmes, J. (2005). When small talk is a big deal: Sociolinguistic challenges in the workplace. In M. H. Long (Ed.), *Second language needs analysis* (pp. 344–372). Cambridge, England: Cambridge University Press.

Meierkord, C. (2000). Interpreting successful lingua franca interaction. An analysis of non-native-/non-native small talk conversations in English. *Linguistik Online, 5*(1). Retrieved from https://bop.unibe.ch/linguistik-online/article/view/1013/1673

Pullin, P. (2010). Small talk, rapport, and international communicative competence: Lessons to learn from BELF. *International Journal of Business Communication, 47*(4), 455–476.

RoAne, S. (1999). *What do I say next?: Talking your way to business and social success*. New York, NY: Grand Central Publishing.

Woerner, B. (2010, March 29). Teaching small talk: Not a small topic [SlideShare slides]. Retrieved from https://www.slideshare.net/bmwTESOL/data homebryantesol-10small-talkteaching-small-talk-tesol-2010-3586491

Woerner, B. (2012, September). Teaching small talk: Not a small topic. *TESOL AEIS Newsletter*. Retrieved from http://newsmanager.commpartners.com/tesolaeis/issues/2012-09-13/1.html

Video Recording on Flipgrid

Laura Giacomini

Levels	*All*
Aims	*Increase fluency*
	Increase engagement using technological tools
	Promote autonomy and self-evaluation skills
Class Time	*30 minutes–1 hour*
Preparation Time	*5–10 minutes*
Resources	*Students' own devices (iPad, iPod, or smartphone with a camera)*
	Internet connection
	Headphones (optional)

I t is a bit challenging to assess a whole group's speaking skills in one day. However, with this twist on a speaking task, a teacher can praise students and correct mistakes in a detailed manner. Students can also be part of their learning process by praising and correcting themselves. In the era of digital storytelling, students are used to recording and posting short, personal videos on the internet. Consequently, recording themselves while doing a speaking task will come naturally to learners. The following procedure is general, so it can be applied to a myriad of speaking activities.

PROCEDURE

Before Class

1. Choose the speaking task that students will complete and share with a video recording of themselves.
2. Decide how students will share their videos. One option to consider is Flipgrid. According to its website, it is the top platform for video discussion. Students can record themselves on video and watch and respond to classmates. Each class has its own account, which may be open or locked. Another option to consider is a learning management system, such as Moodle.

In Class

3. Tell students they will complete a speaking task while recording themselves with their devices. Explain the task that you selected.
4. Upload the video to Flipgrid, Moodle, or another platform, or ask students to send the video by email or as an attachment via any social media used with students.

V

5. You can assess the task outside class, or you can include assessment during class if you want to include self-assessment; have the students view their recording and make a list of strengths and weaknesses they have when speaking in English. It is a good idea to tell students not only to correct mistakes but also to praise achievements. This will promote their autonomous learning and self-monitoring skills.

CAVEATS AND OPTIONS

1. It is important to remind students to speak clearly and in a loud tone of voice so that they can be heard in the video.

2. It may happen that students take longer or start the task all over again several times because they know they are recording themselves. Tell them that the task they are about to do should resemble one in daily life, so they will only have one chance. Otherwise, the authenticity and spontaneity of the activity is lost. Remind students that in real life exchanges, people do not get the opportunity to rehearse conversations or social situations before they happen.

3. If you have an educational platform (e.g., Moodle) and the students are used to uploading materials and contributing, the students could upload these videos and do some peer review or assessment. However, peer assessment should be handled with care and sensitivity.

4. Shadow Puppet Edu is another option to consider. It was created for students ages 6–8 to make slideshows.

REFERENCES AND FURTHER READING

Flipgrid: https://info.flipgrid.com/

Moodle: https://moodle.org/

Numbers Ping Pong With Speech Recognition

Daniel Buller

Levels	*Beginner to intermediate*
Aims	*Practice accurate pronunciation of a variety of numbers*
	Receive immediate and visual feedback
Class Time	*25 minutes*
Preparation Time	*10 minutes*
Resources	*Internet-enabled smart devices with speech recognition app*
	Handout (optional; Appendix)

R

This activity gives students the chance to practice pronouncing numbers while getting instant and visual feedback. When a student says a number, if the app recognizes it, the student receives one point. This activity can be set up as a competition between pair partners or groups. The person or groups with the most points at the end is the winner. Try the dictation app yourself while preparing for class to have more time to deal with technology issues as they come up in class.

PROCEDURE

1. Dictate a list of numbers or ask learners to write a list of at least five numbers. This can be a list of random numbers between 1 and 99,999. For example:

   1) 5   2) 13   3) 3,190   4) 26,000   5) 45,550

2. Review numbers as a class and use choral chants to go over especially difficult areas, such as sixTEEN and SIXty. It might also be necessary to review how to say numbers in the hundreds, thousands, and millions.

3. Demonstrate numbers dictation with a speech recognition app such as iOS Notes or Google Docs. Say a number slowly and with a clear voice (sixTEEN). Check the screen to make sure that the app has understood it correctly and show it to the class. If the app understood it correctly, tell the class you earned a point and write "one point" on the board.

4. Divide the class into pairs and ensure that each pair has their lists of numbers and at least one smart device with a speech recognition app open. Some time may be needed during this step to work out kinks and attend to app or internet delays.

V

5. One partner will say one of their numbers and determine if the app recognized it. If it does, that speaker will mark one point. Then it will be the turn of the other partner who says the same number as the first partner and marks a point if it's understood by the app. The partner with the most points at the end wins.

6. If a pair finishes quickly, ask them to write a list of more challenging numbers to practice with their partners while other groups finish up.

7. Wrap up the activity by going over numbers that were difficult to articulate or understand and encourage learners to practice these on their own.

CAVEATS AND OPTIONS

1. Set students up for success using the app. Before setting learners free on the activity, practice sufficiently offline to minimize frustration that might come up.

2. Bring a list of numbers instead of asking students to come up with their own. This can be used to target specific types of numbers (Appendix).

3. Add an extra challenge by adding information to the numbers with a detail ("1,000 students," "13 percent," etc.).

4. Replace number lists with minimal pairs, new vocabulary, or short phrases. Speech recognition technology can be used in a number of different ways.

5. Set it up as a free practice instead of setting it up as a competition. The competitive aspect of the activity is secondary to the focus on accuracy and engagement.

6. Ask learners to list at least three ways to use this technology to practice outside of class. One of the main values of this activity is showing learners an interesting way to practice on their own.

7. Avoid using Google Translate or Siri for this type of accuracy activity. Those types of apps can be quite useful for other types of speech recognition app activities, like an internet scavenger hunt with no typing allowed. However, these apps often try to do something with the dictated information, such as search the internet, and distract from the accuracy aim of this particular activity.

ACKNOWLEDGMENT

The seed of the idea for using a speech recognition app on a smart phone for pronunciation practice comes from Pete Sharma and Barney Barrett's e-book *Apptivities for Business English*.

REFERENCES AND FURTHER READING

Sharma, P., & Barrett, B. (2013). *Apptivities for business English (e-book)*. The Round.

Pronunciation With Mobile Apps

Hoa Thi Thanh Bui

Levels	High beginner to intermediate
Aims	Practice and distinguish the pronunciation of phonemes \i:\ and \\\
Class Time	Variable
Preparation Time	None
Resources	Smartphones
	Appendix

M obile devices have been integrated into classroom learning for the past few years. Students can use apps on their smartphones or tablets to practice and improve their skills. Teachers can lead the activities or facilitate the students' learning. In this activity, students interact with apps independently, in pairs, or in groups. Students have more time to drill the sounds and receive instant individual feedback with the help of mobile apps. Additionally, it gives the teacher time to go around and correct each student's performance.

PROCEDURE

1. Write the following two words on the board: *seat\si:t* and *sit\sɪt*. Invite some students to pronounce these words. Pronounce the words and make sure that students can recognize the difference. Model the articulation of the two phonemes with the shape of mouth and the position of the tongue.

2. Direct students to open "Sounds: The Pronunciation App" (Macmillan) and tap the sounds \i:\ and\ɪ\. Ask the students to differentiate the sounds as well as the words. Let students practice pronouncing these sounds in pairs. Correct their pronunciation when necessary.

3. Direct students to open "ELSA (Speaking)," click the words in level 1: "Listening Teaser," and sort the words into two columns of \i:\ and \ɪ\ (Appendix). Put the students in pairs and have them check together. Play again and check in pairs and as a class. Then, the students practice pronouncing the target words, comparing their recorded audio and the model pronunciation. Meanwhile, monitor the whole class and assist if needed.

4. Divide the class into two teams. Have team members take turns pronouncing the words with the ELSA app—Level 2 (Appendix). Each student is allowed to speak two or three times if they are not satisfied with the first try. The team that gets a higher score of accuracy will be the winner.

V

CAVEATS AND OPTIONS

1. Some learners may not be able to access the apps via their smartphones. Therefore, they can work in larger groups and share smartphones if necessary. Alternatively, have a backup plan to model the sound by yourself and then demonstrate the use of apps on a mobile device so that learners can practise this at home.

2. ELSA is a pronunciation app with a large number of different levels. Some of these are only available to subscribers, and others are quite complex and not easy for learners to master quickly. However, the first two lessons are free, so this activity takes advantage of using the basic free content of the mobile app in a simple way.

3. It is possible for the students to become distracted when using smartphones in class. Make an agreement with all students to concentrate only on the activity. Monitor carefully and remind students to focus when necessary.

4. For larger classes, students can be divided into four teams. Teams A and B compete against each other, and Teams C and D also compete. The two winning teams go to the final round to become the final winners. The activity can be repeated individually with the students reporting their scores.

REFERENCES AND FURTHER READING

Sounds: The pronunciation app: www.macmillaneducationapps.com/soundspron

ELSA: www.elsaspeak.com/home

APPENDIX

ELSA Speak—Level 1

/iː/	/ɪ/
Eat	Is
Peak	Live
	Sit

ELSA Speak—Level 2

Is Ease It Eat Live   Leave Sit Seat Pick

Sounds Like the Real Mobile Me

Stephen J. Hall

Levels	High beginner to advanced
Aims	Develop pronunciation awareness and reflection
Class Time	1 hour (or less)
Preparation Time	None
Resources	Students' smartphones

Many students may not realize that they do not sound like they hear themselves, as we hear through our skulls and not just through external sounds. A cell phone can provide a recording that can be replayed, shared, paused, and reflected on. Listening to oneself can help us become aware of our own pronunciation and raise awareness of any challenges to being understood by others. Playing back a recording can provide for reflection and also input from peers, which some students find less threatening than teacher feedback. The teacher can then facilitate segmental and suprasegmental awareness through a framework for critical listening and follow up by teaching techniques to address pronunciation needs.

PROCEDURE

1. Check that all students have downloaded a voice recorder app, if it is not already a phone feature.

2. Ask all students to test the recorder using the same phrase, such as, "I am now recording my beautiful voice and listening to sounds and to how my voice rises and falls," or some other short phrase. Have students play it back to themselves to check for volume.

3. Depending on the ability of students, either provide preparation time for cue cards, get them to record at home, or let them record impromptu speaking on a general topic that interests them. Selecting the topic can be very motivating for students. Talking about oneself usually diminishes thinking time, is motivating, and as a favourite topic often promotes greater fluency.

4. For recording, seat students as far apart from each other as possible. Advocate for normal speaking volume. Ask them to record a 2-minute talk on either a given topic or an open topic.

5. Get students to play back their own recording to themselves. They can note down any sounds that are difficult for them. They can also note any words that they emphasised. This can be referred to later in the activity and used for reflection.

V

6. Pair students. If it is possible, pair with students from another first language group. Play back each recording in pairs in a close huddle. The listener should note any words that seem difficult to understand. Spelling is irrelevant. They should also note any words they hear that seem to be important. This helps raise awareness of increased volume (stress), which is often used to increase attention.

7. The speaker can then discuss with the listener. He or she can clarify any challenging sounds or words using the written form if need be. The speaker should then say which words he or she wanted to highlight. The speaker could take note of discussed sounds, words, and tone. Then, discuss the overall feeling about what is said. Then, the students swap roles.

8. Move around, noting sound or segmental difficulties. Also be aware of stress usage or any gaps between students' intentions with intonation and their performance.

9. The framework of sound or phoneme level challenges can be addressed through techniques drawing on what has been heard, but without naming any individuals. Intonation focus on more than individual sounds can be followed up in a later lesson. The focus on either individual phonemes or suprasegmentals can then be driven by real needs, which the students can refer to through the recording.

10. Follow up and comparative work between earlier and later recording provides a record for teachers and students showing progress or areas of need.

CAVEATS AND OPTIONS

1. Some students may prefer to prepare the recording at their own leisure. This provides for a more structured presentation and may motivate practice. Underlining or highlighting keywords on cue cards may assist the use of stress.

2. Students of the same first language may not hear impediments to understanding that listeners from other language groups perceive. There can be first-language accommodation to the known marked pronunciation. However, recording provides data on first-language interference that students may not be aware of—until hearing themselves.

3. Students can record a 2-minute talk and leave it on a web-based site for your feedback. The method can increase the students' comfort level. International comprehensibility is the target.

4. The activity can be focused on just problem sounds or on the wider intonation patterns across an utterance, with a focus on emphasising keywords and rise and fall patterns. This is useful for speakers of tonal languages who need to decrease stress on the less significant words.

5. Speaking and reflecting on how we speak creates a noisy, interactive classroom, so whole class attention signaling needs to be clear.

Improving Presentation Skills With PechaKucha

Suzan Stamper

Levels	*Intermediate to advanced*
Aims	*Develop fluency and presentation skills*
Class Time	*At least 2 (60-minute) classes over 1–2 weeks*
Preparation Time	*60 minutes*
Resources	*Assigned readings*
	Student access to PowerPoint
	Handout (Appendix)

PechaKucha is a style of presentation created in Tokyo in 2003 by Astrid Klein and Mark Dytham for architects to share their creations. A key feature is that a presenter is allowed only 20 slides, and each slide is visible for only 20 seconds (20×20). The slides typically include graphics with only a few—or no—words. In general, the PechaKucha format encourages more planning, rehearsal, and fluency.

This speaking activity was created for an academic English course in which students summarized and reflected on a reading. It adapts the PechaKucha presentation style to encourage students to rely less on referring to slides packed with text and reading long sentences or paragraphs from slides and notes. Using the presentation template (Appendix), each student prepares a short presentation in the PechaKucha style, with a maximum of 10 slides visible for 20 seconds (10×20). This activity supports the development of effective presentation skills, such as fluency, better planning of content included in slides, a clearer focus on main points, stronger transitions, and improved eye contact.

PROCEDURE

1. Before this activity, students are introduced to note-taking and academic skills like finding the main idea, using graphic organizers, noticing cohesive devices, and so on.

2. Divide students into four groups. Give each group a different article to read as homework with instructions to take notes on the article's content.

3. On the Work Group day, Group A students discuss the assigned A reading and its main points. Group B discusses the B article, Group C discusses the C article, and Group D discusses the D article.

4. After students discuss and compare notes for approximately 30 minutes, introduce the PechaKucha format with some examples. Provide rubrics for the PowerPoint (PPT) slides and presentations.

5. Distribute a handout with a presentation template (Appendix) to each student with instructions to draft a presentation that summarizes the assigned article. Advise students to discuss and decide how to best use the assigned number of slides. Examples of helpful discussion topics include

    *   what information should be on the title slide,
    *   how many points will be covered,
    *   how many slides are needed for each point,
    *   how to present the content with a minimum number of words,
    *   how to transition between points, and
    *   what information should be included in a closing slide.

6. Explain that group members can discuss how to best represent the main points in draft slides on the template; however, each individual in the group is required to complete an individual template.

7. (Optional) Check each template before students create the slides in PPT. Advise students at this draft stage about potential problems (e.g., a disproportionate number of slides spent on one point, the use of too many words, not citing sources).

8. Next, provide instructions as needed for creating slides in PPT. Check that students know how to set the automatic advance feature of slides in PPT. (Model this if needed.) Provide students with tips on how to practice with the automatic timing. (The creation of slides can take place in or out of class.)

9. To prepare for presentation day, arrange a time for students to practice in class. They should rehearse several times with the automatic advancing of slides at 20 seconds. (Rehearsals could take place in or out of class.)

10. During the presentations, tell students to start the PPT slides and then move away from the computer; the slides automatically advance. Encourage the presenter to concentrate on eye contact, appropriate hand gestures, body language, and speaking directly to the audience.

CAVEATS AND OPTIONS

1. The official PechaKucha website (www.pechakucha.org) has background information and samples from more than 900 international chapters. A good example is "Life on the Great Barrier Reef" at www.pechakucha.org/presentations/life-on-the-great-barrier-reef

2. The original 20 × 20 PechaKucha format results in presentations that are 6 minutes and 40 seconds long. This activity results in a shorter presentation that is 3 minutes and 20 seconds long. For a different presentation requirement, modify the number of slides.

3. This style of presentation is suitable for a variety of courses. For example, in writing courses, students can summarize their essays or research papers.

4. Though the original PechaKucha style encourages very few or even no words on a slide, this can be adapted to include words, but fewer words. In the reading class example, students were encouraged to include graphic organizers from their notes (e.g., a comparison/contrast was presented with a Venn diagram, a process was presented as a flow chart).

5. Having the students first draft a presentation on a worksheet with a paper template focuses attention on the words and formatting of the slides. Students have to consider how to organize slides. They must plan how many slides are needed for main points, what graphic organizers are appropriate, where words should be placed on the slide, and so on.

6. In Step 6 of the activity, there is a combination of group and individual work. This provides support for the students, but it also ensures that each individual student can be assessed.

7. Give clear instructions to ensure that PPTs are unique to each individual student in wording and design in order to encourage paraphrasing and summarizing skills. In other words, two students are not allowed to turn in the same PPT. Alternatively, you could allow each group to create one PPT for the article with each student individually presenting in separate presentation rounds (i.e., each round with four students presenting one of the four ABCD articles).

Online Visuals and Effective Public Speaking

Kendra Wray

Levels	*High beginner to advanced*
Aims	*Learn the importance of body language, gestures, and voice for presentations*
Class Time	*Variable*
Preparation Time	*None*
Resources	*Computer with internet access and projector/screen or a television*
	Pictures (clip art/Google Images)
	Web links for video clips

One of the greatest challenges with teaching public speaking is helping students move from reading their notes and remaining in one position to relating with their audience and incorporating gestures, movement, appropriate voice inflections, and eye contact. The benefit of this activity is that it relates to a variety of learning styles by helping students see, feel, and experience the differences created by using these public speaking skills. This activity gives students the opportunity to see visual differences between speakers that effectively use these skills versus speakers that do not. It also offers models for the learners to apply and increases their understanding of why the recommended techniques work in public speaking.

PROCEDURE

1. Have the students work in pairs or small groups to discuss what they know about public speaking.

2. Lead a class discussion in which everyone contributes their ideas. Try to get as many details and examples as possible.

3. Watch the video clip from *Bridget Jones's Diary*. (Search for *"Bridget Jones's Diary* Painfully Awful Speech.")

4. Tell students (in pairs or groups) to discuss, "What do you think or feel when it comes to public speaking? Talk about some of your public speaking experiences."

5. Continue this discussion as a class. Most students have some negative feelings about public speaking or some bad experiences, so it's good to take some time to discuss this to overcome the negative mindsets before focusing on how they can improve.

6. As a class, watch two clips from *The Hunger Games: Mockingjay—Part 1*. The first clip is "This is how a revolution dies" and the second clip is "If we burn, you burn with us."

7. Watch the clips in this order and then discuss in pairs or small groups. Then have the groups share their thoughts with the class, addressing these questions:

   • Which clip is better?

   • What makes it better?

   • From your experience, what makes a presenter someone you want to listen to?

8. Using pictures from clip art/Google Images, have the students compare and contrast pictures of public speakers. Ask students:

   • How do you feel?

   • What is the impression the speaker gives? Include body language, gestures, voice, eye contact, and other public speaking skills.

   Some example pictures could include:

Speaker standing behind a podium, head down	Speaker standing with their head up
Speaker standing with a more open posture	Speaker standing with a more closed posture
Speaker hiding behind their papers	Speaker not using notes
Speaker looking at the entire audience	Speaker looking intently at one person

9. Watch the video "Being a Mr. G" and then discuss his use of body language, gestures, voice, and eye contact. This video shows Mr. J. A. Gamache speaking at a Toastmasters World Championship. Other Toastmasters champions may also be watched.

CAVEATS AND OPTIONS

1. For the first step, learners can create a poster about what makes a good presenter and then present it to their classmates.

2. Links can be disconnected at any time for a variety of reasons, so always check them in advance. Other YouTube videos or movie clips can be used as needed/ desired.

3. If access to online clips is unavailable, using downloadable pictures from Google Images or other sources can be just as effective.

4. Some other key areas for discussion:

   — Be aware of one's strengths and weaknesses when speaking.

   — Improve strengths and remember to be yourself.

   — Know weaknesses and learn how to control them.

   — Reflect on who you are with the people you are most comfortable with and learn to bring that to the stage. Public speaking is all about relating with one's audience.

Postpresentation: Peer Feedback and Self-Reflection With Socrative

Valeria Bogorevich and Elnaz Kia

Levels	*High intermediate to advanced*
Aims	*Practice active listening*
	Develop constructive criticism skills
	Promote self-awareness and critical thinking
Class Time	*Variable*
Preparation Time	*30 minutes*
Resources	*Internet access*
	Smartphones
	Directions for the instructor (Appendix A)
	Handouts (Appendixes B and C)

These activities develop skills of peer criticism and self-reflection. Peer feedback not only teaches students ways of improving their own presentation skills but also how to communicate critical comments in a polite manner. Inclusion of peer feedback gives each presenter the understanding that they are presenting both in front of the teacher to earn a grade and for the audience that is carefully listening. In turn, self-reflection helps students develop an important self-regulatory skill that allows them to constructively criticize their own work; develop strategies on how to address a challenge; and identify their strengths, weaknesses, and improvement. It is important to impart both skills (peer criticism and self-reflection) because these analytical abilities are useful for further university education, work, and life, and they can help students direct themselves toward a better future.

PROCEDURE

1. Explain and assign a presentation task. Instruct students to do the work required for the presentation.

2. A couple of days before the presentation, ask the students in what order they would prefer to present and record the sequence.

3. Create a quiz on Socrative (www.socrative.com) following the directions in Appendix A. Instead of questions, there are students' names according to the agreed presentation order.

4. On the presentation day, before a student starts speaking, each presenter asks a classmate to video record the talk using the presenter's phone. (Later, students use these videos for the self-reflection assignment.)

5. Invite the students to give presentations in front of the class using visual aids (e.g., PowerPoint, videos, pictures, or posters).

6. Students, who are the audience members, use the Socrative "quiz" to give peer feedback. Give directions to the class for how to access the website and guidelines for what to comment on (Appendix B). Instruct students to write descriptive comments, such as "It was hard to understand the topic at the beginning of the presentation."

7. Download the comments from Socrative (Appendix A). The file will include student comments sorted by presenters. Email this peer feedback to each student.

8. As their homework, students watch their video-recorded presentations and read peer comments. Then, students fill out self-reflection worksheets (Appendix C) and submit them for grading.

CAVEATS AND OPTIONS

1. One potential problem is that students may be reluctant to leave any comments or leave the same comment for all the presenters. To motivate the students to produce meaningful comments for each presenter, the activity can be graded.

2. Requiring anonymous feedback might lead to offensive, inappropriate comments; however, this can be a good opportunity for you to teach skills of providing constructive, descriptive criticism. On the other hand, requiring names can cause dishonesty and censorship of critical feedback.

3. Peer feedback described in the procedures involves written comments without providing numeric grades; however, students can be instructed to evaluate their classmates by assigning scores using a presentation rubric of your choice.

4. The homework task of self-reflection can be coupled with self-assessment. Students can score themselves using a presentation rubric.

5. In case the students do not have access to smartphones, you can record each student's presentation using a video camera or a smartphone and then share the videos with the class.

6. If there is no access to the internet or smartphones, students can use a paper worksheet with the presenters' names on it. In this case, you will have the additional work of rewriting or retyping all the comments to ensure anonymity; otherwise, the students may be recognized by their handwriting.

7. If you decide against having blind peer feedback, the comments can be given on index cards; you need to make sure that students do not forget to write down each presenter's name on the cards.

V

REFERENCES AND FURTHER READING

Birjandi, P., & Hadidi Tamjid, N. (2012). The role of self-, peer and teacher assessment in promoting Iranian EFL learners' writing performance. *Assessment & Evaluation in Higher Education*, 37(5), 513–533.

SPOKEN ENGLISH FOR ACADEMIC AND PROFESSIONAL PURPOSES
USING TECHNOLOGY

Using Set Summary Phrases to Reference Outside Sources

Evelyn Pierro

Levels	Advanced
Aims	Develop fluency and accuracy when orally referring to outside sources
Class Time	1 hour–80 minutes
Preparation Time	Variable
Resources	Video links
	Handout (Appendix)
	Smartphones and headphones (students use their own)

Participating effectively in a discussion often requires referencing informa-tion that has been learned from an outside source. Referring to outside sources is extremely difficult, however, because it requires spontaneous paraphrasing and summarizing. This activity allows students to reference a video in a discussion by utilizing provided summary phrases. Students benefit from completing this type of practice multiple times over the course of a semester. In each repetition, different videos are used. Here, the example videos are on the topic of co-ops; other videos can be selected to match the focus of a different lesson.

PROCEDURE

Preparation

1. Before the activity, select three videos. (See References and Further Reading to links for the three videos about co-ops.)

2. Consider organizing students' small groups in advance. In this two-part activity, students are divided into groups for Part 1 and placed into different groups for Part 2. The number of groups will depend on class size and the number of videos being discussed. In Part 1, the number of groups equals the number of videos (i.e., three videos result in three small groups). In Part 2, the num-ber of students per group equals the number of videos (i.e., 3 videos results in three students per group). For example, a class consisting of 15 students and three videos would be divided as follows: Three groups of five students with each group assigned one video (Part 1), five groups of three students with each group member having watched a different video (Part 2).

Part 1

3. Assign every group member in each group the same video to watch on their smartphone. (Students should watch the video independently using headphones. This allows students to determine the number of times they watch the video, whether they pause the video, etc.). Tell students to take notes while watching and watch the video multiple times if they wish. (The number of times is based on your discretion.)

4. After the students watch the video and take notes, explain that the group members should discuss and agree on the main idea of the video. Also, tell them to create a list of three to five details that need to be provided when they summarize the video to students who have not watched it. Remind students to work together to paraphrase the information rather than using copied words or phrases from the video they saw. Work with the groups as needed offering suggestions, corrections, and so on.

Part 2

5. Place students into new groups. (All members of the new group must have watched a different video.) Once students are in their new groups, distribute the "Video Information" worksheet (Appendix) on which to take notes. Explain that students take turns summarizing the video they watched while the other two group members listen and take notes on the worksheet. These notes complete the sentences that begin with the summary phrases on the worksheet.

6. Lead a class discussion to allow students to use the sentences they have created. In a discussion about co-ops, for example, ask the class whether it is beneficial for a business to become a member of a co-op. Students share their opinions and use the sentences they created as support. Following is an excerpt from the co-ops discussion for which the activity was created.

> *Teacher*: Is joining a cooperative beneficial to a business?
>
> *Student A*: Yes, it is good for a business to do this because it helps the business become more successful. In a video called "What is a Co-operative?," it says that co-ops help encourage business owners because they feel more important when they belong to a group.
>
> *Student B*: I heard this from my group, too, but a different video said co-ops don't try to make money, so that means co-ops are not good for businesses.
>
> *Student C*: I disagree. In the video "Cooperatives are Everywhere! Take Ownership," the narrator explained that co-ops are created when they are needed. If a business is needed, then it is successful.
>
> *Student B*: But in a co-op, the business owner doesn't become rich.
>
> *Student D*: In the video "Credit Union Cooperative Principles," the speaker says success is not only money.

CAVEATS AND OPTIONS

1. Leave adequate time to find and choose appropriate videos. A search on YouTube on the topic of co-ops, for instance, generated multiple videos. Narrowing down the choices based on length, clear language, and visuals took about 45 minutes.

2. The first time the activity is introduced, it could be done as a whole class activity.

3. Students in a context that does not require formal summary language can be given conversational English phrases.

4. Depending on the objectives for the class, videos about different topics and/ or different lengths may be selected. The videos in the References and Further Reading range from approximately 1½–2½ minutes.

REFERENCES AND FURTHER READING

Cooperative Network. (2015, August 25). Cooperatives are everywhere! Take ownership. [Video file]. Retrieved from https://www.youtube.com/watch ?v=8RCZPrUIU0o

Co-operatives UK. (2015, June 20). What is a co-operative? [Video file]. Retrieved from http://www.youtube.com/watch?v=90FL_bBE4mw

National Credit Union Foundation. (2017). New credit union cooperative principles. Retrieved from https://www.ncuf.coop/news/press/cooperative-principles -video.cmsx